S0-BBM-690

DATE DUE

A POLISH CHAPTER
IN CIVIL WAR AMERICA

POLAND'S MILLENNIUM SERIES

OF THE

KOSCIUSZKO FOUNDATION

A POLISH CHAPTER
IN
CIVIL WAR AMERICA

The Effects of
The January Insurrection
on
American Opinion and Diplomacy

By

JOSEPH W. WIECZERZAK

TWAYNE PUBLISHERS, INC.
New York

Copyright © *1967*, by Twayne Publishers, Inc.

ALL RIGHTS RESERVED

Library of Congress Catalog Card Number: 67-25186

MANUFACTURED IN THE UNITED STATES OF AMERICA

Errata:

p. 12, line 2 .... father .... should read .... mother ....

p. 30, line 2 ....Zablocki .... should read .... Zabolotsky....
p. 30, line 16 .... six .... should read ....five ....

p. 127, line 6 .... sixteen .... should read .... seventeen ....

p. 207, line 5 .... In August, 1864, Czarist authorities captured and hanged .... should read By August 1864, Czarist authorities had captured and hanged....

p. 241, note 51 .... p. 26.   should read .... p. 29.

Addenda:

p. 178 Add: Probably the most recent treatment of the January Insurrection *per se* and American diplomacy is John Kutolowski's "The Effect of the Polish Insurrection of 1863 on the American Civil War Diplomacy," *The Historian*, Vol. XXVII, No. 4, August 1965, pp. 560-577. Kutolowski maintains that: While the battles of Vicksburg and Gettysburg deterred England and France from involving themselves in the Civil War, Poland reinforced their policies of caution; the Insurrection diverted English and French popular opinion from America to Poland; the Insurrection diminished hopes for English and French recognition of the Confederacy; and, American statesmen most responsible for diplomacy were not cognizant of the significance of Poland despite numerous comments from their representatives abroad.

p. 223, between Kalussowski . . . and Leavitt . . . add: Kutolowski, John. "The Effect of the Polish Insurrection of 1863 on the American Civil War Diplomacy," *The Historian*. Vol. XXVII, No. 4, August, 1965, pp. 560-577.

p. 233, note 1 — Add: She was twenty-five years old.

p. 241   Add note: 52 *Ibid.*

E
183
.8
P7
W5

Ha29a69

2619936

SL

FOREWORD

In 1608, one year after the first permanent English colony was established in America, a handful of Poles arrived in the Jamestown colony to help establish the first industries in what came to be the United States. Since that time, the number of Polish immigrants to America has increased, to the point that today from six to ten million Americans are of Polish background. Despite their numbers and the recent awakening of interest in immigration studies, little is known about their contributions to the development of the United States, as indeed little is known about Polish-American relations or about Polish history in general. The Kosciuszko Foundation was therefore pleased to award Dr. Joseph Wieczerzak its 1966 Doctoral Dissertation award for his original study, upon which the present work is based. This award is granted each year to the best doctoral dissertation on a Polish subject brought to its attention during any given year.

Of the mass of materials that have been published on the history of the Poles in America and on Polish-American relations, only a few works have earned the respect of the academic community: William I. Thomas' and Florian Znaniecki's monumental four-volume *The Polish Peasant in Europe and America;* the two biographies of Kosciuszko by Mieczyslaw Haiman, *Kosciuszko Leader and Exile* and *Kosciuszko in the American Revolution;* Jerzy J. Lerski's *A Polish Chapter in Jacksonian America;* Arthur E. Wood's *Hamtramck Then and Now;* Le Roy Fisher's *Lincoln's Gadfly, Adam Gurowski;* and Metchie Budka's edition of Niemcewicz' American diaries entitled *Under Their Vine and Fig Tree.* We are confident that Dr. Wieczerzak's *A Polish Chapter in Civil War America* will join their ranks.

5

The Kosciuszko Foundation tries, among its many objectives, to promote a knowledge of Poland's cultural heritage and of the Polish contribution to the development of the United States. It was pleased to assist Dr. Jerzy Jan Lerski in completing his education and later in making possible the publication of his study on the Poles in Jacksonian America. It was likewise pleased to make possible the publication of Dr. Metchie Budka's *Under Their Vine and Fig Tree* through its award of its first Doctoral Dissertation Award, in 1964. Today it is equally proud of the assistance it has given Dr. Wieczerzak in carrying out the research for his dissertation, and of its part in assisting in the publication of this work. Hopefully, when a sufficient number of such monographs becomes available, a much needed synthesis of the Polish contribution to the development of the United States will be prepared.

The Foundation is likewise proud to include this work in its Poland's Millennium Series, which now includes Marian Kukiel's *Czartoryski and European Unity 1770–1861;* Jerzy J. Lerski's *A Polish Chapter in Jacksonian America;* the monumental two-volume *Kosciuszko Foundation English-Polish, Polish-English Dictionary,* edited by Kazimierz Bulas, Francis Whitfield and Lawrence Thomas; and the *Introduction to the Polish Language,* by Sigmund Birkenmayer and Zbigniew Folejewski.

We are likewise pleased to cooperate with Twayne Publishers in publishing this work, especially in light of its great achievement in inaugurating its *Polish Authors Series.*

New York City
October, 1966

STEPHEN P. MIZWA
PRESIDENT
THE KOSCIUSZKO FOUNDATION

In Grateful Appreciation

To Professor Ludwik Krzyzanowski, who first suggested the topic of the dissertation upon which this book is based, and then served as mentor, guide, teacher, taskmaster, and father confessor through many trying hours.

To Professors Rita W. Cooley and Edwin G. Olson of New York University, who gave much of their time in reading the original manuscript and made several very valuable suggestions.

To Professor Feliks Gross and Colonel Roman Michalowski of New York University, who aided me as I took my first steps along the path of graduate studies and who inspired me to stay on it.

To my parents and my sister Irene, for their patience, understanding, encouragement, and occasional prodding.

To the institutions that have allowed me free access to their storehouses of invaluable material: The National Archives of the United States, The Library of Congress, The New York, Boston and Brooklyn Public Libraries, The New York Historical Society, the National Library in Warsaw, the Library of the University of Warsaw, the Czartoryski and Jagellonian Libraries in Cracow, the Ossolineum in Wroclaw, the Library of the Society of the Friends of Learning in Poznan, the Library of the Polish Academy of Sciences in Kornik, the Institute of History of the Polish Academy of Sciences, the Institute of History of the University of Warsaw, the British Museum, and the National Library of Ireland.

To the Kosciuszko and Wanda Roehr Foundations, for giving me financial assistance in my post-doctoral research, which led to an expansion of my dissertation, and to the Polish Academy of Sciences for generously providing me with shelter, stipend, and assistance during the time spent in Poland to complete that research.

7

To my most gracious Polish advisers: Professor Stefan Kieniewicz, Dr. Krzysztof Groniowski, Dr. doc. Irena Koberdowa, Professor Henryk Wereszycki, the late Prof. Adam Lewak, Mrs. Krystyna Murzynowska, Dr. Florian Stasik, and many others.

To Mrs. Barbara Johnson and Mrs. Esther Bookman of the Peggy Sweet Typing Service, who not only typed my manuscript but also made some sound editorial suggestions.

To Dr. Eugene Kusielewicz of the Kosciuszko Foundation and to Mr. Erik J. Friis of The American-Scandinavian Foundation for applying generous coats of polish to cover many rough spots in my writing.

To the friends, associates, and acquaintances who provided a receptive ear into which I poured my story of the Polish January Insurrection and Civil War America.

And, to my wife Dorothy, for her patience and understanding during the first days of our married life, which we shared with the proofs of this volume.

TABLE OF CONTENTS

INTRODUCTION

The influence of one nation upon others are very difficult to trace with any degree of exactitude. They are always so intimately mingled with domestic elements as to make it well-nigh impossible to discern the definite limits between foreign and native. Material influences can be based on the basis of objective evidence. Mental influences, however, are often so subtle as to evade observation. Sometimes they may come with such a shock that they cannot be mistaken. In other cases, they may conceal themselves under national slogans; even illusions may play their part.[1]

At first glance it would be extremely difficult to detect any influences exerted by nineteenth-century Poland on nineteenth-century America. Two of the major means of direct contact and channels of influence, commerce and diplomacy, did not exist between the two nations; while the United States was growing into youth and early maturity, Poland was politically dead, its body dismembered and divided among Austria, Prussia, and Russia, three absolute powers which themselves had little contact with and scarcely any influence on America. Yet, there were two intangible factors that often more than made up for the lack of official relations and which helped to forge the links in a chain of influence and to create a friendship based largely on sympathy. The two factors were example and sentiment. They came into being almost simultaneously with the birth of the United States and with the death of the exhausted Polish Kingdom.

The names of Kosciuszko and Pulaski were well-known among Americans of the late eighteenth and early nineteenth centuries. Kosciuszko, the engineer who fortified Saratoga and West Point, enhanced his popularity in American minds by returning for a brief visit to his Revolutionary War associates after his release from prison in 1796. He had been freed by the Russian czar whose father, in 1794, had crushed the first Polish revolution and the struggle for independence which Kosciuszko had led. The sentiment for the more dashing Pulaski was reinforced by the dramatic circumstances of his death at Savannah in a cavalry charge and to some extent by the simple fact that the combination of letters in his name was not beyond the ability of Americans to pronounce, as was so often the case with his compatriot's.

The sad example of political anarchy which had preceded Poland's dismemberment served in one area as a deterrent to the delegates who met at the American constitutional convention. It forestalled the establishment of an elective monarchy or a lifetime presidency in the United States.[2] In turn, the United States Constitution of 1787 partly inspired the representatives at the Four-Year Diet who drafted the Polish Constitution of May 3, 1791, a few years before Poland's dismemberment.[3]

The combination of Kosciuszko, Pulaski and the partitions provided capital for a substantial "sentimental legacy" of pro-Polish sympathies which was stored in the minds and hearts of the American public through the earliest decades of the nineteenth century. The legacy accrued sizable dividends from poetic and fictional sources. Chief among these was *Thaddeus of Warsaw*, a novel by an Englishwoman, Jane Porter; it was based slightly on the life of Kosciuszko and caused many tears to be shed for its heroic but non-existent Polish exile, accepted as real by many American readers.[4]

In 1830 and 1831 the Poles were to make their first major draft on the "sentimental legacy." In November 1830 cadets in Warsaw, who had formed a conspiratorial group, struck a blow against Russian authority. Their rioting mushroomed into a revolution which was to last nine months and was to involve full-scale battles between a Polish Army and Russian units.

In America, the November Insurrection inspired a wave of Polonophilia. Scarcely a day passed without sympathetic mention of Poland in the newspapers. Editors heaped scorn upon Poland's partitioners and castigated England and France for their reluctance to declare war on Russia. Polish dances were taught in New York dancing schools, a plethora of amateur poetry and fiction on Polish themes made its way into print. Hundreds of American youths offered to fight alongside the Polish insurgents. Further inspired by a stirring appeal from the pen of the most successful American writer of the day, James Fenimore Cooper, Americans formed aid committees which collected thousands of dollars for the Polish cause at numerous public meetings. Unfortunately, the funds arrived at their ultimate destination after the insurrection had been crushed. Instead of being used for the purchase of arms it was distributed among wounded veterans who found their way to Western Europe.[5]

The agonies of the November Insurrection were prolonged for more than a decade after its final defeat. There were needless executions, occasional atrocities, arrests and, above all, mass deportations to Siberia of an untold number of insurrectionists. As late as 1843, American readers could still find in their newspapers lurid accounts of such acts of retribution. Furthermore, the actual entry into the United States of hundreds of the former Polish insurgents made the plight of Poland more vivid in American eyes.[6]

Soon afterwards, however, the links in the chain of Polish-American sympathies were to be weakened and the "sentimental legacy" was to be depleted by suspicion and friction. Of the Polish veterans who found themselves on American soil, at least 235 had been literally dumped from Austrian vessels completely against their expressed wishes to remain in Europe until the time was ripe for another revolution. Most of them were officers of the landed gentry class, and their negative attitude toward the United States was aggravated by disillusionment when they tried to come to terms with the social crudeness of the Americans, and the natural ruggedness of their new surroundings. They vainly sought an Old World status as well as the comforts and the refined living which were not to be found in Jacksonian America. They sought intellectual pursuits and professions from which they were invariably barred by a formidable language barrier. The American army was at its lowest strength, and thus they could not even find the only alternative employment which they considered honorable.[7]

On the other hand, Americans whose rugged individualism and social egalitarianism had reached a high point during the presidency of Andrew Jackson, were becoming resentful of foreigners whose concepts of republicanism were tainted with aristocracy and class discrimination. They were soon confounded by or even caught in the crossfire of quarreling between factions formed among the Polish exiles, and they learned that factionalism and power struggles among the insurgents had been nearly as much a factor in bringing on their defeat as the Russian armies. The Polish exile in the flesh sometimes turned out to be a far cry from Thaddeus of Warsaw.

From the 1820s to the mid-1840s Americans generally felt sympathy towards all European revolutions. Such orators as Daniel Webster helped to foster this feeling by equating the goals and ideals of such revolutions with the American War of Independence. A final sympathetic crescendo was attained in 1850 when the United States Congress invited the Hungarian leader Louis Kossuth for a visit. After being transported from Turkey aboard an American warship, Kossuth toured the United States and spoke at numerous gatherings, including a special banquet tendered by Congress itself. He was to disappoint American liberals, however, and in particular the New England abolitionists, by cautiously refraining from taking a stand on the slavery question. The American public soon learned from these embittered groups that Hungarian landowners had not been averse to repressing Slovak, Croatian, and Rumanian peasants even during Kossuth's short-lived revolutionary regime. Americans were also to be apprised of the unpleasant fact that the Polish revolutionaries of 1830-31 had not acted to abolish the institution of serfdom which existed in their country.

Within a year of Kossuth's visit, there was a change of attitude in the American government. President Millard Fillmore set the tone in his Annual Message to Congress in which he devoted a full paragraph to clarifying policy towards European revolutionary movements. He stated that the United States had an "imperative duty not to interfere in the government or internal policy of other nations." Although Americans might "sympathize with the unfortunate or oppressed everywhere in their struggles for freedom," he pointed out, American principles forbade their participation in "foreign contests." His concluding sentence was to give as much comfort to Russia as to the Austrian government, which had just raised strong objections to the Kossuth visit: "We instigate no revolutions, nor suffer any hostile military expeditions to be fitted out in the United States to invade the territory or provinces of a friendly nation."[8] Thus, revolutionary leaders, and potential leaders, realized that the only support their movements could expect from the New World was moral support; that the admonition in George Washington's Farewell Address against "foreign entanglements" and the opening words of the Monroe Doctrine noting that involvement in "the wars of the European powers" did not "comport" with American policy, had received new reinforcement.

Finally, but no less importantly, the "sentimental legacy" of American sympathies toward Poland was affected by developments in direct American-Russian relations. At first, these were diplomatically correct. Aside from Poland and the fact that the Monroe Doctrine had been inspired by Russian expansion into areas along the Pacific coast of North America claimed by the United States, there was little cause for friction between the two nations. Soon after the promulgation of the Monroe Doctrine both Russian and American commercial interests looked forward to an increase in trade and to a treaty that would lead to a mutual paring down of tariffs. The Polish November Insurrection delayed negotiations on this treaty and an impulsive Russian chargé d'affaires in Washington almost sabotaged it by lodging several undiplomatically worded protests and requests to the Jackson government to curb pro-Polish editors or at least to have them print a "correct" version of the story supplied by him. While the government did not do this, it is a fact that at the suggestion of the Minister to St. Petersburg, James Buchanan, Jackson persuaded the editor of the Washington *Globe*, who was a friend of his, to soften his criticisms of the Czar, and that in his inaugural address of 1834 he singled out the 1832 trade treaty with Russia as being a symptom of growing American-Russian friendship.[9]

In the 1850s the course of American-Russian relations moved further in the direction of cordiality. This was to some extent a result of the outbreak of the Crimean War. Russia, the arch-villain of the Polish November Insurrection, was now cast by American journalists in the heroic role of the champion of Christianity fighting "the unspeakable Moslem Turk." Great Britain and France were assigned supporting villainous roles. Feelings against the former had run high over fishing rights and territorial disputes with Central American republics, and it was even easier for Americans to despise the regime of the arbitrary Napoleon III. An abortive scheme by a group of Polish exiles in New York to send an expedition to the Crimean front via Siberia earned them the label of troublemakers violating American hospitality.[10]

During the Crimean War, and in the years which immediately followed it, several Americans passed through Poland on their way to the Russian capital and recorded their observations. A young army captain by the name of George McClellan journeyed through Poland on the way to the front as an official observer. In a letter which he wrote to his brother, he commented that Polish villages had a filthy and repulsive appearance, that the Poles seemed unpleasant, unintelligent, and even degenerate, and that he found it difficult to understand how such people could have waged historical struggles.[11]

In the late 1850s the American reading public learned of conditions in the Russian-ruled part of Poland from two chapters in a book written by Bayard Taylor, a professional traveler and a rather less professional poet. Taylor first admitted to his readers that during his visit he had had few opportunities to converse with Poles. Then, almost simultaneously, he jumped to the conclusion that they were "gradually acquiescing to the rule of Russia." The few who had spoken to him, he added, had admitted, "if reluctantly," that the new Czar, Alexander II, was making changes for the better and pursuing a policy which "had given him much popularity among them." Taylor concluded his chapters with a prophetic statement which seemed to suggest that everything could not really be settled in Poland by the liberal policy of the Czar alone. "The feeling of nationality," he noted, "survives . . . long after a nation is dead and buried. The Jews in Poland call themselves Jews, and the Poles in Russia will call themselves Poles, centuries hence."[12]

That the liberalization policy of the new Czar did not cover everything was more than hinted at in one of the rare allusions to Poland in American diplomatic correspondence of the same period. In acknowledging the receipt of a letter to a not yet existing American consulate in Warsaw, the Minister to the Russian court, Thomas Pickens, cautioned that "everything connected with Poland" was "under the strictest surveillance" of the Russian authorities.[13]

Polish nationalism would not permit the acquiescence to Russian rule which Bayard Taylor had mentioned. Alexander's liberality reached its peak in the aftermath of Russia's defeat in the Crimean War, but it did not pacify his Polish subjects. Neither did the improved economic conditions and the internal improvements instituted in Poland. By the 1860s there were patriotic demonstrations for complete independence, followed by incidents which brought on repressions, and these in turn led to a new tragic insurrection in the first days of 1863.

Thousands of miles away, and at almost the same time, events in America built up to an equal tragic climax in a Civil War. The Polish January Insurrection, as it came to be called, and the American Civil War were to have a historical nexus—a tie which has long been neglected or minimized by historians. One element in this nexus was the fact that the very existence of trouble in Poland did not escape notice in the divided American press. Even with a score of domestic problems, American editors in the North and South were to devote much space to comments on Poland. Their comments, unlike the editorials of the 1830s, were not solely those of dispassionate but sentimentally inclined distant observers. They were tempered with ambivalence and with various considerations. For, as it turned out very soon after the outbreak of the insurrection and the war, the Poles were fighting a government which alone among the major governments of Europe looked favorably on the Union cause. Moreover, some of the more conservative Polish leaders, grouped together in the so-called "White" faction, were to seek the intercession of England and France in their struggle; these were the two powers which the Union feared might actively intervene in the Civil War in support of the Confederacy. This ambivalence, with the pro-Polish "sentimental legacy" and sympathy for independence on one side and gratitude to a friendly Russia on the other, was to have repercussions on the American scene in areas besides public opinion. It was to enter the realm of diplomacy and even that of charity when Polish exiles sought financial help for their cause.

These and other factors will be taken up, with documentation, in the chapters which follow. It is hoped that they will provide some insight into the American mentality and opinion at a critical time in the history of the United States; that they will bear out in part the quotation from a work by Halvdan Koht which opens this introduction and, finally, that they will contribute somewhat to the understanding of American mentality in general, even at the present time. It is my contention that native Americans (of whom I am one), perhaps more than any other people, allow themselves to fall into pitfalls of naiveté even while they present an image of severe practicality to the rest of the world. They also tend to seek crusading causes, to strongly categorize in terms of good and bad even when such categories are utterly impossible. This is my thesis. Some might call it my prejudice. Whether the reader concludes that it is thesis or prejudice, I hope that this book will stimulate further thought and reflection. If so, the purpose behind my writing it will have been fulfilled.

A POLISH CHAPTER
IN CIVIL WAR AMERICA

CHAPTER I

1861: THE TRAGIC PRELUDE*

ON MARCH 6, 1861, John Appleton, the United States Minister to Russia, drafted a routine dispatch to his superior, Secretary of State Jeremiah Black. The dispatch was a thirteen-page, very detailed report on Czar Alexander II's Serf Emancipation Decree, which had been proclaimed three days earlier. On the eleventh page of the report, there was a paragraph which digressed to another subject. It noted:

> You will see from the enclosed *clip* which I cut from the *St. Petersbourg Journal* of March 2d that there has been some trouble recently in Warsaw. The difficulty may have been more serious than it is represented to have been in this account. We have had rumors of Polish discontents for some time past. They were distinctly manifested, it is said, during the Warsaw Conference, when there was a marked absence of the nobility from all public demonstrations. Whether the disturbances on the 13th and 15th of Feb. had a distinct political character or not, it is impossible to say.[1]

The half-column clipping which Appleton attached to his dispatch was supercaptioned PARTIE OFFICIELLE, a certain indication that it was an official government account of the "trouble" in the former Polish capital. It attributed the disturbances to a group of evilly inclined individuals (*"une bande de gens malin-tentionnés"*). It listed the total number of casualties as six dead and six wounded. However, one of its concluding phrases, *"la tranquilité était rétablié,"* must immediately have evoked shudders in any one acquainted with more recent Polish history. The phrase was frequently used to conclude Russian reports on the

21

arrests, excesses, and reprisals that followed in the wake of the saber-wielding cavalry detailed to crush popular demonstrations under the hoofs of their charging mounts.

Two days later Appleton penned his next dispatch. Its dozen pages were again mainly devoted to Alexander's emancipation decree. He proffered an unenthusiastic analysis of its results and limitations, and also attached a clipping from the *Journal de St. Petersbourg* with the full text of the decree. And again, Poland was the subject of a paragraph of comment. This was a considerably longer paragraph, calling attention to clippings from the *Journal* on "the late troubles in Poland." Noting that "the difficulty in Warsaw was more serious than it was first represented," Appleton made a special comment on the latest casualty figures. "Instead of six killed among the people," he informed Black, "there was probably ten times that number, and in proof that this sacrifice of life was wanton and unnecessary, it is said that not one soldier was killed or wounded."[2]

Thus, the first American diplomat to report on the freeing of Russia's serfs, simultaneously told the story of how the "Czar Liberator's" proconsuls on the western fringes of the Russian empire had reacted to other demands for freedom with murderous brutality. And, partly because of Alexander's actions in Russia, Appleton was to be unduly optimistic about his conduct toward the Poles. The dispatch contained another clipping from the *Journal*, setting forth the Czar's reply to Polish leaders in regard to their petition for a constitution. "The Emperor chooses to regard the request as inopportune," Appleton paraphrased the text, "but promises to do his duty to all his people." Then, in reassuring terms he added that there was hearsay information to the effect that Alexander had already "made some concessions to Poland in a conciliatory spirit."[3]

What were the concessions? Appleton included no details about them. In fact, he had absolutely no inkling of what they might have been and, instead, had to suggest more distant sources of information. He told Black that he could undoubtedly find out more, and find it out sooner from London journals, for it was extremely difficult to obtain reliable information "upon any political subject" in the Russian capital. Half-apologetically, he concluded: "The accompanying extracts contain nothing important, perhaps, which has not already reached you. I feel bound, nevertheless, to send them."[4] Appleton's reason for the dearth of facts had already been given by his predecessors in this post. In the future, it was to be referred to time and time again by his successors.

Exactly a month later, Appleton drafted his next dispatch and addressed it to the new Secretary of State, William H. Seward. It was half the length of his previous dispatches, but it dealt mainly with a matter of immediate interest to his government. In compliance with Seward's instructions, he had given the Russian Foreign Minister, Alexander Gorchakov, a copy of President Abraham Lincoln's inaugural address, which pleaded for preservation of the American Union. He also sounded Gorchakov out on the possibilities of Russian recognition of the newly formed Confederate States of America. Gorchakov answered his query first with a vague comment to the effect that "His Majesty was not unmindful of the friendly relations which had so long subsisted between the two countries," followed it with a practical consideration—that Russia realized that the United States was 'the only commercial counterpoise to Great Britain in the world,"—and ended with a frank admission that "while things continued as they were, the commerce between the Confederate States and Russia would not be interrupted." This was sufficient indication that while England and France traded with the Confederacy, the Russian government would do likewise.[5]

The emancipation of the serfs was now looked upon as being of secondary importance. In two sentences Appleton noted that it had "produced little excitement," and that the imperial ukase implementing it was "so complicated that no one seems to understand it."[6] In the final paragraph he alluded to the situation in Poland in language which was far from optimistic. "Notwithstanding the concessions of the Emperor," he began, "there have been renewed disturbances of a serious character." He enclosed several clippings from the *Journal de St. Petersbourg* detailing the new events and the concessions. He warned that the accounts "must be received with some allowance" and that "other accounts present the difficulties as more serious, and the loss of life as much greater." He concluded:

The government has now taken very stringent measures to prevent future outbreaks, and once more "order reigns in Warsaw." Unhappily tho, it is the order inspired by fear, and enforced by the presence of an army. Soldiers are in possession of all the public places, the shops are all closed, the streets almost deserted, and the city threatened with a state of siege. It may be doubtful whether the Imperial concessions have been received with as much favor as they deserve.[7]

The opening and concluding phrases of the paragraph reveal an impatience on Appleton's part with the Warsaw Poles. He could not understand their continued stubbornness. Although his American idealism might have made him sympathetic toward the demonstrations, his American sense of practicality made him favorably disposed toward the magnanimity of an autocrat who had just given evidence of his benevolence at home. The "imperial concessions" which he had made, did, indeed, seem to offer the Poles a substantial measure of self-rule; a Council of State was to hear their grievances and suggestions, and a Commission of Public Instruction and Religions was to initiate educational reforms and ease restrictions on the Catholic Church. Also provided for were popularly elected provincial and local assemblies. Perhaps Appleton thought that as a result of further generous decrees Russian Poland could move still closer to national autonomy, even toward eventual independence, without bloodshed.

Whatever thoughts on Poland the outgoing minister might have had, they were at least a month behind the actual course of events. For, as he was drafting his last dispatch and preparing to return home, a "rational" group in Alexander's Polish provinces had accepted the concessions. The group was led by the Marquis Alexander Wielopolski, a nobleman who, as early as 1846, had placed Poland under the moral protection of Alexander's father, Nicholas I, calling him "the most generous of our enemies."[8] On March 27, Wielopolski had been simultaneously appointed head of the Commission of Public Instruction and Religions, member of the Czar's Council of Administration, organizer of the Council of State and the local councils, director of agrarian reform and of Jewish emancipation, head of the Departments of Justice and the Interior, and adviser of the Russian Governor General of Poland. For all practical purposes, he became virtual dictator of Poland. By April, he began work on a series of ambitious projects which included the reorganization of Polish society through agrarian reforms and a strengthening of the urban classes, the re-Polonization of education and administration, and a general restoration of political order within the framework of czarist control. Through such projects, he sincerely hoped to have Russia's Polish provinces amalgamated and restored to the autonomous "kingdom" status which had existed between the 1815 Congress of Vienna and the defeat of the Polish November Insurrection of 1830-31.

American diplomatic correspondence contains no commentaries on the results of the Wielopolski program, the main reason being that there was a change of ministers. The reserved Appleton was replaced towards the middle of 1861 by a blustering Kentucky abolitionist, Cassius Marcellus Clay, who had worked actively for Lincoln's election. Clay's initial dispatches were filled for the most part with unsolicited suggestions on the conduct of Civil War, peppered with comments on international diplomacy, with particularly vile criticisms of England and "Catholic" France, and frequent panegyrics upon the "Czar Liberator." During the balance of the year he only mentioned Poland once, namely, in a request for the establishment of an American consulate in Warsaw. The request had absolutely no connection with political developments in Poland and was made merely because the city was to be the western terminus of a railway connecting it with the Russian capital. Had it been approved, the United States would have had a good listening post in a center of future revolutionary activity.[9]

Appleton's remarks to the effect that news of the Polish events would reach his superior sooner and in greater detail from London, were well substantiated. In the "Received" column of the

State Department's *Register of Despatches,* the date April 6 is entered for the dispatch that he had written March 6; April 26, for the dispatch that he had written March 20; and May 17, for the dispatch that he had written April 20. In American newspapers, which reprinted most of their foreign news from Western European journals that arrived by mail steamer within a fortnight, the first items on the February outbreak in Warsaw appeared in mid-March.

To say that the news from Poland came to America at an unfortunate juncture would be an understatement. Circumstances made the importance of the news not merely secondary, but tertiary. It was completely eclipsed by ominous national news. Seven states had already severed the ties that joined them to the Federal Union. On February 4, six of them had formed the Confederacy. In the inaugural address which he delivered on March 4, Lincoln pledged to use all the power given him to "hold, occupy and possess the property and places belonging to the Government." A few weeks later, attention on both sides of the newly formed dividing line focused on Fort Sumter, a small piece of Union property in the harbor of Charleston, South Carolina. There, the pledge was to be put to its acid test.

Secondly, the news of the unrest in Poland came as a sort of "rider" tacked onto the news of Alexander's emancipation decree. This was the arrangement not only in bulletins but also in most editorials. Thus the Polish events were not only overshadowed by the sensation created by the liberation but were also frequently tied to it. In the case of those Northern journals which were violently in favor of Negro emancipation, the news from Poland was likely to be greeted with resentment.

Typical of the comments that the moderate Northern press made on Poland was an editorial which appeared in the *New York World* of March 25 under the very general caption "Nationality." The editorial opened with an observation on nationalism: "The greatest movement of this age is a resultant of two forces: one impelling toward isolation, the other toward aggregation; the former the spirit of individual liberty, the latter the spirit of nationality." It then noted how the nationalistic spirit had prevailed in Germany and Switzerland, in Hungary, which was in the process of securing a patent of rights from the Austrian emperor, and in Italy, whose unification was nearing its completion. It continued:

Finally, it has inspired abased, dismembered Poland to raise her humble head and cry out that she, too, has an individuality; that although her territory has been dissevered and partitioned, her nationality has remained intact; and that she claims if not all her rights; at least the right to her existence.

The next paragraph was given over entirely to Poland. It put both the stubborn Poles and their Russian ruler in the same heroic spotlight. It doubted that mere force, unless it were applied "with an exterminating harshness," could crush the Poles, whose aspirations "for a national rehabilitation" seemed to animate their entire "race," from the "distinguished gentlemen" who sat in meetings of the Agricultural Society in Warsaw "down to the humble peasant who drives or drags a plow." But the editorial writer could not discern such harshness "among the heroic motives of the philanthropic ALEXANDER." Finally, the *World's* editor, the anti-Lincoln Manton Marble, compared the Polish question to the situation in Hungary; he pointed out the analogy between two empires facing a similar domestic problem as one among other domestic problems. He saw Alexander involved in disputes with his own nobles over the liberation of the serfs, while the serfs themselves began to "stammer the accents of freedom." He reasoned that if Alexander would take a cue from the Austrian ruler—who had granted autonomy to Hungary—and make political concessions to the Poles, stopping short of complete independence, he would be able to preserve his empire intact and win the Poles' support. But he questioned Alexander's power to withstand the protests of the powerful Russian nobles, who could block implementation of the liberation decree and perhaps even depose him. "In his present position," Marble reasoned, "he [Alexander] cannot but bethink him of the fate of certain of his predecessors."

The emancipation of the serfs, which Marble linked to the Polish situation, he ascribed to Alexander's liberalism as well, but in so doing he probably overrated the liberalism. It is true that the Czar had favored agrarian reform in Poland since the beginning of his reign. At a conference with Polish landowners in 1856, he had sympathized with an enlightened faction whose aim was to work in that direction, and who were later to form the Polish Agricultural Society. At the same time, however, he had warned them against nationalistic aspirations with the admonition *"Point de rêveries, messieurs, point de rêveries."* Despite the editorial's title and its optimistic prediction that "this principle of nationality, like that of individual liberty, must triumph in the end," its author did not consider another possibility: that national autonomy with close ties to the imperial center might not lead to independence, but that it might perpetuate and make stronger the bonds of dependence, a situation which was indeed to occur in the case of Hungary vis-à-vis Austria.

The editorial's final paragraph made an interesting observation on the relationship between the question of nationality and the American domestic imbroglio. It viewed the Southern secession, a movement that had resulted in the *de facto* existence of a new national entity, as an action taken counter to the principles of nationality, and, therefore, not at all animated by the same spirit that was stirring among the Poles. It noted:

And now, while we see throughout the civilized world this enthusiastic outburst of nationality, how it aggravates our sorrow and deepens our humiliations as we turn our eyes upon our own country and find the national spirit in one part of it apparently extinct—at most a feeble spark ready to be stamped out by the remorseless feet of selfish demagogues. Told by those whom we once called our countrymen, with whom we have triumphed and for whom we have made sacrifices, that we never had a country; that we never were a nation; that our Union which we thought glorious, supreme, enduring, was only a business association.

Marble's rival, the aging William Cullen Bryant, who editorially and personally had helped to increase American sympathy for the Poles at the time of their November Insurrection three decades earlier, now showered paeans of praise on the Russian Emperor and his act of emancipation, equating it with the great liberal movements of history. His only allusion to the recent events in Poland appeared in a two-column encomium to Alexander entitled "The Great Event of the Age," which appeared in his *New York Evening Post* on March 27. Quite ironically, this reference to Poland was included in a few charitable comments reserved for the nobles who had opposed the Czar's action. Bryant noted that the Russian nobility had been "justly alarmed" at "the revolutionary tendencies of the Poles and Hungarians" and for this reason were "justly reluctant" about any plan to give their serfs freedom.

The then fledgling *New York Times*, edited by Henry J. Raymond, a young Vermonter and protegé of the fiery Horace Greeley, printed the first editorial to consider the Warsaw disturbances a primary rather than a secondary or tertiary subject. Entitled "Poland and Russia," and appearing in the March 29 edition, it began on a high note of sympathy for the Poles:

> The "muffled" movement in Poland, unanimous and resolute as it assuredly is, and spreading with formidable celerity from the centre to the borders of the land, is significant of a most serious and self-reliant sentiment—one truly national in its character, and intelligently cognizant of the moral sympathy of the times, as manifested in the healthy progress of liberal ideas throughout Europe.

However, subsequent paragraphs swung the editorial to the side of Russia and into a pattern followed by the *Times'* sister journals with even more vigor and more poetic zest. The editorial continued with such gems as: "the same Czar who glorifies his dynasty by the emancipation of 45,000,000 [*sic*] serfs, claims additional lustre for it by bestowing a separate Council of State upon the Kingdom of Poland. . . . Alexander steps out of his dreary traditions with his hands full of progress, and his heart full of sympathy. . . . The world moves, and Poland and Russia may have approached near enough to read kindred ideas in each other's political countenance." Who, then, was to blame for the spilling of blood in the streets of Warsaw? The editorial's answer

absolved the "Czar Liberator's" lieutenants of all guilt by pointing an accusing finger at General Zablocki, the commander of
the city's Polish gendarmerie. It stated that one of his men had
fired the first shot into the crowds and had thus provided the
Cossack cavalry with an excuse for charging in to restore order
and, in the process, to accidentally kill several of the demonstrators.

Most of the Northern journals were so filled with news of
the Southern secession that they neglected to give their readers
sufficient detailed accounts of the other demonstrations in Poland
and the events which led up to them. These demonstrations had
been precipitated by a procession on the occasion of the anniversary of the 1831 insurgent victory at Grochów, which served
as a silent protest for national rights; further demonstrations in
Warsaw while the Polish Agricultural Society was meeting; the
killing of six demonstrators, who subsequently were given a
martyr's funeral, their cortege winding through Warsaw's streets
and their thorn-covered coffins being led by clergy of all faiths,
an emotion-charged atmosphere prevailing throughout. Only
two New York papers mentioned this aspect of the story: The
Tribune of March 23, which termed the event an *émeute* and
included the names of the victims, and the *Times* of March 25,
whose account was pieced together from items in German and
Swiss newspapers under the erroneous caption "The Revolt at
Cracow." The straightforward hour-by-hour narrative in the two
newspapers had a greater impact than any of the editorial rationalizations or the occasional dispatches from special correspondents in Western European capitals, who, in addition to playing
up the emancipation and Alexander's liberalism, were particularly concerned with Europe's reactions to the Southern secession.

The North, especially New York City, had large concentrations of literate European immigrants whose leaders were, for
the most part, veterans of various revolutions and insurrections.
Editors of foreign-language newspapers were generally exiled
liberals. Unlike their native-born counterparts, they disassociated
the news from Poland from the news of Alexander's emancipation
of the serfs and greeted the former as the first rumble of a

republican revolutionary upheaval which, they hoped, would rock the entire European continent. In addition, a spirit of fraternalism linked the various immigrant nationalities in America, and, when the first news of the Warsaw disturbances arrived, there appeared in the New York *Evening Post,* on March 26, a letter to the editor in which the writer mentioned that during his childhood in Europe he had been taught to pray daily for Poland. He discussed the aid which exiled Poles had just given his own homeland in its successful bid for independence, and then appealed to the citizens of his adopted land in these words:

The United States (North and South) owe some obligations to Poland; her children fought side by side with the men of '76. Having had a share in the building of this mighty temple of civil and religious liberty, it would be well for the present American generation to return to Poland some token of their sympathy and gratitude.

The "token" was to be in the form of material and financial aid of the kind that committees of distinguished Americans working together "without distinction of political party or religious creed" had just collected for the revolutionaries in his own country. Finally, the writer noted that March 25, 1861, the day on which he was writing his letter, marked the thirtieth anniversary of the recitation of a special litany for freedom in all Polish churches. He cited the litany in its entirety to remind his American friends of Poland's new sufferings.

The author of the appeal was G. F. Sechi de Casali, a former *Garibaldini,* who was editor of New York's Italian Journal, *L'Eco d'Italia.* There was no reaction to it in the press, and it may well be assumed that it fell on deaf or deafened ears. However, it was a precursor of future appeals and activities to be carried out on behalf of Poland by various nationality groups after the full-scale insurrectionary struggle began.

By mid-April, when the tensions over Fort Sumter had finally resolved themselves tragically into the Civil War, Poland was driven even further into the background as far as American editorials were concerned. But the war was to have international repercussions. There were fears in some circles that England

and France would intervene on the side of the Confederacy. Coincidentally, the two powers were also sympathetic to the Poles and certainly not averse to seeing them break off from the Russian Empire. In some instances, bitterness towards France and England was very evident in items in the Northern press dealing with Polish developments. For example, the *New York Daily News*, a journal that was later to turn strongly pro-Southern, in its April 26 issue printed an editorial entitled "Poland," in which it was asserted that the recently reported stories of disturbances in Warsaw had been purposely exaggerated in the British press "not from love of liberty or sympathy with struggling freemen, but exactly the reverse." It claimed that the British Consul in Warsaw was "sheltering and encouraging the Polanders," and concluded its first paragraph with the warning: "Let no one suppose for a moment that this Polish rebellion is not the next thing to a lie—a gross exaggeration."

Following these strong words, however, there were several mildly sympathetic remarks about the Poles. "It must not be supposed for a moment," the second paragraph began, "that we do not feel for the subjection of the gallant Poles. . . ." This was followed by several allusions to the past struggles of the Polish nation for its freedom, and this reservation:

But it is not reasonable to suppose that they would leave their motives liable to be questioned by breaking into rebellion at the very hour a great cloud of slavery rises from the nation which governs them. It would not be natural for patriots to rise in rebellion, and call the Czar a tyrant, just at the time that millions of serfs are proclaimed free. Poles are too sensible to run the risk of judgment which such a cause would insure. Nor can it be said that the Emperor, who voluntarily liberates an empire of men, unable to assist themselves, would continue to hold others, powerful for their own case, in painful subjection.

Again the balance of editorial sympathy tipped in favor of Alexander and against the Poles. The *News*, which boasted on its masthead that it had the second largest circulation in the

Union's largest city, threw its readers morsels of cynicism that must have dulled their sentiments in regard to the Polish cause.

How did the Southern press react? One might readily surmise that the pro-slavery, pro-states' rights editors of journals in the Confederacy would have made capital of the Warsaw disturbances; that they would have identified their cause with the cause of the potential Polish rebels; that they would have put the "Czar Liberator" and his enthusiastic Northern admirers in a hypocritical light. However, a glance at Southern opinion reveals that there was no editorializing of such a nature. In fact, there was hardly anything but editorial silence.

Even before the outbreak of open hostilities, the South was morally on the defensive. Its editors devoted many columns of editorial space to justifications—or desperate rationalizations—of slavery, of states' rights and, especially, of the act of secession. Xenophobia was one of the pillars of their argumentation. The way in which it was used is illustrated in the following example:

In an editorial entitled "The Spirit of Nationality," the editor of the New York *Express* had concluded that such a spirit would prevent the people of the South from continuing their separate political existence and would soon lead them back into the Union. On May 5, the indignant editor of the Richmond *Daily Dispatch* retorted with an editorial bearing the same title but embodying a completely opposite viewpoint. First, he accused "the driveller of the *Express*" of having no acquaintance with the citizens of the Confederacy and no knowledge of the true nature of their struggle, because, contrary to his suppositions, the Southern fight was *for* nationality and not *against* it. "The struggle of the South," he pointed out in his blistering conclusion,

is the struggle of Italy against Austria; of a Confederation of independent states, occupied by a homogeneous people, against foreign oppressors, who have violated the common league into which they have entered, and threaten us with cruelties and barbarism compared with which the so-called despotism of Russia is mercy and compassion.

Other Southern journals adhered to the same line of argument, and it was to be reiterated frequently throughout the war. The Southerners considered themselves a native "homogeneous" people defending themselves against a North controlled by fanatical New England abolitionists bent on imposing alien ideals upon them; they were also convinced that subservient to the abolitionists was a motley band of ex-foreign revolutionaries whose immigrant followers constituted the bulk of invading mercenary forces. Some substance was given to this reasoning when hostilities broke out, for among the Federal units in the first wave sent southward there were entire units composed of German, Irish, Italian, Hungarian, even Polish—volunteers.

A consideration of the concluding words in the *Dispatch's* editorial gives a clue to another reason for the failure of the Southern press to make capital of the Polish situation. It was a reason rooted in basic human nature rather than in history or politics. To Southerners on the military defensive the sufferings of the faraway Poles might have seemed terrible, but their own immediate plight seemed inestimably worse. Why then, some of the Southerners reasoned in print, should an excess of attention and sympathy be showered on the former—and the lesser—plight? This feeling prevailed and even increased in intensity when the Polish troubles erupted into a national insurrection and the fortunes of the Confederacy, almost simultaneously, ebbed to their lowest point. This development will be dealt with in subsequent chapters.

There were in the Southern press a few notable exceptions to the rule of journalistic indifference and apathy in regard to Poland. Like their Northern counterparts, the major newspapers below the Mason-Dixon Line had special correspondents stationed in Western Europe. Their principal task was, undoubtedly, to "feel out" European opinion on formal recognition and sympathy towards their cause. Yet, another prime topic in their letters was the Polish situation as it was discussed in various gathering places on the continent. In two obvious instances the initial tone of reporting of the Warsaw disturbances, as well as the tone of the correspondents' analyses and their prognostications on Poland's future status was so sympathetic to the Poles that they must have elicited more than a modicum of pity from readers. In both instances, the correspondence emanated from Paris. One series appeared in the staid *Richmond Daily Whig;* the other in the less restrained *Charleston Courier*. Typical of their content is a letter which appeared in the *Whig* of May 1 on the subject of the czarist order disbanding the nationalist Polish Agricultural Society. With bitterness that went far beyond the limits of dispassionate reporting, the correspondent commented that the order was bad in itself, but:

When to this is added the murder of a large number of inoffensive citizens, who had manifested no symptoms whatever of an alarming character, we are reluctantly driven to the conclusion that the Russian Government does not intend, and never has intended, to make any change in the arbitrary course it has always pursued in Poland, since the partition of that unfortunate kingdom, and so often marked by violence and bloodshed.

Basing his final observation on a conversation which he had with a Russian exile, the correspondent ended his letter with a statement that Czar Alexander had never really intended to make any concessions to the Poles; that he was determined to maintain the harsh *status quo* if only to show them that he was still an autocrat. He saw Alexander's hopeful-sounding though vaguely worded reply to the Polish petition for reform as a good tactical maneuver which would give him ample time to dispatch more troops into potentially rebellious areas in order to forestall further risings.

Northern readers might have drawn similar inferences about the Czar's policy without guidance from editorials or correspondence but from the terse news bulletins which began to appear in their daily papers with greater frequency. Throughout April and May the bulletins noted that there were large-scale troop movements into Poland. They mentioned new disturbances as far east of Warsaw as Kiev. And they also noted that many leading Poles were dissatisfied with the czarist rescript of concession. Readers of the *New York World*, for example, could find in the

April 1 edition of the paper a report that as of March 15 the Russian army garrison in Warsaw had been increased from 5,000 to 20,000 troops. In their paper on April 30 they could read of the arrival in Poland of three Russian generals to command an estimated total of 100,000 men, with more "pouring in." In one instance, at least, this sort of news elicited a brief comment of an editorial and rather poetic nature. The "Foreign Gossip" column of the New York *Evening Post* of May 16 opened with the following prefatory statement:

Poland, after suffering the despotism of Russia for a generation is now displaying all its former heroic character. 'The odor of its nationality' blossoms sweetly even 'from its dust.'

For a moment, it seemed as if the venerable Bryant was about to rekindle some of the editorial fire that he had lit for Poland in 1831. However, even if there were any spark of such fire within him in 1861 it would have been quenched by the cold water of new rumors. Bryant, and his less liberal colleagues, soon gave full play to a story to the effect that the Warsaw disturbances as well as other troubles in Poland were fomented by agents of Napoleon III in order to cause embarrassment to his liberal imperial rival, and to keep Russia occupied with internal problems while he fulfilled his expansionist ambitions in other parts of Europe, especially in Italy and on the Rhine. This oft-told story was occasionally linked to widespread speculations that the Western powers would intervene in the Civil War on the side of the Confederacy. Thus, when the New York *World* of May 20 cast doubt on the plausibility of such an intervention, it strengthened its argument by assuring its readers that the ambitious Napoleon could not count on an important friendly nod from Alexander, because the Russian government, "having traced the threads of the . . . national agitation in Poland to the Tuileries," spurned his friendship and was "seeking consolation in the arms of its old allies, Austria and Prussia."

By the middle of 1861, the spurt of news from the Polish scene began to ebb in the American papers and was displaced by items dealing with the Civil War. The Wielopolski program received no editorial notice in the North or in the South. On infrequent occasions, a space filler item would appear in an out-of-the-way column to remind readers that the Polish story had not yet been concluded. When old Mikhail Gorchakov, the Czarist governor of Poland, died, a semi-eulogistic obituary was printed in the New York *Evening Post* of May 26. Among other complimentary statements, the obituary noted that:

His greatest praise is not the skillful slaughter of Poles at Ostrolenka [in 1831]—but that in spite of it, he was more nearly loved by them than any governor the usurping power had ever given them. He was a thoroughly humane and warm-hearted man—all this in spite of a life-long despotic training.

Although its assessment of Gorchakov was fair, the article failed to take into consideration Gorchakov's role during the Warsaw disturbances of 1861. Furthermore, it did not consider the possible consequences which his death was to have on the fate of Poland. The stern but levelheaded governor had wisely restrained his strong hand, in spite of orders from St. Petersburg to apply it vigorously, and had entrusted to a committee of Poles the maintenance of order during the tense period following the disturbances. And it was partly at his suggestion that Wielopolski was allowed to head the uneasy Polish government. After Gorchakov's death, the situation in Poland was to worsen. His successor, who could not cope with the new troubles, committed suicide.

In the South, the publication of a letter in the *Richmond Daily Whig* of June 5 had a triple irony behind it. Addressed "To the refugees in America from foreign lands," it was an appeal to foreigners to enlist in a special brigade of twenty companies which its writer was in the process of organizing for the Confederate Army at Richmond. The letter bore the signature "Caspar Tochman, Major of the Polish Army of 1831." The first irony was that the letter appeared almost in the wake of several Southern editorials which attacked the North for using "foreign troops." The second irony, which was probably at once apparent to most readers, was the fact that it had been written

by Tochman. In the 1940s and 1850s his activities had made him
well known in the eastern United States. From 1840 to 1844
alone, he had delivered over a hundred lectures on Poland's
plight before audiences which totaled over 250,000. His lecture,
"Poland, Russia and the Policy of the Latter Towards the United
States," was a scathing denunciation of the alleged friendship
of the czarist regime towards the American Republic and was
first published in 1844. The Polish-Slavonian Literary Society,
which he had helped found, included among its members such
prominent Americans as historian Jared Sparks, Harvard College
President Josiah Quincy, Albert Gallatin, Jefferson's Secretary of
the Treasury, and a young New York senator, William H. Seward.
Indeed, many Americans came to think of Tochman as an unofficial Polish ambassador to the United States.

While practicing law in Washington, Tochman became a
good friend of the then Secretary of War, Jefferson Davis. In
1852, he established residence in Virginia. When the Civil War
broke out, he openly espoused the Confederate cause (1)
because he feared "an amalgamation of the races," (2) because
he felt that the Federal Government was violating provisions of
the American Constitution regarding states' rights, and (3)
because he felt that his oath of citizenship obligated him to
be loyal above all to his home state. He gave these reasons in
his reply to a resolution in which he had been castigated by
former comrades-in-arms now belonging to the Polish Democratic Societies in France and England. The resolution demanded
an explanation of his motives for "deviating" from the Constitution and censured him for raising troops for the slaveholding
Confederates.[10] Here, then, was the third irony—and a double
one at that. The one person who, better than anyone else, could
have acted as a propagandist and spokesman for Poland among
Americans in the critical days to come, had deliberately chosen
the "wrong" side in their fratricidal struggle. His erstwhile colleagues, already stigmatized by some segments of the American
press as the Napoleonic agents stirring up trouble in Poland to
discredit the "Czar Liberator," were the very people who severely

brought him to task for betraying the Constitution of the United States!

New demonstrations and disturbances, the formation of two rival nationalist factions, the conservative gentry-controlled "Whites" and the revolutionary urban-centered "Reds," Wielopolski's vain maneuvers to stem the revolution, new repressions by Czarist officials, and many other significant developments in Poland, occurred without editorial notice in the press of Civil War America. The remainder of the story, which had begun with the Warsaw disturbances and was to be the prelude to a more important story—that of the January 1863 Insurrection— was not fully told to Americans; when many Americans thought about Poland and Russia it was Alexander's magnanimity and liberalism that would first come to mind.

The locale for the conclusion to the unfortunate prelude which has been sketched in the preceding pages, is the same as that of its opening: the American legation in St. Petersburg. The complex unfolding of events in Poland inspired one remarkable commentary on the part of Cassius Marcellus Clay. The commentary began as a complaint against the Northern journalists' "great ingratitude" towards Russia as allegedly manifested in their attacks on her "home policy." The attacks, Clay noted, were often "in juxtaposition with a faint acknowledgment of our gratitude for the friendly avowals which she has made before the world in our behalf." Then, specifically citing Poland as the matter of Russian "home policy" which the journalists unduly criticized, he let loose with the following "analysis":

The same causes which destroyed Polish Independence—the unbending bigotry of the Catholic clergy—impedes her progress now. I have carefully read all the *New Powers* with which the Emperor Alexander invested the Poles: and I am (radical though I be thought) fully convinced that they give as much self-government, as is consistent with the integrity of the Russian Empire: and amply sufficient for that discipline in the management of affairs, by whole masses, which is consistent with wholesome progress. But why are all these liberal advances of the Emperor rejected? Because the Polish people would have at last become Russianized and in consequence made part of the *Greek Church,* as fast as time and association could efficiently accomplish that purpose! Hence the opposition of the Catholic clergy: the closing of the churches and the delusion and revolt of the people! The same causes, which have kept the Spanish provinces in America from all stable progress, have kept up the disunity of Poland with the Russian Empire. And when our people are ready to join the Catholic propaganda, in putting down a liberal government in Mexico—in destroying all the fruits of the blood of liberals shed for 40 years—and in setting up a "conservative" Catholic King over the fallen Republic—then ought they also to denounce Russia for her Polish policy—and not till then.[11]

Most likely, American journalists were not aware of the unfounded indictment which Clay leveled at them. It was not the policy of the State Department to release the contents of diplomatic dispatches, and it was not likely that Secretary Seward would have permitted an unofficial leakage. The Secretary himself made no comments upon it beyond a routine acknowledgment. In all probability, he gave consideration to its source, and did not take it with any seriousness. (Clay had already gained notoriety among his colleagues as a "noisy jackass," and on several occasions he had carried his petty grievances over Seward's head directly to his "friend" Lincoln.) All this was fortunate. Clay's first vituperative remarks on Poland were safely confined to the precincts of the State Department and had no influence on American opinion. Nevertheless, they are included here because they make for a sad but appropriate *finis* to this prelude, and because they are indicative of further "analyses" to come from Clay when the Poles were involved in their insurrectionary struggle for freedom.[12]

CHAPTER II

1863: DIVIDED AMERICA
REACTS TO THE POLISH INSURRECTION

LIKE ITS unfortunate prelude, the story that followed also opened on a note of emancipation. The date was January 1, 1863. The emancipator was Abraham Lincoln. The emancipated were Negro slaves. Loudly greeted in the cities of the Union with cannon salutes and the pealing of church bells, Lincoln's Emancipation Proclamation was received with some editorial misgivings. And it was sadly ironical that several of the shortcomings which the editors immediately noted in the proclamation were very similar to shortcomings which they had overlooked almost two years previously in the Emancipation Decree of Czar Alexander II. Some noted that the proclamation was an extra-constitutional measure; that it was the act of a desperate administration to compensate psychologically for military failures which had plagued the North throughout the previous year.[1] In 1861, however, they had not noted that the Alexander's Decree also had a psychological-tactical basis that overshadowed its seeming magnanimity; that its aim was to stem peasant discontent and the growing influence of exiled revolutionaries, as well as to arouse peasant loyalty and play the lower classes against the powerful nobility, which constituted a threat to Alexander's power. Other editors correctly noted that emancipation was not abolition; that it freed slaves only in *certain* states or parts of states that the Union armies occupied, or would occupy in the future; that it did not put an end to slavery in the few loyal

41

"border" states; and that the Lincoln administration's plan for emancipation in those states rested on the principle of compensation to the slave owners for loss of property.[2] In 1861, the very same editors chose to ignore or to minimize the fact that the "Czar Liberator" intended to reimburse his nobles for the loss of their serfs; they also ignored or minimized the much more unfortunate fact that the vaunted decree did not free *all* of the serfs in the Czarist realms, and that it did not apply to household serfs (i.e., those who did not work in the fields) nor to serfs in Poland.

On the other hand, the positive impact of the Emancipation Proclamation on distant public opinion was at least of the same magnitude as that of the Emancipation Decree. The decree had earned for Russia the sympathies of distant American liberals. The proclamation earned for the United States the sympathies of distant European liberals, among them Giuseppe Garibaldi, Victor Hugo, and the exiled Alexander Herzen. Unlike many of their American counterparts, the European liberals were staunch supporters of Polish independence.[3]

Although one of the primary reasons for the promulgation of the Emancipation Proclamation was to change the Civil War from an almost meaningless sectional struggle of attrition to a quasi-religious crusade against slavery, its initial impact on the military front was slight. The year began with relatively minor and costly Northern victories, mainly in Tennessee. But most of the Union troops, uniformly in low spirits, were in winter quarters along the Rappahannock and Potomac Rivers, recovering from the severe defeats inflicted upon them the previous summer and fall by outnumbered but stubborn Confederates. The ultimate victory might still have gone to the Confederacy. Napoleon could still afford to entertain ideas of leading a possible European intervention. The South could still hope for the moral victory that European recognition would constitute. These crucial matters, in addition to another matter under heated discussion in the halls of Congress—that of military conscription—provided overworked editors with a surfeit of material for their comments.

Coincidentally, another conscription was already being carried out. That conscription took place in virtually forgotten Poland. At first glance, it would hardly provide much grist for the busy editorial mill, especially when first reports calmly indicated that the conscription had "passed off without disturbance." Yet, within a few weeks the Polish conscription generated a series of cataclysmic events, news of which rippled across the Atlantic and was translated into printed words. In the process, the original emotional import of the events was thoroughly diluted. Nevertheless, the words were to be seen through eyes that also smarted from the fire fueled by a burning domestic issue—the Civil War—and when the Polish situation came to be interpreted editorially by American journalists, their personal and immediate feelings manifested themselves in their interpretations.

The first reports of the new troubles in Poland reached the United States on February 13. Several foreign newspapers dating back to January 28 arrived on that day on the *Etna,* a steamer which had completed a twelve-day crossing from Liverpool to New York, and on February 14 the reports appeared in the foreign news columns of journals in New York, Philadelphia, Washington, and Boston. In most captions, the word "insurrection" appeared. This made it immediately apparent to readers that the events detailed in the few paragraphs beneath were not merely temporary outbreaks of national passion and similar to those that had occurred two years previously, but that they were indeed part of a full-scale struggle for independence, perhaps on the scale of the events of 1831.

The opening sentences of the various accounts noted that the military conscription in Poland, which had began in mid-January, had precipitated general uprisings. Most of the reports did not go into further detail and, therefore, did not indicate that the conscription had been applied almost exclusively to city youths and thus was a stratagem adopted by the shaky Wielopolski regime and the Czarist authorities for the purpose of removing the most probable supporters of the growing "Red" conspiracy from the urban centers harboring them. Little mention was made of the manner in which the conscription had been carried out: how the young Poles had been awakened at gunpoint in the middle of the night, had been rounded up in groups by the gendarmerie and carted off to military garrisons. Yet, every account seemed to emphasize the fact that on the night of January 22 many Russian soldiers, while asleep in their billets, had been killed by outraged Poles, and almost every account used the words "a second St. Bartholomew's massacre" to describe the event. In addition, many of the papers noted that peasants and large landowners were not involved in the insurrection which immediately ensued.[4]

In a majority of America's east-coast journals this first news item from Poland was followed by the full text of a speech which Alexander had made to his officers on the St. Petersburg parade grounds on January 25. In it he had made the forgiving statement, "Even in the presence of these atrocities I will not accuse the Polish nation." None, however, printed the text of the Manifesto of January 22 which had been issued by the initiating force behind the insurrection, the secret National Government of Poland. This document called the people to arms, promised peasants freedom from feudal obligations to their landlords, offered them land, and proclaimed "all sons of Poland without regard to religious belief or birth, status of origin, free citizens of the nation."

In some instances, the American newspapers gave credit to the European journals which they had utilized as sources for their first accounts of the outbreak of the Polish January Insurrection. The sources included the German *Breslauer Zeitung*, the Austrian *Wiener Presse*, the English London *Times* and *Daily News*. Most often, however, credit was given to the *Journal de St. Petersbourg*, the mouthpiece of the czarist regime; that newspaper was by then pro-Union to the point of suppressing reports of Northern defeats, as well as pro-Emancipation Proclamation to the point of devoting an entire page to its praise. And the most unfortunate term, "a second St. Bartholomew's massacre," it turned out, had been coined in St. Petersburg by the editor of the *Journal*.

Almost a week elapsed before the Polish side of the story made its first appearance in the American press. This time, credit was given mainly to French and Belgian journals that were usually inimical to the Union cause, and whose editors were among the foremost proponents of European mediation in the Civil War under Napoleon's auspices.[5]

As could be expected, very few of the American journals reacted to the news from Poland with immediate editorial comments. One significant exception was the *New York Tribune*. The outspoken Horace Greeley ran his first editorial on the subject in mid-February along with his first news account of the January Insurrection. Writing with dramatic flair, reminiscent of his famous plea for emancipation ("The Prayer of Twenty Millions" editorial of August 20, 1862), he began with the cry, "Unhappy Poland is once more in arms against its oppressors."[6] In stirring language he elaborated on the details of the struggle as they had appeared in the news columns, and reminded his readers that it was a revolutionary movement led by an old revolutionary veteran, General Mieroslawski.[7]

However, the editorial ended on a note of discouragement, very much like the 1861 editorials dealing with the Warsaw disturbances. Greeley concluded:

Great and universal as the sympathy of the civilized world with the wrongs inflicted upon unhappy Poland is, the recent insurrection will be almost unanimously regretted. Under the actual circumstances there is little, if any, hope of success. Had peace been maintained, it is certain that the Polish nation would have made immense progress, not only in material prosperity, but also toward the recovery of its independence. The Austrian province of Galicia had already a Polish Provisional Diet, which might have become an important center for the political aspirations of the entire nation. All Europe has so far advanced in civilization that the extermination of nationalities, especially if they are so powerful as the Poles, is now counted among the impossibilities. Poland of whose existence as a nation even the noble Kosciusko despaired, had become sure of a resurrection. This new outbreak, we greatly fear, will postpone the realization of the ardent national wish.[8]

Obviously, Greeley's old sympathies towards the "Czar Liberator" had manifested themselves anew. The man who had prodded the Lincoln administration to take immediate military action and who had been the first to take up the battle cry "Forward to Richmond!"[9] could only hope that the despairing population of Russian Poland would wait for its freedom to come by a process of evolution—of constitutional development forced by the slow hand of a "liberal" autocrat and his less "liberal" underlings.

The same day, Joseph Beach, editor of the more moderate *New York Sun,* also printed an editorial. It was more brief and less dramatic than Greeley's, but it also held out more sympathy for the Poles who had been "stung to madness by a forced military conscription which penetrated families and seized husbands, sons and brothers at the discretion of the police, turned upon their oppressors and killed them."[10] But again, there was a note of pessimism. Beach held that the insurrectionary movement was "destitute of order and unity of action" and expressed his belief that "the result may be easily anticipated, though it is doubtful whether it has been suppressed as easily as the Russians represent."[11] In his concluding sentences, he allowed himself some wishful thinking, and, probably for the first time, the events in Poland and the American Civil War were linked in an optimistic context:

The Poles who fled to the woods may form the nucleus of armies destined to shatter Russia and all the thrones of Europe. If the fatal phrase "order reigns in Warsaw" fails in its full significance, we may reasonably hope that the news of Poland being in arms may arouse once more the Democracies of Europe to a diversion in favor of that country and of ours.[12]

The calmer pro-Lincoln *New York Times* seconded the feelings of the *Sun* editorial, though with somewhat less enthusiasm. Editor Raymond presented a lengthier analysis of the background and causes of the troubles in Poland and pronounced the movement a "genuine national uprising provoked by an unjust conscription," and not as the Russian authorities would have the world believe, a "St. Bartholomew's Day, a devil's holiday staged by young hotheads whose object was the division of the nation's lands."[13] Raymond also considered the insurrection in connection with the Civil War. However, in his conclusion there was skepticism rather than hope. He contemplated and reflected on the possibility of the insurrection spreading into Austrian and Prussian Poland as well as to Hungary, something which he believed, would make for "a European complication of the first order."[14] Such a revolution, he deduced, would also reopen the Eastern Question and "the still unsettled condition of Italy" and would "supply the French Emperor with a problem so knotty that it would leave him little time and less heart for the cortemplation of *our* troubles here, and would probably consign his mediation schemes to one of the highest pigeon-holes in the Cabinet."[15] In his final sentence he cautioned: "But we must not flatter ourselves that he will meddle with Polish affairs unless they are forced upon him."[16]

Two days later, the Philadelphia *North American and United States Gazette,* a journal which was highly respected for its thorough coverage and analysis of the news and was widely read by educated and mercantile elements throughout the United States,[17] printed an editorial entitled "The Outbreak in Poland," which was considerably longer and more perspicacious than any of the editorials published in the New York papers. In its opening passage the writer groaned at noting that the world had "been pained once more by one of those periodical but futile insurrections which cause so much misery to unhappy Poland." The editorial castigated the Poles for not having learned "wisdom from adversity" and for operating under delusions that the free nations of the world would sympathize with them and "one day or another interfere in their behalf." This "visionary faith" plus "a furious hatred of everything Russian," it stated, was all that animated Polish revolutionaries and made them "plunge madly into war, without the least reflection as to the probable consequences." By doing so, it further commented, they run contrary to the times, for "the civilized world has come to the conclusion that making war without a reasonable prospect of success is a crime, and what is worse . . . a blunder."

The *Gazette* editorial also gave a backhanded compliment to the Russians for not exterminating the Poles, "though they long have had it in their power to do so." It implied that the South would also lay down arms when it found no hope for success, even though Southerners talked loudly about resistance to the death. Finally, it turned again to the Poles and advised them as follows:

Let the Poles then, learn wisdom in time and endeavor to make the best of the hard lot they are called upon to endure. Mere wanton, reckless rushing to arms will only heap disasters upon them. It is not that we do not sympathize with them, nor wish they had another chance of becoming a nation, and of making a better use of their independence than they did when they were one. But it is not a light matter to disturb the peace of the world; still less is it right to do so without any prospect of benefit.[18]

Thus, the editorial writer, who might have been the editor himself,[19] began by making his sympathy give way to his sense of practicality, and as he brought his lengthy first paragraph to a close, he even made the Poles the villains in their own tragedy. Confident—perhaps overconfident—of an ultimate Union victory, he could readily condemn the Poles, and, by parallel implication, the Union's adversaries, for being foolhardy enough to be potential losers! His strong criticisms of Polish romantic quixotism were a new extension of criticisms which American editors had made as far back as 1831 and were to make over and over again in years to come. American practicality never seemed compatible with Polish romanticism, even when national freedom was a goal of the romantics. And he was not the first, nor the last, American journalist to suggest that the political sins of egoistic Polish fathers were being visited upon their oppressed children, even though such sins had been committed nearly a century before. Both of these lines of negative reasoning were to be frequently employed by the press in Civil War America.

The second paragraph of the *Gazette's* analysis was in marked contrast to the first. "On the other hand," it began, "we must say that the Russian government appears to be actuated by unusual animosity towards the Poles."[20] It elaborated on this new theme by putting most of the blame for the outbreak of the insurrection on the shoulders of the Russian viceroy, Grand Duke Constantine, "to whom the government of Poland had been entrusted." But it did not completely exonerate Alexander, who, though good "in many aspects" could "not overcome the annoyance he experienced during his visit to Warsaw [in 1862] when the Polish nobility avoided his presence as much as possible, and when they came into it, presented daring demands for liberty." Constantine was blamed for being "especially obnoxious to the charge of goading the Poles to revolt, by extreme harshness in his administration" and for being behind the enactment of the "terrible" conscription law.[21]

Further on, the editorial writer pointed out that the conscription had "been held in *terrorum* over the heads of the unhappy people for more than six months." He noted that a recruitment which had not been applied in Poland since the time of Nicholas I, had been reestablished by Constantine "in a novel and fearful manner" (i.e., he drafted recruits exclusively from Poland's urban areas). "Perhaps the object of this is to civilize the semi-barbarous portions of the Empire," he wavered in making a sarcastic excuse, to which he added: "It may be a cunning policy, but it is decidedly a cruel, and we should think, an unsafe one. In the event of a foreign war, the Polish conscripts will assuredly desert to the enemy; and in time of peace they will spread dissatisfaction with the government all over the districts where they may be quartered."[22] The writer then went into the details of the "cruel proceedings" which had brought on the insurrection, quoting entire passages from letters written by the Warsaw correspondent of the London *Times*: "At midnight police agents and soldiers commenced the work" . . . "In the absence of the young man, his parents were seized as guarantees for his appearance" . . . "In the first haul, which lasted until nine o'clock in the morning, twenty-five hundred men were carried off" . . . "The conscripts were seized . . . and locked up in the citadel" . . . "The anguish of wives and mothers surrounding the prisons, bewailing the loss of their husbands and sons. . . ."[23] Readers could easily draw their own inferences from the details, and could come to their own conclusions as to whether the desperate Poles could really have continued to "make the best of the hard lot" they were "called upon to endure."

Finally, after stating that many of the hunted youths had taken to hiding and fighting in the woods, that they apparently had received no aid from the peasants, that the nobility did not have time "to turn out and assume the lead," he noted that the Russian authorities had "acted with energy and cruelty," and asked bluntly:

But what is to be the end of all this? Does the Emperor suppose that by cruelty he will convert the Poles into loyal subjects? He may provoke revolt after revolt, and still crush the insurgents as fast as they may rise up, but he will not derive the more benefit from the oppressed kingdom. Unless Poland be conciliated, the agitation must go on, year after year, until it brings some calamity on the Russian Empire. One revolt after another may be put down, but sooner or later some conjecture will come wherein Europe will be found arrayed against Russia, and then the hostility of Poland will be fatal to its sovereign. Why should not the Emperor conciliate his unhappy appanage instead of driving it to the confines of madness? We are the more induced to ask this question as it appears that Alexander II is acting in opposition to the advice of his most enlightened counsellors. [24]

The last few sentences of the editorial discussed the steps which the writer thought the Russian government would have to take in order to carry out the "pacification" of Poland. The first, he surmised, would be the removal of the Grand Duke from his post as viceroy in Poland; the second would be "to find scope for the ambition of the nobility, the priesthood, and the landed proprietors, who are the most steady enemies of Russian despotism." [25] For the latter step he saw only one possible alternative— extermination.

The closing words of the editorial's concluding paragraph formed a never-to-be-fulfilled prophetic coda:

. . . The Sarmatian and Slavonian races will one day form a dominion extending from the Balkan mountains to the Baltic and from the Vistula to the Theiss, and on the ruins of the old Turkish Empire will rise a Christian power which will limit the spheres of usefulness and the capacity for evil of the Czars of ancient Muscovy. . . .[26]

And like a drawn-out musical symphony the editorial ended on its opening theme. Its final words advised: "Poland must wait for that consummation."[72]

Within a fortnight after the Northern journals had made their dire pronouncements about the futility of the insurrection, they printed editorials written in a slightly more hopeful vain. In several instances, the text of the Polish January 22 Manifesto appeared alongside their new comments. The mainstay of their clouded optimism was a series of reports that the Polish insurgents had given a good account of themselves in their first engagement with the Russians. This appeared all the more amazing to them because the Central National Committee, the "Secret National Government" which had issued the call to arms, had been ill-prepared. It had a badly equipped fighting force which, at best, might have totaled 10,000 men, while its Russian adversaries had 100,000 first-line troops. The Committee's funds were meager, its leadership was confused, and it had no strong assurance of popular support, especially among the long-neglected peasantry.

On the same day, four of New York's leading dailies, the *Sun*, the *Herald*, the *Tribune*, and the ultraconservative *Journal of Commerce*, carried editorials which informed their readers that the Polish revolutionary movement was spreading. The *Sun* and the *Herald* reiterated their earlier hopes that the European powers would become so involved with the Polish question that they would abandon all thought of intervention in the Civil War. Their hopes were prompted by a degree of justifiable anxiety. Their news columns noted that Napoleon's emissaries were at the moment trying to sell England and Russia on the idea of mediation to stop the American war, while England's Foreign Minister, Earl Russell had expressed the view that his government would wait until spring to see what developments would occur in the military sphere.[28]

The *Journal's* editor, David Stone, exercised a bit of mental fence-straddling. He had words of sympathy for the insurgents and their cause, but in the very same paragraphs he noted that Russia had kept aloof from Napoleon's mediation scheme, and also included words of gratitude for the friendship which she had manifested towards the isolated Union. Finally, he expressed a wish that the Russian government would enact administrative reforms as it had enacted economic reforms; unless further reforms were carried out in such parts of the empire as the Kingdom of Poland, "the peace of the whole continent of Europe will always be endangered."[29]

On the last day of February, the *North American and United States Gazette* voiced ideas similar to the comments made by the journals in New York, but with some unique variations. Its second page contained another long analysis, which opened with the words, "Nothing has taken the civilized world more completely by surprise than the great insurrection in Poland. . ."[30] After telling how the warfare in Russian Poland had spread into "whole provinces of the country," it noted that there were large concentrations of Prussian troops in areas near the border, and discussed the possibility of Austria becoming involved in collusion with France, on the side of the insurgents. The motive for such a move, it suggested, would be to weaken Russia and to allow Austria to make up "somewhere" for the territory that she had lost in Italy during the Sardinian War of 1859. "It is essential to the success of the scheme of French military ascendancy," it commented tartly, "that the immense power of Russia should be crippled." It contended that the Crimean War had been undertaken for that purpose but had succeeded only partially in accomplishing it, and "this Polish insurrection looks very much like a new effort in the same direction." Bluntly, it added, "We suspect that French agents and money were at the bottom of it."[31]

Since Napoleon was the chief potential European enemy of the Union, a statement such as this could hardly have made new friends for the Polish insurgents among the *Gazette's* scattered readers. However, the editorial writer dutifully added that distance and "very imperfect information" made it impossible to form any judgment as to the prospects for the continuance of the revolutionary movement. "Alone the insurgents can hardly hope for success," he concluded, "but if Austria or France should help them, the war would soon assume gigantic proportions in which case France would have to abandon her Mexican enterprise."[32] Moreover, he hopefully noted, "Should the European affairs continue to become complicated, as they have of late, foreign intervention in our own civil war will not only become improbable, but impossible."[33]

In the northernmost metropolis of the Union, the *Boston Daily Courier* related the Polish Insurrection to the Civil War in language that was saturated with irony. An editorial of February 28 claimed that if a "rebellion" had broken out in Poland three years ago,

. . . it would have made no little impression on the people of this country, and called forth strong and general expressions of sympathy. We should have had, very likely, public meetings, at which a good deal of schoolboy declamation would have been ventilated. Orators would have talked of Sarmatia and John Sobieski and Kosciusko, and quoted largely from the "Pleasures of Hope." The Czar of Russia would have been denounced in good set terms. Poetry would have been written, or at least that which goodnatured persons are content to call poetry. Perhaps a flag would have been presented by somebody to somebody. But now a change has come over the spirit of our People.

In the same tone it pointed out that the price of cotton had since then gone up at the same rate that the price of rebellion had gone down, and that "new importations" of rebellion "are received with as much disgust as a cargo of codfish in a catholic [*sic*] port at the end of a rigorous Lent." It concluded that although it was "a pretty sight" to see neighbors' houses aflame with rebellion, an American homestead afire from the same cause was no longer picturesque. "Three years ago," its opening paragraph concluded, "a rebel, as such, was a fine fellow; now he is a monster, with no rights at all except the right to be hanged."[34]

Such bitterness continued through two more paragraphs, both of which were peppered with sarcasm against foreign revolutionaries who had emigrated to the United States. "Three years ago," it was noted in the second paragraph, "every man who undertook to overthrow an established government became at once, and for that sole fact, entitled to our sympathy and admiration: but now, if a play were composed at the Boston Theater by a company composed of rebel exiles—every one with ten consonants in his name—we fear that there would not be enough [*sic*] in the house to pay the expenses." [35]

The final paragraph talked of the school, its stern teacher being named experience, which Americans had been attending since 1861. There they had learned that the Southern rebellion might not be the first uprising in which the rebels were wrong. The young men to be entrusted with the future destiny of America, it commented hopefully, might receive an "abiding impression" from the lessons to be drawn from the Civil War. "We trust," it concluded, "that they will be made to feel how solemn and tremendous is the responsibility under which men are acting when they set the ball of revolution in movement, and that a man may be a conservative without having either a bad heart or a small mind." Its last words were particularly strong: "We trust that the time will come when a foreigner arriving among us will be required to show some other passport to our favor and confidence than the fact that he has tried to overthrow the government under which he was born, and miserably failed in the attempt." [36]

In histories of journalism the *Courier* is classified as belonging to the traitorous Copperhead press. [37] Its editor and owner, George Lunt, tended to sympathize more openly with the Confederate cause as the war continued. Since government sedition laws and threats of mob attack prevented open expression of such sympathy, he, like others of his ilk, "became less bold and more crafty." [38] Lunt operated under the cover of conservatism and tended to use double-barreled irony. Using such irony as a veil, he took every opportunity to attack the Lincoln administration's conduct of the war. One of his favorite targets was Secretary of State Seward and Seward's diplomats, particularly Cassius Clay. A flagrant example was the paper's January 24 edition in which an editorial referred to Clay as a "tongue-ruffian" for suggesting that the United States seize Canada and stir up revolts in Ireland and India to prevent British intervention in the Civil War. In light of such facts, it is understandable why the *Courier* lashed out against rebellion in such strong language. The February 28 editiorial had been written with tongue very much in cheek. A clue to this might have been found in the ironic ending of the first paragraph: "Three years ago, a rebel as such, was a fine fellow; now he is a monster, with no rights at all except the right to be hanged."

A *Courier* editorial reviewing European diplomacy and printed less than a month later, disguised its position much less. While doubting that the insurrection would affect the course of the Civil War, it noted that:

One thing we hope this attempt of a gallant people to achieve their independence will effect in this country; that is to silence forever the tyrant's doctrine that rebels have no rights. Rebels are rebels, whether their cause be right or wrong. They, and they alone, must judge whether it justifies resort to arms, and abide the result. The rebellion in the South must be treated in the same manner, and the laws applicable to it are the same as if it had sprang up in Poland, Hungary, Venice, Ireland or Canada.[39]

Making a direct reference to the insurrection, the same editorial voiced optimism in regard to the Polish insurgents' chances. "If they be left alone," it stated, "we by no means despair of the success of the Poles. Russia, to-day, is not the Russia of 1830. The Crimean War exposed her to many weaknesses. . . ."[40] Among the chief weaknesses alluded to was the alienation of the nobles brought on by Alexander's liberation of the serfs. This, too, might have been a covert Copperhead remark; the *Courier* opposed *slave* emancipation and made frequent derogatory references to "nigger" troops in the Union armies and printed derogatory "nigger" dialogues exaggerating the effects of the emancipation.[41]

When Copperhead editors compared the Polish Insurrection and the American Civil War, they would stress the subject of conscription. They occasionally pronounced the insurrection a revolution against conscription, and referred to it frequently in their editorials in opposition to the draft that was about to go into effect in the North. Two items from an arch-Copperhead weekly, Samuel Medary's *Crisis*, of Columbus, Ohio, illustrates their technique. The first item was extracted from another Copperhead paper, the *Chicago Times*, whose Washington correspondent wrote on February 15 that a member of Congress had remarked: "If the people of Warsaw are resisting the conscription, will not the people of America do the same? Are our people less free than the people of Poland? Or is the fate of Poland to become ours?"[42]

The second item was extracted by Medary from the *New York Express*, a paper described by Frank Luther Mott as being strongly Democratic but not disloyal.[43] It was an account of the outbreak of the Polish Insurrection, to which Medary added a conclusion that *all* conscriptions are odious unless "they touch the Popular heart, for Popular purposes, in a Popular war."[44]

What were Southern reactions to the first news of the Polish Insurrection? Through February and most of March there was nearly complete editorial silence in the South on this subject, and there was no speculation as to the effects of the insurrection on the Civil War. Leading Southern newspapers confined themselves to news reports of the events in Poland, the first such reports reaching the readers of Richmond's *Whig* and *Daily Examiner*. The latter sensationalized it as much as any foreign news could possibly be sensationalized in the Civil War era. It headlined the event in bold upper-case letters:

REVOLUTION IN POLAND—GENERAL UPRISING AND AT-TACK ON THE RUSSIAN TROOPS—THEY ARE STRANGLED IN THEIR BEDS AND SHOT DOWN IN THE STREETS—TER-RIBLE SCENES, &C.[45]

However, both journals gave credit to their source, which turned out to be the *New York Herald* of February 14 (ultimately, of course, the source was the notorious *Journal de St. Petersbourg*). The Charleston, South Carolina, papers did not print the news until the following week. The leading journal in that city, the *Mercury*, printed its first account on February 28, an account which was third or even fourth hand, since it had been taken from the *Richmond Whig*.

The *Whig* also included a rather brief editorial entitled "The Polish Revolution," which pertained less to the insurrection itself and more to what it saw as Northern hypocrisy. Its inspiration came from a speech made by New York Tammany politician John Van Buren, whom it termed "The Prince of political harlequins." Van Buren rejoiced over the possibility that the Polish struggle would divert Napoleon's attention from the Civil War. "It is a noteworthy sign of the times," the *Whig's* editorial writer observed, "that the subjects of Lincoln cannot rejoice over the effort of a long suffering and gallant race to free themselves from the fetters of usurping Despots on any other than the ignoble account that they (the subjects of Lincoln) may reap some incidental advantage from it." Had the Polish "revolution" occurred three years previously, he added, "all Yankeedom would have gone crazy in their admiration for the noble 'rebels' while curses mountain-high would have been heaped upon Russia." At the moment, however, they could not "anaethemize Russia without calling down imprecations on themselves"; they could not "applaud the intrepid and liberty loving Poles, without giving aid and comfort to the Southern 'rebels.'" [46]

Several weeks later, the *Daily Express*, published in Petersburg, Virginia, elaborated on the same theme and with more ironic sarcasm. "Before the war with the Confederate States began," it opened, "the intelligence of the uprising of a downtrodden and brave people like the Poles would have been hailed with acclamation by the American people": [47]

. . . The warmest sympathies would have been manifested for the insurgents—public meetings would have been held and the most patriotic speeches would have been the order of the day. Every encouragement would have been given to such a movement for the overthrow of despotic authority, and the most enthusiastic admiration would have been publicly expressed through the land for the patriotic spirit which exulted the Poles to rise in arms against a government which they hated. In no section of the late union would this feeling have been more actively and more warmly developed than in the Middle and Eastern States. Especially would it have blazed forth in the *New England States,* where European revolutions were considered as glorious popular outbreaks, tending to the subversion of tyranny and the promotion of the cause of free institutions. Had this Polish insurrection broken out two years and a half ago, every northern rostrum would have thundered with plaudits to the gallant Poles, and every victory which they would have achieved over the Russian forces would have awakened the most gratifying emotions in the popular bosom of Yankeedom.[48]

The editor of the *Express* had no doubts that the true sympathies of the people in the North were with the Poles. However, he saw two "potential reasons" that prevented them from "speaking a word in favor of the revolutionists on the Vistula, however deeply in their *hearts* they may feel for them in the fearful struggle into which they have rushed." First, he pointed out that the Russian Czar was the only friend that Lincoln had among Europe's crowned heads, "and as he is a very powerful Potentate, and as his government is, like the Lincoln one, a pure despotism, there cannot be but friendship between them." Therefore, he contended, Lincoln "and his subjects" would carefully avoid any act which "would give umbrage to the Czar and thereby hazard the loss of his good will." Second, he saw a "still stronger consideration" in the similarities between the Polish and the Southern struggles. He termed both "revolutions from a hated hateful Union . . . for the establishment of distinct and independent nationalities." And, he noted, since both Russia and the North were endeavoring to achieve the same end by the same means, Northerners could "show no sympathy for the Polish rebels without, in so doing, manifest it equally for the Southern rebels."[49]

The conclusion of the editorial was filled with taunts aimed directly at the Northern press. The editor stated that he looked in vain through Northern journals "for any amicable greetings to the Poles—any favorable notices of their cause—any satisfaction at their successes—any commendation of their purposes." All that he could find were discussions of the probable influences of the situation in Poland on the cabinets of France, England, Austria, and Sardinia. He stated that the Northern newspapers viewed the Polish Insurrection "altogether in its *exterior* aspects and not at all in the light of its intrinsic merits," and that even the New York *Herald,* "once so hot an advocate of the Poles and so outspoken about their wrongs, has not a nod of approbation for them now that they are striking for vengeance and liberty." The *Herald,* he pointed out to his readers after an exclamatory "Oh no!" was "content to calculate the chances of the insurrection so absorbing Louis Napoleon's attention as to prevent his pressing further any plan that he may have formed for mediation or other interference in the American war."[50]

In his neatly drawn analysis, the incensed editor of the *Express* gave little consideration himself to the "intrinsic merits" of the Polish struggle. Furthermore, he did not admit that the Confederacy also had reasons to view the insurrection in its "exterior aspects" and, perhaps, to even wish its being put down. Actually, the further intertwinement of the Polish question with European politics and diplomacy might have had adverse effects on the recognition of the Confederacy as well as on mediation and on Southern hopes for Napoleon's intervention in the Civil War on the side of the Confederacy. This was not overlooked by his colleague of the *Daily Richmond Examiner.* As the spring thaws began and full-scale warfare was about to resume on the Potomac, the *Examiner's* editor made a most heartening appraisal of the South's chances for military success. While he saw a diminution of hopes for French intervention in the Civil War, he advised his readers that the Polish Insurrection would give Napoleon an opportunity to "balance the power of Russia." On guard against Napoleon, Russia would avoid any form of involvement in the Civil War on the side of the North. To his thinking, the lifting of "the last shadows of intervention" meant a clear field of battle from which the South would emerge as the victor.[51]

The Richmond *Sentinel,* on the other hand, was so skeptical of the reports from Europe—which it extracted from Northern journals—that it added a critical bracketed note to items dealing with the initial Polish military successes and with Napoleon's temporary setbacks in Mexico. The note cautioned the readers that "U.S. newspapers, for obvious reasons are disposed to magnify" both events, and statements obtained from them should be received in the South "with proper allowance."[52]

At about the time the news from Poland reached the South, public sympathy there towards England was at its lowest. The papers began to print the correspondence between Earl Russell and Confederate Commissioner James Mason concerning both the Federal blockade of Southern ports and recognition of the Confederate government. Russell's response was not only negative but it was also stated in a supercilious manner. When the full text of the notes was finally published in the *Richmond Enquirer,* its editor took occasion to label Great Britain "next to the Yankees, our worst and deadliest enemy."[53] Southern ire was brought to its boiling point when the British consuls in Richmond and Mobile, whose exequaturs had been issued before the Civil War by the United States, were found to be actively engaged in securing exemptions for large numbers of Queen Victoria's subjects from service in the Confederate forces.[54] With all this to occupy editorial space, the Southern journals did not at first make any comparison between the diplomatic slights to their government and the possible diplomatic recognition of the Polish "rebel" government. Such comparison was to be made in a matter of weeks.

The growing Catholic press, almost entirely confined to the North, and almost completely in the control of Irish immigrants, reacted most positively to the news from Poland. Immediately, the New York *Irish-American* in a tersely phrased editorial wished Godspeed to the insurgents. Its accounts of various St. Patrick's Day banquets indicated that Poland was almost on a par with Ireland in its ability to evoke sentimental feelings. *The Pilot* of Boston printed a long and eloquent editorial entitled "The Uprising in Poland." It sanctioned revolution against tyranny as the employment by the Deity of human agents to act "in the amendment of His laws," because "it is on human agents they are broken."[55] Such quasi-theological justification of revolution was also a "cover" for justification of the Southern rebellion. (In subsequent issues, *The Pilot* expressed outrage against what it alleged to be desecrations of Catholic churches in New Orleans and Charleston by Union troops.)

In the closing sentences of *The Pilot's* editorial the Poles received a blessing while the Irish were verbally prodded. The Poles were justified in revolting, it concluded, for "Moral force is of no value with a despot." "Why do not the Irish imitate the Catholic Dalemations?" it asked; "Britain is worse than the Czars and Irish rights are as sacred before heaven as Polish rights."[56]

And in the same city, *The Liberator,* the leading organ of the abolitionists, maintained complete editorial silence on Poland. Its opinions were confined to the Emancipation Proclamation and were hardly concerned with anything else, even if that anything else was associated with the Civil War.

CHAPTER III

AMERICAN OPINION TAKES SIDES

AS SHOWN in the preceding chapter, American editorials began to express cautious sympathy for the Polish insurgents after the writers of such editorials had become sufficiently convinced that the January Insurrection was actually taking hold throughout Russian Poland and that it was assuming the character of a genuine revolutionary movement. Since they tended to be influenced by the sad precedents set by the failure of the November Insurrection and by more recent Polish history, their caution was somewhat intensified and their sympathies were apt to waver. Therefore, any events that occurred abroad or at home, and that had an intrinsic, extrinsic, even a dubious, connection with the insurrection's outcome, would show on the barometer of opinion. The editorial writers would either stimulate such opinion in a sympathetic direction or prevent it from taking any direction at all.

Several of the stimulating or inhibiting editorials followed each other in a rapid and confused succession in the very first months of the insurrection. In fact, the pro-Polish stance taken by most of the papers in early and mid-March was reinforced to a significant degree by the sensational nature of some of the first Polish victories. Most sensational to the American press was the battle of Wachock. Around this small town near Kielce, a force of about a thousand insurgents, which soon grew to three thousand, withstood a two-pronged assault by a much larger Russian force and held out until it was victorious. Wachock, misspelled in many ways, won an honorable place in the columns of American newspapers. Occasionally, that place was in close proximity to the name of a Mississippi town—Vicksburg—the scene of a Northern victory and a long siege just about to commence at that time.

The commander of the Polish insurgents at Wachock, General Marian Langiewicz, a forty-five-year-old veteran of Garibaldi's campaign in Italy, became the heroic subject of several one-paragraph biographies, as did the commander of the Federal troops around Vicksburg, a forty-one-year-old veteran of the Mexican War, General Ulysses Grant. But the biographies of the former had one colorful element which those of the latter lacked. Langiewicz' aide-de-camp was a woman![1]

A second stimulant of pro-Polish sympathies in American editorial circles stemmed from the promulgation of the notorious Alvensleben Convention. The convention, an agreement signed between Russia and Prussia, allowed Russian troops and agents to cross freely into Prussian Poland in pursuit of fugitive insurgents. Its announcement on February 8 brought liberal tempers in Western Europe to a feverish pitch. Rumors of the convention trickled into the United States via England from about mid-February, but they were not strong enough to merit editorial notice. When official confirmation finally reached America, March was on the threshold of its second week.

Several American editors were immediately convinced that the Alvensleben Convention definitely moved the Polish question from the limited realm of Russia's domestic affairs to the sphere of international affairs. Early in March, the editor of the New York *World*, in an editorial entitled "The Polish Question," noted that the stir created by Poland, "the Niobe of nations," would result in Russia's isolation from the rest of Europe and the Prussian government's isolation from "the liberal sentiment of Germany."[2] There was a note of regret in the statement that the peaceful status quo of Europe was about to be disturbed, but the statements which followed might well have been written with a sigh of relief:

So dangerous and delicate it is, not only in what it exacts but in what it involves, that its consideration and manipulation must arrest, if they do not for a long time to come suspend, any intended action of the great Powers in regard to affairs in our country; and it is very far from impossible that the tyranny of a Russian viceroy and the dogged incapacity of a Prussian king, may contribute very seriously to the defeat and overthrow of the great conspiracy against the future of the American people with which we ourselves are now contending by saving us from the vast and definite complications of a powerful European intervention in America.[3]

Ten days later another editorial in the *World*, entitled "Prussia and Poland," expressed almost diametrically opposed sentiments. It hypothesized apprehensively that the convention would be countered by an Anglo-French alliance, and such an alliance would give the friendless Napoleon sufficient confidence to proceed with his scheme for "mediation" in the Civil War. It also gave vent to the same kind of critical impatience with Russia as American editors had once exclusively reserved for the Poles when their manifestations of discontent also had threatened the peaceful European status quo. It accused the Russian government of being shortsighted in its past policy towards Poland and for allowing its own internal problem to become an international affair.[4]

Other New York journals preferred to maintain an optimistic outlook, at least as far as America's prospects were concerned, and to reserve all their pessimism for the Polish insurgents, The *Times* commented that the convention might bring Napoleon into a war over Poland, not for altruistic reasons but rather with the expectation that a victory over Prussia would gain him coveted territory on the west bank of the Rhine. Such a war, the *Times* believed, would force Napoleon to limit his activities to the European continent and to cease his pressure on Mexico. It also noted that even if the recent events were not to result in a European war, they would "give his restless mind work" and leave it no time for "unhealthy broodings over American affairs."[5] Less than a week later the *Times* took an even stronger tack when it commented:

This insurrection probably wards off all danger of foreign intervention in our affairs. Whatever Napoleon may have *wished to* do on this side of the Atlantic and whatever he might have tried to do under other circumstances, he will probably be compelled to look out mainly for his own security. An attempt to crush liberty and establish monarchy in Mexico and to overthrow the Republic of the United States and establish a slave-holding despotism on its ruins will be rather more than he can manage while the sounds of a Polish rebellion are echoing in the ears of the French nation. His philanthropic purposes on this continent must be postponed. The grand schemes disclosed in his letter to General Forey must be deferred. He will have to avail himself of some other opportunity to check the progress of the United States and to reassert the supremacy of the Latin races in America.[6]

An editorial in the *Herald*, entitled "Complications Produced by the Polish Revolution," treated the news of the Alvensleben Convention from still another optimistic angle. First, it noted that the Polish struggle had aroused the *people* of France and England to such an extent that pressure would be put on the governments of the two powers to take action on behalf of the Poles. Second, it saw a very positive connection between the Polish and American "insurrections" and concluded:

To us the Polish insurrection is fraught with immense importance. It puts an end to all probability of forcible intervention by any European power, and thus brings home to the rebels the fact that alone and unaided they must face the overwhelming power and resources of our government. . . . Thus, as it were by providential retribution, a truly wronged and tyrannized nation, rising to break its fetters, by that very action defeats the hopes of a rebellious horde which has wickedly endeavored to overthrow the most free and enlightened government with which a people were ever blessed.[7]

Similar opinions were expressed by the *Herald* a week later in an editorial captioned "Important Results of the Polish Insurrection." It voiced a very strong belief that the initial successes of the Polish insurgents and the popular sympathies for Poland evoked by the Alvensleben Convention were acting together to force Napoleon immediately to take his stand "on the side of the despots or of the people."[8] It concluded that he would probably choose the latter alternative, in order to ally himself with a popular cause and thus "wipe out some of the odium of the Mexican venture" and also because of his fear that if he associated himself with despots he would soon be contending with another revolution in France.

The *Herald's* editorial writer held out very little hope that England would be involved on behalf of the Poles, except, perhaps, in the diplomatic sphere. However, he did not entirely exclude the possibility that future events might "force" that power to align itself with France and take some drastic action which would eventually involve almost all of Europe in a war, and would be of "momentous" importance to the United States in so far as an intervention was concerned. A few days later, the *Herald* was to project its wishful thinking to such an extreme that it saw the French *advance* on Puebla in Mexico as a preliminary step to Napoleon's *withdrawal* from North America.[9]

In Philadelphia, the customary eloquence of the venerable *North American and United States Gazette* was given full scope when it analyzed the new developments. It ran three editorials, very close in time, to keep up with its New York contemporaries. The first, entitled "France and Poland," reviewed France's past policies in regard to Poland. While it excused the revolution-threatened *ancien régime* of Louis XVI for not having acted to prevent the dismemberment of Poland in the 1790s, it attacked Napoleon I for not restoring her independence and for turning his back on the Poles in order to curry favor with his erstwhile ally, Alexander I. Hypercritically, it noted that France had refrained from action in 1830 and 1831 when Poland had been involved in revolution, but she had helped Spain, Portugal, and Belgium in their revolutionary struggles. In his brief comment on the latest situation, the editorialist put forth two interesting desiderata which he evidently considered to be interrelated:

> Let us hope he [i.e., Napoleon III] will actively "intervene" in behalf of Poland. Nothing would do immortal honor to France more than the liberation of that heroic nation; and we should not object to the "rectification" of the Rhine frontiers as price of it.[10]

The second editorial speculated about intervention. Its title, "The Polish Trouble and Its Interest for Us," well indicated its thesis. It began in a self-righteous vein and castigated some of "the over quick journals of New York and other cities" for minimizing the insurrection "in their usual summary style," while it boasted that the *Gazette* immediately had foreseen its "vast consequence" in having "relieved" the Union of an "impending" intervention. "We could not help feeling amused," its opening paragraph concluded, "at the manner in which these shortsighted journals at first denounced all efforts of Americans to sympathize with the unfortunate Poles."[11]

In its second paragraph, the *Gazette* editorial expressed satisfaction that Northern newspaper writers were at last realizing that the safety of the Union depended not upon any sentiment of justice or honor on the part of European nations but rather upon whether those nations had their hands full with their own troubles or were at liberty to interfere in American affairs. Since the beginning of the war, it concluded with certainty, it had been apparent "that the monarchies of Europe regard the great republic with a jealous eye, and would rejoice at any event which would dismember our territories or humble our power." That Russia was no exception, it added with blunt finality, could be gathered from her reply to a joint mediation proposal which Napoleon had submitted to his European neighbors in 1862.[12]

The Russian reply to Napoleon's proposal was no secret to American newspaper readers. It had been widely published, and even a layman might have detected that the Russian attitude towards the United States was based on diplomatic expediency rather than altruism, and that the reply left a neat opening for Russia's participation in a possible future mediation scheme.[13] However, with the sole exception of the *Gazette*, the Northern press preferred to delude itself further by stressing Russia's alleged friendship. The delusion was maintained at a cost which was often paid in the currency of American sympathy towards the Poles. Was the currency worth anything? The next two paragraphs of the *Gazette* editorial seemed to give a good answer:

The natural sympathies of humanity are with the struggling Poles. As we have no interest in maintaining the thing called the European balance of power, we are perfectly free to give at least the expression of our sympathy to the poor Poles. When Mexico was so direfully threatened by the European allies, it was deemed very dangerous for us to raise our voices against it. We did so, however, and the expression of our people has been of great value in encouraging the Mexicans in their unequal conflict. Instead of our running any risk with France by this course, we have assisted the Mexicans to prevent all possibility of French intervention in our struggle.

So it is with this Polish question. It is to our interest that this insurrection should become as formidable as possible. Russia, Austria, Prussia, France and England cannot stir to molest us while this contingency threatens a general European war. So, far from thinking the rebellion abortive, we are inclined to regard it as much more auspicious than any popular rising of late years in Europe. It appears to be based on a feeling of desperation which does not admit of submission unless in the event of absolute subjugation, of which there is no present prospect, and the National Committee, well knowing the awful fate that awaits them in case of failure, are making efforts so comprehensive, so sagacious and so determined, that we think they may succeed.[14]

The remainder of the editorial concerned itself with the Polish situation per se. From it, readers might have gathered why the *Gazette* was so optimistic: It had a profound but somewhat naíve confidence in the Polish leadership, particularly in Generals Klapka and Dembinski, both of whom had made their mark during the 1848 Hungarian Revolution. This optimism was further strengthened by the fact that the insurgents had "got rid by suicide of a leader, Gurowski, who was believed to have been insane, and was evidently incompetent."[15] In its final sentence, the editorial noted an awareness of Prussian involvement on the side of Russia, but wrongly stated that Prussian troops had "entered Poland to assist the Russians." Its sole comment in regard to this aspect of events was merely a wishful "there are some things which the greatest military Power cannot achieve, and we hope, as we believe, that the crushing of Poland is one of them."[16]

The third and final editorial in the *Gazette's* series, which was headed "The Aspect of Europe," elaborated in more detail on the

Alvensleben Convention and speculated about its possible ramifications. It began by telling readers that a critical period had begun in the history of Europe, that "it will be the mere turn of a straw that shall decide whether there will be a universal war or a prolonged peace," and that "the spark which now threatens to fire the train is the insurrection in Poland."[17] Its tone turned very pessimistic as it expressed fears that without outside aid the Poles would not stand up long against the enormous power of Russia. There would only be a repetition of 1830, it predicted. The Poles would achieve a few successes at first, "the reaction" would come as it did in the November Insurrection, "and order would again reign in blood at Warsaw."[18]

Here the *Gazette* was contradicting itself and following the reasoning of those New York journals it had so roundly castigated. "But in the present case," it added in the next sentence, "the foolish and mischievous King of Prussia has contrived to rouse the indignation of all Europe by interfering on behalf of the Russians." This action, it prognosticated, would set off a chain of diplomatic if not military activity. Napoleon would capitalize on the situation by insisting on an adherence to those provisions of the 1815 Vienna Treaty in which Russia had pledged to guarantee the Poles under her rule a constitution as well as "a nationality." Next, it predicted, England and Austria, not to be outdone by the French Emperor, would join in the protest, and the Polish struggle would "at once assume the dimensions of a European question." The editorial hopefully concluded that both the Czar and the Prussian king would give in "without much resistance." The Czar would make concessions because "internal complications" caused by his emancipation of the serfs would not allow him to wage a full-scale war; the Prussian monarch, because he was in an unstable position vis-à-vis his subjects who demanded reforms. "If so," the editorial writer added as an afterthought, "the Polish question will be settled for a time, and a brave but unhappy people will be relieved by peaceful diplomacy from the cruelties of their Cossack rulers."[19]

The *Gazette's* editorialist also speculated on the possibility of Russia's resistance to diplomatic pressures and of her resorting to "an appeal to the sword." He felt that in such a case the Western European powers would surely make "a demonstration in favor of Poland" in support of the 1815 Treaty. Such action, he noted, would be legitimate even for Austria because she had just been released by Minister Gorchakov himself from her obligation under the Convention of Münchengratz to join Russia and Prussia in putting down revolutionary movements in Poland.[20]

The use of the term "demonstration" might have led at least a fraction of the *Gazette's* reading public to hope that a joint *military* action of the powers against Russia was about to materialize. But it was to be a very weak action, formed of the nebulous substance of diplomatic reproach rather than of the solid material of military threat. It is safe to say that such a "demonstration" would have disappointed most editors on the American side of the Atlantic, as it would certainly not have reduced sufficiently the potential for intervention in the Civil War. However, in his next paragraph the *Gazette's* editorial writer bypassed this consideration and even commented in a complimentary tone on the "demonstration's" pacific character.[21]

The editorial also focused on other international complications, such as the problem of guaranteeing the succession to the throne in Belgium, a change in Spain's government which seemed to portend its renewed participation in European politics, weaknesses in the new Italian government, and the disintegration of the Turkish Empire at the expense of the rise of small Balkan states. Pausing at the Balkan disturbances, and recalling the height of Poland's territorial expansion centuries before under her Jagellonian dynasty, it commented that "Reconstituted Poland would certainly sympathize with these oppressed nationalities, and not seek to absorb them, as Russia does." Furthermore, if "the Poland of Jagellon" were to reappear on the map of Europe, she would be certain to interfere with Russia's designs on Constantinople.[22]

Finally, after some more verbal headscratching over the European puzzle, the editorial expressed a vague hope that "in the long run" the people would be the gainers, and a specific wish "for the reconstitution of Poland as a nationality, even though it be under the sovereignty of Russia." This, it concluded in fine, would be "a great step toward the ultimate rendering of justice to that long-suffering nation."[23]

Later, the *Gazette* printed detailed extracts from French journals in a column captioned "The French Press on Poland." It noted Napoleon's apparent wavering in the matter of intervention in Poland, and commented that perhaps he was "waiting for something to turn up" across the Atlantic. It also reported the rumors about his diplomatic "tool," Minister of State Count Alexander Walewski, who was the illegitimate son of the first Napoleon and a Polish Countess, being groomed for the Polish throne even though it was unlikely that the Poles would accept him.[24]

The news from France provided at least partial inspiration for another *Gazette* editorial, entitled "The Dubious Friends of Poland." This time, the editorial writer sounded like a rank cynic. England and France were not likely to give the Poles any material aid, he predicted in his opening sentences, in spite of all their "diplomatic pother," the Poles were their own best friends. "When they have proved by their keen-edged scythes and stout hearts that they can help themselves," it ruefully concluded, "these self-constituted arbiters will be very ready to help them by furnishing them with some dunderhead of a Dutch or French prince for a king."[25]

In a digressive note, the same editorial stated that:

The suicide of General Kurowski, a Polish leader who lost a recent battle, is no great loss to them. He was a brother of the conceited person of the same name who has figured in the United States somewhat notoriously, and is said to have been himself rather crazy. The Poles will be fortunate if they can get rid of all inefficient generals so easily.[26]

This allusion was incorrect. Kurowski was not related to Count Adam Gurowski, a renegade Polish exile who had disassociated himself from his confreres in the 1830s, had secured employment with the State Department as a reader-translator of foreign newspapers, and was at that time most unpopular in pro-Lincoln quarters because he had just published his *Diary*, a collection of scathing attacks on the administration, especially on its mild stand on abolition and its alleged incompetence in the military sector. Ironically, Gurowski, soon after the 1830 Insurrection, had espoused Panslavism under Russian domination. As will be shown in a subsequent chapter, he was definitely opposed to the January Insurrection.

In Washington, the *Daily National Intelligencer* saw legal parallels between the proposed allied "demonstration" and Seward's stand against Napoleon's mediation offer. In an editorial entitled "Non-Intervention," it reminded readers that "some of the principles of public law" which the Polish Insurrection had "called into fresh exercise and recognition" were principles "such as have bearing on the relations of our own domestic war to foreign governments."[27] It pointed out that while Napoleon abstained from "any claim to deny to Prussia the right to take precautionary measures for the preservation of domestic tranquility in Prussian Poland," he did deny the legitimacy of Prussia's entering into an agreement with Russia for the purpose of facilitating military movements and "the dispositions taken by the latter for the suppression of a revolt which . . . is purely a domestic question . . . and with which Prussia, notwithstanding her proximity, and the similarity of the interests which are imperilled by the insurrection, has no right to interfere." [28] It felt that when Seward rejected Napoleon's mediation offer he was merely applying to America's domestic affairs when "the same wholesome doctrines which France had already affirmed in regard to the insurrection of the Poles against the Russian Government."[29]

The *Daily Evening Traveller*, a faithful pro-administration Boston journal, printed a three-column review, "Poland and the Polish Question," which indicated that its editor was torn between past sentiment and current hopes. At one point he commented that while the Polish cause was just and the actions of the Russian government justified armed resistance by the Poles, Americans should judge the Czar's course of action as they would judge England and France in a similar situation. He elaborated by saying that if the Russians were to put down the Polish Insurrection, American opinion should react no differently than it would to the suppression of an Indian revolt by the British or of an Algerian revolt by the French. Further on he put the entire blame for the failure of the November Insurrection on the two Western powers, and, because of that failure, he claimed, they had no right on legal or political grounds "to send the mildest of notes to Russia about Poland."[30] His concluding paragraph was in the nature of a cautious admonition:

As to the moral right of Western European Powers, with or without the aid of Austria, to interfere in Polish affairs, that is another matter. It is one, too, that we Americans cannot blindly admit and support at this time, no matter how much we may wish success to the Poles, who have always been admired in this country, and concerning whose rights and wrongs there has [sic] never been two opinions in the United States. If England and France have the right to interfere in the dispute between Russia and her Polish subjects, on moral grounds, have they not the same right to interfere between our government and the secessionists? The secession war has produced ten thousand times more evil to the world outside of Poland, than has followed from the Polish outbreak; and we could not well admit the right of intervention in the one instance and deny it in the other: We must remain silent for the time.[31]

The influential *Philadelphia Inquirer,* which boasted a circulation of over 60,000 and also supported the Lincoln administration, used the example of Poland for a moralistic editorial ominously captioned "Poland and the United States—A Warning," which appeared alongside extensive articles on the siege of Vicksburg and a contemplated Union invasion of Kentucky.[32]

After a solemn opening, referring to the inscrutability of "the ways of Providence" and a statement that "the suppression of a rebellion in the New World may depend upon the rise of an insurrection in the Old," it traced, in four long paragraphs, Poland's history from the year 1385. It called the attention of readers to the disunity that prevailed among her ruling classes, and attributed her partitions and her current troubles entirely to such disunity. Finally, it expressed satisfaction that Poland was in the news once more. "At this solemn crisis in our own history," it commented, "it is well that the history of Poland's folly and Poland's fate has been brought more distinctly before us." And, as a conclusion, it presented its "warning"—an admonition to the citizens of the embattled Union to resist "any dismemberment" and to "prevent it at any cost" lest they also suffer the fate of the Poles.[33]

Of all the Northern journals, the *New York Sun* was most overtly sympathetic to the Poles and most contemptuous of the Western powers. As soon as it received hints of a possible intervention in Poland, it devoted considerable space to editorializing on what its prospects might be. One edition, for example, contained comments on "Poland's Danger." It theorized that the only solid aid that Poland could expect from the outside world would come from professional revolutionaries in Western Europe who might be able to filter into Poland provided Prussia kept aloof. "If this result should be accomplished," it noted, "Lord Palmerston, Louis Napoleon and the Austrian Emperor may be foiled in their treacherous attempt to stifle liberty in Europe by a hollow friendship with Poland."[34]

The *Sun*, alone among all major New York journals, gave an editorial endorsement to a preliminary meeting which was to be held by Polish sympathizers in the city. In it there was also a definite note of scorn, that "The ardent sympathy of our people may go far towards saving the Polish revolution from falling into the desperate clutches of Lord Palmerston and the French and Austrian Emperors."[35]

A moving appeal to arms signed by Langiewicz inspired another *Sun* editorial, "The War in Poland." It mentioned several insurgent victories and began with a hopeful thought that "the spirit of the Polish people will go far to make up for the lack of more effective weapons." It wavered between doubt (". . . we cannot doubt the ultimate triumph of the Russians over the brave men who defy the well-armed battalions that are sent against them:") and, again, hope (". . . it seems highly probable, from the tenor of the news, that better times are to dawn upon the down-trodden peoples of Poland.")[36]

The phrase "tenor of the news" was an allusion to the fact

that the Poles were spared some criticism in the United States that intervention by the European powers again seemed possible. In the *Sun's* view, they would not sustain the revolution but would rather strive to confine it through "gradual concessions," and thus also would dampen the revolutionary spirit spreading among the peoples of the domains of the Western rulers particularly those of the Habsburgs.[37]

A few of the *Sun's* readers might have been aware of the background for the eloquently worded Langiewicz proclamation, its ardent declaration of "liberty and political equality of all sons of Poland, without distinction of belief, of conditions or of birth," and its promise of "the giving, under conditions, of the landed property, subjected . . . to rents or charges, to the rural population, with indemity to the proprietors, who will be saved from harm out of the funds of the state." They might have noted similarities both in intent and content between the Polish document and Lincoln's Emancipation Proclamation. Both were issued in order to transform stagnating, attritional warfare into ideological warfare. Both were drafted in attempts to arouse the apathetic and neglected lower strata of their respective populations. Both pledged a limited emancipation. Finally, in addition to their domestic application, both documents were undoubtedly issued to elicit sympathy from a sensitive but cautious public opinion abroad.

Even without additional details, some of the *Sun's* more astute readers might have gathered that things had not been going well in the insurgent ranks, and that a prime shortcoming of the 1831 Insurrection, quarreling among the leaders, seemed to be manifesting itself in 1863. The absence of Mieroslawski's name from the proclamation must have prompted some to conclude that the older, less popular, and less aggressive general was being replaced by his own protégé, the military man of the hour, who had the influential backing of the wealthier, conservative "Whites." In this, too, there were some elements of similarity between the insurrection and the Civil War. The American public had become accustomed to reading quite frequently of Lincoln's replacing or shifting "slow" army commanders. It is not unlikely because of such unpleasant similarities. But, as far as can be determined, none of the anti-administration journals took advantage of the opportunity to make odious comparisons.

Nevertheless, at least one New York newspaper did use this issue for an editorial attack. The paper was the *Journal of Commerce*, which called its readers' attention to what it termed the "Polish indulgence" in "traditional factionalism" by "men of whom we expected better things . . . given over to folly and ambition." Its criticism was tempered with further regret and trepidation about the prospects of the unfortunate turn of events for the United States "because this Polish question affects the policy of both France and England toward us."[38]

When the American journals finally printed some details of the power struggle between the insurgent factions and of Langiewicz's succession to the dictatorship of the National Government, they also carried reports of a "peace mission" sent by Grand Duke Constantine to the Poles. The mission carried a truce offer and a promise that Constantine would endeavor to seek the restoration of the Kingdom of Poland to its 1815 status of limited autonomy under a constitution. The information was extracted from a letter that had been dispatched by the London *Times'* Posen (Poznan) correspondent under the date of March 13. The correspondent commented that Constantine's offer was immediately rejected by the wary Langiewicz and by the "upper strata" of Poland. He also noted that "Warsaw capitalists" had said that the 1815 constitution was "no longer the panacea by which the cure would be effected." News columns of the same journals carried several vivid accounts of insurgent military successes, including some victories in Lithuania, beyond the boundaries of the "Kingdom."

From these items, American readers could readily gather that the Polish Insurrection, like the Civil War, had reached a point of no return; that just as the North would not be likely to accept anything short of total surrender by the Confederacy, the Polish insurgents were not likely to accept any offer which would give them boundaries less extensive than those of the old pre-partition kingdom. The possibility of a peaceful solution of the Polish question through the "magnanimity" of Alexander—and for this many American editors had once hoped—had been almost completely ruled out.

Before the editors could properly sort out the numerous items that were pouring in from the Polish scene and could draw some conclusions for the benefit of their totally befuddled readers, they were in receipt of additional and more startling news. On March 21, Langiewicz and his troops had been cornered in a battle; after putting up a desperate defensive action, he had been forced to flee across the border into Austrian Poland and had immediately been interned. While a majority of the American journals lamented this event, and their editors concluded that the insurrection had been dealt its death blow, there were a few who did not completely despair, even though the reasons for their feelings of assurance were of a somewhat dubious character.

The *New York Sun,* which carried the complete story of Langiewicz's internment, thought the Austrian government was actually throwing a "protective aegis" around him.[39] In its "Foreign News Summary" the *North American and United States Gazette* included a very odd statement: "We learn that this reverse will prove fatal to the cause of Polish liberty in one sense, though in another it will not—for the Emperor Alexander has offered to recognize the nationality of Poland and to grant her a constitution."[40] Obviously, the *Gazette's* editor had either not read or had refused to believe the account of the rejection of the Russian offer as it had been printed in the rival *Philadelphia Inquirer* less than a week before. The Copperhead *Crisis* even turned defeat into victory by printing a brief comment under the emphatic caption "Good for the Poles!" and stating that "the Emperor of Russia, through the sympathies of Europe in behalf of the Poles, has concluded to grant Poland a *Constitution* and more liberal government."[41] Most likely, however, the pro-Southern Medary had a dual motive in printing this capsule editorial; his optimistic misinterpretation of the Polish situation gave him a good opportunity to make a veiled reference to the Confederates' argument that they were struggling for states' rights. His second, and concluding sentence—"So the Poles have gained something by their revolution."—might also have been a covert message of encouragement to the American rebels in their "revolution" against the North.

Some of the American analyses of Langiewicz's defeat struck a realistic mean between optimism and pessimism, for there was still much incoming news to indicate that the clandestine National Government could carry on the insurrection. Some of the reports to this effect emanated from Poland itself. Others arrived in optimistically embellished form from the Western European capitals. The New York *Spectator*, for one, took up such a line of reasoning in an editorial entitled "The Surrender of Langiewicz." It also devoted considerable space in the same column to a discussion of a pro-Polish sympathy meeting that had been held in Manchester, England, a city which was not only a strongly proletarian center but also the site of mass meetings in favor of the Union cause. This particular meeting had been addressed by Count Andrzej Zamoyski, the exiled former head of the Polish Agricultural Society. He had proposed that England break off all diplomatic relations with Russia until the Polish question was resolved, and that she immediately recognize Poland as a belligerent nation. This prompted the *Spectator's* editor to make a reference to British diplomatic flirtations with the South and to conclude that:

The semi-official greeting which was extended to the slave-holding confederacy before it struck a blow on behalf of disunion will not be tendered to a people whose separate nationality and constitutional rights have been solemnly guaranteed by the treaty of 1815 . . . not even after months of heroic valor and endurance.[42]

As April passed its mid-point and May appeared on the calendar, the flow of news from Poland slowed down. However, a certain inertia kept the name of the struggling nation in American journals. Some of the items printed during this period of lull included background information which allowed readers to mentally "catch up" with the situation. Outstanding in this respect were several articles appearing in the *North American*

and United States Gazette. Exemplifying this journal's thorough-
ness was an article "Poland and the Poles." It gave an excellent
review of social conditions in Poland, based largely on various
chapters in *The Polish Captivity*, a book published in 1863 by
the English journalist Henry Sutherland Edwards.[43] Probably
for the first time many American newspaper readers learned of
the social conditions leading up to the insurrection, of the
restrictions on personal freedom placed upon the Poles by their
Russian rulers, and of the various boycotts and demonstrations
which the Poles had conducted in protest.

Unfortunately, one conclusion reached by Edwards was made
invalid by immediate events. This was the conclusion that "party
feeling, the curse of Poland" was "fast disappearing." In the
second half of the article, the *Gazette* reprinted extracts from
documents published in London newspapers which indicated
that Mieroslawski's nomination had come from the White-orien-
ted Paris Polish Committee, that Langiewicz had taken advantage of Mieroslawski's "sudden and serious illness" to proclaim
himself dictator, and that Mieroslawski had protested the usurpa-
tion but had refrained from involving the insurgents in a Polish
civil war. "We can only infer from this," the article commented,
"that whatever may have been the heroism of Langiewicz, his
ambition was likely to, and perhaps may, have fatally com-
promised the designs of the national government." To this it
added: "If this be so, we may cease to regret his downfall,
though we cannot but deplore the reverses to the Polish arms
which occasioned it."[44]

Thus, the *Gazette* removed the name of Langiewicz from its
very temporary occupancy of the vault which held America's
"sentimental legacy" toward Poland. The removal was followed
by the usual comments on Polish factionalism, along with a
nouveauté from Edwards' book—that Kosciuszko did not utter
"Finis Poloniae!" when he fell in battle against the Russians in
1794, but on the contrary, that "he was willing to acquiesce in
the avowed project of the Emperor Alexander the First for reunit-
ing Poland as a separate constitutional kingdom under the sceptre
of the Czar as king." It also noted that the Polish hero wrote a

letter to the Emperor to that effect, thus making precisely the same request that Count Zamoyski had made of Alexander II in 1861.

In its conclusion the article cited a portion of Kosciuszko's protest to France's Count Ségur when he found that Napoleon I was about to betray Poland:

With my death on the field of battle, or otherwise, Poland could not and would not *end*. All the Poles have done since then in the glorious Polish legions, and all they will yet do in future to recover their country, must be regarded as proofs that though we, the devoted soldiers of this country, are mortal, Poland is immortal.[45]

And for its own part, the *Gazette* concluded and questioned:

This noble sentiment animates the Polish heart at the present time, and will continue to do so to the last. Why is it that Europe leaves so gallant a people to the mercy of the oppressors, when they might so easily be raised up to the bulwark of civilization?[46]

CHAPTER IV

THE INSURRECTION
VIEWED BY AMERICAN DIPLOMATS

> So, firmer based, her power expands,
>> Nor yet has seen her crowning hour,
> Still teaching to the struggling lands
>> That Peace the offspring is of Power[1]

THE LINES cited above form the twelfth stanza of a fifteen-stanza ode to Russia entitled "A Thousand Years." Composed in September, 1862, they had not been written by a pro-Russian Slavophile nor by a Russian Panslavist, but by an American who was the secretary of his country's legation in St. Petersburg. The versifier who seemed so enamored of Russian power was Bayard Taylor. During the most critical period in Civil War diplomacy, from the fall of 1862 to the spring of 1863, Taylor, as chargé d'affaires ad interim, was in complete charge of the legation. He had the responsibility of feeling out the Russian court on its attitude towards the Union and its stand on the all-important question of European intervention in the war. Additionally, through conversations with diplomatic representatives of the Western powers, as well as through his own analyses of the Western European press, he was to give his superior in Washington a fuller picture of the attitudes of the European governments in regard to the same questions.

The beginning of 1863 found Taylor writing lengthy and, at times, semipoetic, accounts of the favorable reaction to the Emancipation Proclamation evidenced by the czarist court and the Russian newspapers. In one such account, which he wrote late in January, he devoted several pages assuring the worried Seward that there was no foundation to rumors of "an increasing intimacy between Russia and France, and a possible combination on their part for interference in American affairs." Taylor had brought the rumors to the personal attention of Gorchakov, and the Foreign Minister had given his government's word that it would never undertake any diplomatic mediation unless it had the consent of *both* sides. Although the Russian statesman had added professions of friendship for the Union, he had also told Taylor that his government held no hostility "towards the people of the South." Before the chargé put his signature to the dispatch with its comforting news, he added in very routine fashion: "The internal condition of the Russian Empire continues to be very satisfactory."[2]

In February and March, Taylor sent Seward three more dispatches, but none of them made mention of the events which were then transpiring in Poland, and which had, in fact, begun the day after he had commented on the "very satisfactory" internal condition of the Russian Empire. Subsequently, after having sent a dispatch enclosing an intercepted note from the Confederate State Department to its prospective Commissioner to Russia, Lucius Quintus Cincinnatus Lamar, he took occasion to draft still another dispatch. Its principal topics were the Russian attitudes towards the Emancipation Proclamation and the naval battle between the *Monitor* and the *Merrimac*. On the ninth page were Taylor's first comments on the Polish Insurrection, preceded by two excuses for their lateness—an illness which had incapacitated him for a fortnight, and his lack of a secretary. Taylor agreed with official Russian assertions that the insurrection had been precipitated by the discovery of a revolutionary organization, and that the conscription was "but a pretext for an outbreak which would have been very powerful if its beginning had not been prematurely forced upon the insurgents." He concluded, as had some of the American editors, that the Polish struggle would draw the attention of Europe away from America's struggle.[3]

Obviously, Taylor did not see anything momentous in the insurrection, and, just as obviously, he could secure little information about it. In his next report, however, he told—and admitted —more. First, he noted that the Russian government was satisfied with the joint Congressional resolution rejecting Napoleon's offer to mediate in the Civil War. Then, he complained that he had considerable difficulty in obtaining correct information on the Polish situation, but that the jealousy between Mieroslawski and Langiewicz had deprived the revolutionary movement "of that coherence which at one time promised important results." Poland, he reported, was filled with scattered bands of insurgents who dispersed at the approach of larger Russian forces and reorganized rapidly at other points. "The rebellion has lost all chance of success." He concluded, "I do not send you the floating rumors, because those of one day are contradicted by those of the next, and nothing seems to be certain, except that the Imperial troops, in spite of reverses which are carefully concealed from public knowledge here, are gradually gaining ground."[4]

Taylor pronounced a verdict of futility on the insurrection, and was certainly more firm in his pessimism than the home press. He correctly noted that the new Polish struggle was more in the nature of guerrilla warfare than of the conventional warfare which had marked the previous insurrection. He then proceeded to inject his own opinions, first as to the possibilities of intervention by the Western Powers, and next as to the Poles' "national character":

. . . The propitious moment for intervention has passed, and the storm of windy words in the English Parliament and the French Senate will blow over without harm or help to one side or the other. If the Poles will but learn from this experience that neither of those nations acts from sympathy, or gives assistance without an equivalent, it may lead them to relinquish attempts which are only calculated to retard the progress of Russia towards a future more just, grand and free, than they, with the discordant elements of their national character, could ever reach through separation from her. History teaches us truer [sic] lesson than that there is no resurrection for a nation once dead.[5]

Again, Taylor's dire pronouncements went to greater extremes than did those of the American journalists. His comments on Russia's future were almost a prose version of his earlier poem. On the other hand, his comments on the Poles were a mixture of painful truth and extreme practicality, just a step short of the open bias displayed by his erstwhile chief, Cassius Clay. Here it might be interesting to cite the concluding sentence of a statement Taylor had made in 1859 and which he completely contradicted in 1863: "The feeling of nationality survives, however, long after a nation is dead and buried. The Jews in Poland call themselves Jews, and the Poles in Russia will call themselves Poles, centuries hence."[6]

Before the end of April, Taylor gave Washington some information about the repercussions that the events in Poland were having in Russia itself. He advised Seward that the insurrection continued to "occupy public attention almost to the exclusion of every other subject," and then commented that it had been "unexpectedly prolonged" even though the extent of Polish resistance was "undoubtedly exaggerated in the English and French papers." Although he had heard that the Russian army had been put on a war footing, and that the strengthening of the Baltic fortifications at Kronstadt was being vigorously carried out, he assured Seward that the measures were "precautionary rather than menacing" and that the fear of an active intervention by England and France had subsided. With information such as this emanating from an on-the-spot source, it is doubtful that the United States government could have entertained even a slight hope that the European war which was sometimes wished for in the American press would eventuate.

Another section of the dispatch dealing with Poland contained some of Taylor's observations on Alexander's "Easter Manifesto" of April 12. Taylor did not cite the document in its entirety, but instead quoted only the paragraph dealing with the amnesty the Czar had offered to all those subjects of the Kingdom who were "implicated in the recent troubles" and would "lay down their arms and return to obedience" by May 1. "Humane and generous as is the tone of this manifesto," Taylor added, "the general impression here is that it will not produce much effect." He believed that the insurrection had assumed a religious as well as a political character and that there were "probably no two sects in the world so uncompromisingly hostile to each other as the Latin and Greek Churches." He reiterated his belief that the Polish struggle was futile, but that the insurgents might "continue for some time yet, to encourage the hopes of their sympathizers in other parts of Europe, and thus agitate the political atmosphere of the Continent."[7]

As Taylor aptly pointed out, the *tone* of the "Easter Manifesto" seemed "humane and generous." However, he did not fathom the motives and intents behind it. He was not aware that they were governed by very practical considerations. For one, the manifesto followed immediately in the wake of the first hints of possible European intervention in the insurrection, and, in all probability, it was issued as a countermove to forestall or discredit any such action. For another, it had several psychological motives behind it. Alexander hoped that it would remove the stigma of recent Russian actions: The conscription, whose true background had soon become known; the Alvensleben Convention, which had stirred up world opinion and agitated Western diplomats; the reprisals against the families of the insurgents, just then publicized in Western journals and aired in the forums of Western opinion; and the atrocities, knowledge of which were just beginning to reach the West. Failing to discern these motives, the neophyte diplomat had also neglected to note that lieutenants of the "forgiving" ruler had already expropriated the property of insurgents and had absolutely no intention of returning it.

In his concluding paragraphs, Taylor evaluated the effects of the insurrection on the once lively interest which the more sophisticated inhabitants of the Russian capital city had taken in the Civil War. He first stated that the American struggle had, as was "natural during such a crisis relapsed into secondary importance." This comment was followed by a partially reassuring: "While on the one hand I am relieved from the pressure of adverse opinions, on the other hand I encounter not an absence, but a suspension of active sympathy by the anticipation of possible events here."[8] Unfortunately, he did not specify the sources of the adverse opinion, but, obviously, his very mention of its existence indicated that alleged Russian sympathies for the Union were not as unanimous as some gentlemen of the Northern press would have had their readers believe.

At other European listening posts, United States diplomats gave rather scanty evaluations of the insurrection. In their view, it, most logically, took second place to the still all-important question of a possible intervention in the Civil War. The first report came in February from an exasperated William Dayton, the Minister to Paris. Dayton, who had been trying for days to see French Foreign Minister Drouyn de L'Huys in regard to Napoleon's mediation note, had to inform Seward that he had been unsuccessful because the Polish insurrection had "driven American affairs out of view for the moment." "A disturbance on the continent, especially in Central Europe, is so near at hand," he prophesied, "and touches so many of the crowned heads of these countries, that distant events fall out of sight until these more immediate troubles are settled." But Dayton could not give Seward any inkling of Napoleon's feelings in regard to a possible intervention in Poland. It seemed to him that nothing was "publicly known of the views of his Majesty" even though the French press had "almost universally" condemned Russia and had already expressed its sympathies for the plight of Poland.[9]

More than a month later, it fell to Dayton to convey to the French Foreign Ministry the harsh resolution which the United States Congress had passed as a retort to Napoleon's mediation proposal. Despite the document's tone and its implication that the Union would consider intervention tantamount to a declaration of war, Drouyn de L'Huys accepted it with seeming calm. He told the American Minister that he had already been made aware of its contents by Henri Mercier, his own Minister to Washington, and asked him to forego the customary recitation of its contents. De L'Huys was "evidently not disposed to go into any conversation on the subject," Dayton noted in his dispatch, and, attempting to explain this mood, he noted that the French diplomat's mind seemed to have been occupied "with Poland and its complications."[10] Thus it was that Poland fortuitously blunted what otherwise might have been a hectic interview marked by bitter words from French officialdom.

In London, Minister Charles Francis Adams viewed the French mediation offer with decided skepticism. "The wish for French intervention is father of the thought," he wrote Seward at the end of February. He assured the Secretary that even rumors of the end of the Union's blockade of Southern ports, cherished by "malevolent parties," left no impression whatever on a British public opinion which was strongly in sympathy with the North. He interjected a comment that sympathy with the Poles would be in complete harmony with "what is called the traditional policy of France, and with the current of popular sentiment," but that he doubted that it would be expressed in a general war. Efforts to arrive at some form of peaceful settlement would increase and would be successful, he felt. This would give the Union an "interval" to improve militarily so that it would be able to withstand not only the Confederacy but also any European intervention.[11]

Adams thus threw cold water on the fiery American editorials which had mentioned the possibility of a European war over Poland, but, like the editors who had written them, he saw a definite advantage accruing for the Union from the insurrection, namely, the advantage of time. His attitude remained calm even after he learned of the signing of the Alvensleben Convention. He also voiced agreement with what he thought was the prevailing opinion in France—that Napoleon still did not contemplate any "immediate action."[12]

There was some irony in the fact that the most anxious reports on Poland did not come from diplomats stationed in the key Western capitals but from Stockholm, where J. S. Haldeman, the Minister to Sweden and Norway, noted a widespread fear that a general war or revolution throughout Europe might ensue from the troubles in Poland. In one dispatch he described the visit of "a large number of Poles" headed by a leader of the exiles, Wladyslaw Czartoryski. He noted that the Swedes had welcomed the group with great enthusiasm, that the press, which was "very violent," had urged the government to take the initiative and use the occasion of Russia's preoccupation with Poland to "rescue Finland from the Russian Bear." A Swedish King, Charles XII, had saved Poland from the grasp of Peter the Great, Haldeman recalled, and now, it was claimed, another and better occasion offered. He believed that the reigning king, Charles XV, was in accord with the enthusiasm for Poland, but that his ministers were very much in favor of strict neutrality.[13] None of these items were mentioned in the press in America.

Seward had made a few interesting comments on Poland in three of the notes which he had sent to his ministers. On April 8, he had acknowledged a report by Dayton on the policy of the French government in regard to the Polish question. The report had not seemed to be a source of enlightenment to the Secretary of State. He stated that it was in accord with expectations which had prevailed in the United States "in view of the parliamentary expositions and diplomatic notes" that had already arrived. Then, he added a concluding paragraph which betrayed his personal feelings:

If advices which have outstripped your despatch are to be credited, the revolution has come to an end even sooner than was anticipated in Paris, and the gallant nation whose wrongs, whose misfortunes, and whose valor have so deeply excited universal sympathy in Europe is again left to the magnanimity of the Czar. There are many traits in his character which persuade us to hope that he will concede to the Poles rights and privileges which they have been unable to recover by force.[14]

Such feelings on the part of an official spokesman for the Lincoln administration were almost a mirror reflection of the feelings of many of America's editors. Alexander's Emancipation Decree had, indeed, created a "sentimental legacy" in the United States which now outweighed the anterior Polish "sentimental legacy." In a second note to Dayton, written on April 24, Seward indicated that Lincoln himself was following the situation in Poland. But, once more there were words of praise for Alexander.

Again, he thought a possible solution of the Polish problem would be due to Alexander's magnanimity rather than the efforts of the insurgents or the intervention of the Western powers, and he wrote:

The Emperor of Russia seems to us to have adopted a policy of beneficient reform in domestic administration. His known sagacity and his good dispositions encourage a hope that Poland will not be denied a just share of the imperial consideration if, as seems now to be generally expected in Europe, the revolution attempted by her heroic people shall be suppressed.[15]

The same ambivalent pattern was followed in another note which Seward wrote the same day to James Harvey, his Minister to Portugal. Again there was an expression of sympathy for the Poles; and again there was an expression of trust in the Czar's magnanimity. This time, however, there was also a favorable comment on the actions of the Western powers:

The people of Poland are subjects of a traditional sympathy, which is co-extensive with civilization. In no country is this sympathy more intense than in the United States. Since the European states, which have taken the cause of that heroic people into consideration, have concluded to confine their action upon it to an appeal to the magnanimity of Russia, it is earnestly to be desired that this very pacific form of intervention will not be fruitless. The noble character of the present ruler of Russia I think warrants an expectation that, while he is so diligently and so generously ameliorating the condition of the Russian people generally, he will not hesitate to bestow the boon of freedom to his unwilling subjects in Poland.[16]

Interestingly, in none of his three comments on Poland did Seward allude to the effects which a possible European intervention in Poland might have on the probability of a European intervention in the Civil War. Whether the omission reflected a complete absence of such considerations from his mind, or whether it was intentional, cannot be gauged from diplomatic correspondence or even from his private writings. Yet, since it is certain that he consulted newspapers in regard to the Polish situation, it seems most unlikely that he had overlooked the many editorials which had already dealt with this aspect of the situation. For that matter, it seems unlikely that he in his own thinking could have overlooked it. That Seward was not pusillanimous in his attitude on intervention in the Civil War is evidenced by a memorandum which he had sent to Lincoln in 1861 and in which he had advocated a "foreign-war panacea" to keep the Union intact. (He had proposed that: (1) the government demand immediate explanations from Spain in regard to its occupation of Santo Domingo, and from France in regard to its intentions in Mexico; (2) the government seek explanations from Russia and Britain regarding their stand on intervention; (3) agents be sent into the Central and South American republics to stir up "a vigorous continental spirit of independence" against European intervention; and (4) Lincoln convene Congress to declare war against Spain and France if they did not offer "satisfactory" explanations.)[17]

Significantly, one key listening post was silent during the early phases of the insurrection. That post was Vienna, where the American Minister was the historian John Lothrop Motley. In the several items of official correspondence that passed between Motley and Seward during the first four months of 1863, there were several evaluations of events in Europe, but none of them concerned Poland. Yet, what Motley failed to write Seward officially, he discussed with his mother in private correspondence. His feelings on the insurrection, on intervention, and on Russia, were all made vividly clear in a letter he wrote her in March. He told her that he was happy that attention in Europe had been "somewhat diverted" from American affairs by events in Poland. However, he felt that even though the insurrection would last for months it would be crushed, for there would be no intervention on the part of the Western powers. Sarcastically, he concluded: "There will be a great deal of remonstrating and a great talk about liberty and free institutions on the part of that apostle of liberty and civilization, Louis Napoleon."[18]

In another paragraph of the same letter, Motley expressed regret which showed that he, too, was under the spell of Czar Alexander's alleged liberalism and friendship with the Union. "I feel very much grieved," he wrote, "that our only well-wisher in Europe, the Russian Government, and one which has carried out at great risks the noblest measure of the age, the emancipation of 25,000,000 slaves, should now be contending in arms with its own subjects, and that it is impossible for us to sympathise with our only friends."[19]

Two months later, when Motley wrote to a friend, the wife of the British diplomat Lord William Russell, he cut loose with such language of contempt for British and French diplomacy vis-à-vis Poland as was not likely to be found in polite reports. "I take it for granted," he opened, "that no sharper instrument than the pen will be used by the 'two powers'—and that they will shed nothing more precious than ink this year—which can be manufactured cheap in all countries." He noted how the French Ambassador to the Austrian court had gone to Carlsbad for six weeks to drink of the resort's curing waters, and the English Ambassador had gone to the country, and the Austrian Minister was "ailing for some weeks," while Europe's journalists campaigned on paper. "The poor Poles are shedding something warmer than ink," he reminded Lady Russell, "and I can't say it seems very fair to encourage them to go on, if you can't help them with nothing harder than fine phrases which have small effect on Cossacks or parsnips." With bitterness, he added that what was termed "moral influence" in diplomatic jargon was "a very valuable dispensation," but that gunpowder came nearer the mark.[20]

In his private correspondence, Bayard Taylor also made non-diplomatic observations in regard to the insurrection, quite contrary to the careful dispatches he had sent to Seward. At the beginning of May, he wrote his wife that the opposition of England and France had "united all the discordant elements in Russia and given her great internal strength." To this he added that the Polish Insurrection could yet prove a benefit to Russia, then advised his wife that Lord Napier, the British Ambassador to the Russian Court, had assured him that there would be no war between Britain and the United States.[21]

A few days later, Taylor wrote about a reception that had

been held for the diplomatic corps in the Russian capital. Like Motley, he assumed an attitude of caustic cynicism towards the diplomacy of the European powers. He epitomized it in one sentence: "Russia sat between France and England, and all three acted as if there was no such thing as Poland."[22]

And in Taylor's personal correspondence there is more than a hint of the friction which had existed between him and Clay, together with comments on the truly low esteem in which the ill-mannered Cassius Marcellus had been held by the czarist court. When Clay made his departure, the relieved Taylor wrote his mother and sisters: "I am glad of it, for (between ourselves) he is immensely gassy. I don't think there is the slightest danger of his being reappointed: he is utterly unfit for the post."[23] Unfortunately for Taylor, and more unfortunately for the Polish cause, Clay *was* reappointed after he had had his brief stint in military service. Just as the turmoil in Poland reached its height, Taylor submitted his resignation and took his family to Königsberg in Prussia. Ironically, the railroad journey traversed Lithuanian territory that had been under harassment by Polish insurgents. After he had escorted his family and returned to await Clay's arrival, he wrote his wife that he had heard that the insurrection was spreading along the Prussian frontier and in Lithuania, and that things "looked very black"; he also mentioned that the rebels had been active along the rail line between Kovno and Vilna the night before they had passed through there. The incident was never reported in his dispatches.[24]

The Confederate side, too, had listening posts in Western Europe, but there were none in Russia; the quasi-diplomatic agents of the Confederate government submitted reports in the form of dispatches to their Secretary of State, Judah P. Benjamin. The Polish Insurrection was a subject about which they also wrote, and it soon became more important to them than to their enemies because it affected European recognition of their government.

The first mention of the insurrection in the Confederate diplomatic correspondence was made by Agent Henry Hotze in London, in a dispatch dated February 14. He regretfully informed

Benjamin that the Conservative opposition in the British Parliament was not much of a help to the cause of Southern recognition because: (1) the Conservatives were never very effective as an opposition party; (2) England's traditional policy was not to recognize insurgent powers; and (3) England was staunchly opposed to the provisions regarding blockade in the Paris Convention of 1856. He struck a further note of disappointment in a terse comment that the British press had already manifested sympathy for the Poles while it had been slow in according such sympathy to the Confederacy, a sympathy "with which they have so often deluded apparently well-founded hopes."[25]

A few weeks later, A. Dudley Mann, the Confederate Commissioner to Brussels, ventured his opinion on the Polish Insurrection. He saw little hope for the Poles' success. In a discussion of possible French recognition of the Confederacy, Mann surmised that Napoleon would have to recognize the insurgent Polish National Government, hopeless as its future might be, if he chose to recognize the Confederate government. However, he felt that if Napoleon did not recognize the Confederacy there was hope for his rapprochement with the Union. The Union might even be amenable to supplying Napoleon with arms for his armies in Mexico, Mann thought.[26] Further in the same dispatch, Mann informed Benjamin that "almost everybody seems to be clamorously ardent for the re-establishment of Poland," and that manifestations of sympathy were "as earnest and general in Stockholm as in Lisbon," but, that as far as he could see, the only hope for Poland lay in the possibility of ameliorations decreed by Alexander.[27]

In the same dispatch Mann maintained that six months previously Napoleon could have done anything he chose for Southern interests "perhaps without much risk" and that "all Europe would have cheerfully followed him"; that his recognition, coupled with the Confederate victories at Fredericksburg, would have had the same effect "as if an additional force of 100,000 efficient men" had entered the war on the side of the South. Now, in order to become once more the master of the situation or to restore his alleged image as "an invincible warrior and a far-seeing statesman," the Emperor needed a swift triumphant march of his armies into Mexico City as well as an end to the unrest in Poland brought about if necessary through the force of Russian arms. As long as neither eventuality materialized he would not dare to aid the South directly or indirectly, in spite of his "reported good intentions." In his conclusion, Mann held out more hope for Mexico than for Poland. Yet, like some of his Northern counterparts, he saw the possibility of "important ameliorations" to be effected by Alexander in the government of the Kingdom.[28]

The Confederate Commissioner to London, James M. Mason, was trying to secure European armed protection for cotton purchased or owned by neutrals in the Confederate States. He found, however, that the British Cabinet had "an absolute determination to refrain from any act which the United States may choose to consider objectionable." He thought that under different circumstances Napoleon would have taken some active steps at once. Mason also noted that the Emperor's ill-starred expedition to Mexico and "the complications thrown around him by the recent outbreak of revolution in Poland" hampered him at the moment.[29]

The other member of the Mason-Slidell duo filed his first dispatch to deal with Poland late in March. It, too, had an air of misgiving and cynicism. From his Paris post, Slidell complained to Benjamin that it was the English government that prevented a "practical solution" of the Polish question. England was pursuing a "selfish and tortuous policy" towards Poland, he stated, and it was the same policy that she had pursued towards the Confederacy. Her leading statesmen and journalists clamored for France to take the initiative in acting on behalf of the Poles, but they were slow in uniting behind the French government even when it suggested nothing more than diplomatic protest. Slidell hastened to add that Frenchmen were suspicious of English aloofness. They surmised that the English would be happy if France were at war with the Union government while they would remain neutral.[30]

To supplement his report, Slidell attached a copy of a speech given in the French Senate by Billoult, the Minister Without Portfolio who had succeeded Walewski, and whose special function was to explain and defend Napoleon's policies and views on all matters connected with foreign affairs. The address had included a resumé of the Polish situation, as Slidell pointed out to the Secretary of State; that it also had contained a few remarks on the Civil War with expressions of friendship for the South might have given a new glimmer of hope to the otherwise friendless Confederacy.

Benjamin, too, began to see a glimmer of hope for Jefferson Davis' government, especially after the Union had refused Napoleon's mediation offer and the belligerent congressional resolution had been presented by Dayton to the French foreign minister. But Benjamin remained adamant on his government's policy of no mediation without recognition, and thus, in effect, he too turned down Napoleon's offer. In a note to Slidell reiterating this policy, he commented that the tone and overtones of Seward's rejection might have inclined Napoleon to immediately recognize the Confederate States of America, in retaliation if for no other reason. Furthermore, he noted that King Leopold of the Belgians, who was the father-in-law of Maximilian, Napoleon's future puppet Emperor of Mexico, was urging his French ally to take the initiative in the recognition of the Confederacy. Yet, before he put his signature to the note, Benjamin extinguished any glimmer of hope with a pessimistic conclusion. The Confederacy could not rely on any such course of events, he wrote, more especially for the reason that the Polish Insurrection was growing to "increasing proportions" and was threatening to lead to complications in Europe which might involve the French government and render it "averse to any hazard, however remote, of difficulties with the United States."[31]

In sum, the comments made in their diplomatic correspondence clearly indicated that as far as Benjamin and his commissioners were concerned, the Polish Insurrection had happened at an unfortunate, if not an altogether fatal, juncture. Even though the Southern journals leveled criticism at the North for its lack of sympathy for the Poles and for its friendship for

Russia, to the South Poland constituted a definite intrusion that also enmeshed itself into European diplomacy and helped prevent the recognition which, together with a last minute intervention, might have preserved the Confederacy for a longer time, or might perhaps have salvaged it from utter defeat.

The Polish struggle might have affected the Confederacy's future in still another way. Despite some of the righteous pronouncements of its newspaper editors, the South was by no means against securing a diplomatic foothold in St. Petersburg. In September of 1862, Benjamin gave Lucius Lamar his commission to the Russian capital and instructed him to seek recognition for the Confederate States "in accordance with international law as equals." Lamar was instructed not to plead for any favors which would make his government seem to be on an inferior level. He was to mention that the Civil War had been caused in some measure by Europe's refusal to arbitrate, and Jefferson Davis was well aware that there was no intention to interfere on the part "of the humane and enlightened ruler" who "presided over the destinies of Russia."[32]

As late as March, 1863, Lamar was in London waiting for the Confederate Congress to confirm his appointment. Meanwhile he assured Benjamin that the Russian government would accept his credentials, for although it was inclined to favor the cause of the United States, it did not harbor any feelings of hostility towards the South. To bolster his argument, Lamar wrote that a member of the Russian legation in London had told him that "when the true nature and causes" of the Civil War would be made known, and, *especially* when *the Emperor* was "made to see" that it was "not a rebellion but a lawful assertion of sovereignty," the South could "reasonably expect his more active cooperation with the views of the French Emperor."[33] Implied in this statement was the thought that Alexander hesitated to look upon the South in a favorable light because he believed, or was led to believe, that it was engaged in a war of rebellion. And with the Poles engaged in a war of rebellion against the Russian government, he could hardly have been expected to show any sympathy for rebels on the other side of the world, unless they could convince him that they were not rebels.

Early in April, Cassius Marcellus Clay sailed from New York for Russia. When he arrived and once more presented his credentials to Alexander, he delivered an address in which he stated:

The more intimate relations which steam, the press and the telegraph have introduced among the nations heighten the natural interests and increase the conventional claims which each has upon the other for mutual comity, protection, and to advance of civilization. Whilst the people of the United States cannot, in consequence of these facts, be indifferent to passing events in other nationalities, they are aware that a cautious reserve as to uncalled-for intervention in the internal organizations of the several peoples is demanded for the peace of the world.[34]

Clay's reference to "passing events in other nationalities" was, without doubt, a hidden reference to the Polish insurrection. His concluding phrases were intended to assure Alexander of the fact that the United States would not intervene in this movement. They stemmed from a new development. American policy had moved from a rather dispassionate observation of the Polish struggle to the very brink of direct diplomatic involvement.

CHAPTER V

THE UNION CHOOSES
NON-INVOLVEMENT

BY APRIL of 1863 the serious tensions between the governments of the United States and France had been somewhat alleviated. Napoleon's cabinet had finally come to realize the futility of attempting to foist any mediation scheme upon the Lincoln administration. It had scrupulously honored the Union blockade of Southern ports, ineffectual as that action might have been. Confederate privateers were not allowed to bring their prizes into French harbors, and Federal letters of marque and reprisal were honored by French officials. No vessels, it seemed, were being secretly built for the Confederate navy in French shipyards, in marked contrast to the activities in English shipyards. In spite of Napoleon's intervention in Mexico and the sharp criticisms launched against the North by the government-controlled press, to all outward appearances, France and the United States were achieving a mild rapprochement. Certainly, they were on friendlier terms than were England and the United States.

On April 9, Minister Dayton had a lengthy interview with French Foreign Minister Drouyn de L'Huys. Their cordial discussion centered mainly on the topic of letters of marque, and Dayton emerged a satisfied man. Before he departed, however, he expressed a hope that the Foreign Minister would "seasonably" apprise him of anything of special interest to the Union government. The Minister gave a cheering assent and then immediately introduced a completely new subject. He informed Dayton that France, England, and Austria were "about to express their views or wishes" to Russia concerning the Polish situation. He assured him that the three powers "had substantially agreed upon the character of representation they would make; that everything would be in the mildest form, with no attempt at pressure, &c." He added that France was going to invite other powers to join in the diplomatic demarche. Would the United States also join?

Dayton parried this "sounding out" in a correct and adroit manner. He replied that Poland was a concern of European policy only, and that although the United States had "a general interest" in her, such interest was altogether subordinate to its interest in the affairs of "our own country and continent." Thus, he fell back on the spirit and letter of the Monroe Doctrine, which France herself was already violating in Mexico. He immediately recalled the very recent and unsuccessful attempt to employ the same maneuver against the American Union. He believed that the latter had failed because Napoleon had tried to go it alone. A joint declaration would strengthen a similar maneuver vis-à-vis Poland, but the French ruler would nevertheless get credit for having taken the initiative.[1]

Seward was obviously satisfied with his subordinate's handling of the French approach, and probably thought that Dayton's reply would close the matter as far as the United States was concerned. He made a routine acknowledgment of the dispatch without any comments whatsoever.[2]

However, the French Minister did not give up hope. On April 23 he sent a note to Henri Mercier, his representative in Washington. Its tone was diplomatically correct and was devoid of any emotionalism. The note's opening sentence was matter-of-fact: "Sir: Events in Poland have awakened preoccupations common to all cabinets." The next paragraph contained a few dispassionate background notes: The Polish Insurrection, whether viewed from the standpoint of humanity or with political interests in mind, inevitably claimed "the solicitude" of Europe's powers. The disturbances that were "periodically renewed" in Poland attested to a "permanence of difficulties which time has not smoothed away" and were bound to involve "dangers." Therefore, in order to remove these "difficulties" and "dangers" the three powers had decided to present "in concert" to the Russian government "the reflections which this state of things suggests."[3]

The next few sentences were scarcely less vague. Mercier was advised that the three powers had drafted their notes to St. Petersburg. A copy of the French note was attached to his instructions. "In preparing this document," Drouyn de L'Huys advised him, "our aim has been to make ourselves as much as possible the faithful interpreters of general opinion. We have refrained from every order of ideas which had been peculiar to us; we have not offered any observation which the other courts could not appropriate as theirs." He expressed a hope that in view of this, other cabinets besides those of the three powers would feel free to "voluntarily support the manifestation near the court of St. Petersburgh."[4]

Lastly, Drouyn de L'Huys instructed Mercier to read the explanations to Seward and to leave with him a copy of the French note to Russia. He hoped that the United States would either draft a similar note or present "analogous considerations" to the Russian court. "The good relations which exist between the government of the United States and the court of Russia," he pointed out, "cannot but give greater weight to counsels presented in a friendly form; and we rely entirely on the cabinet of Washington to appreciate the measure in which it will be able most satisfactorily to open its views to the Russian government." On this note of near flattery Drouyn de L'Huys hopefully rested his case.[5]

The French note to St. Petersburg that was shown to Seward was, indeed, very general and was couched in the mildest diplomatic language. It was by no means a plea for Polish freedom. It was, rather, an expression of worry over "lively preoccupations in the midst of a repose which no near event seemed likely to disturb." Its purpose was to call upon the Russian court's "solicitude" to "the inconvenience and the delays" which the insurrection had engendered. The "solicitude" was not for the Poles but for their neighbors who suffered "an agitation the recoil of which makes itself felt throughout Europe."[6]

The final statement of the document contained an appeal to Alexander's "liberal dispositions," of which his reign had "already given such striking testimonials," to "devise means for placing Poland in conditions of lasting peace."[7] It seems very unlikely that it could have been possible to draft a milder note. It seems highly doubtful that any note could have done less for Polish morale; and it seems equally doubtful that the contents of any note could have been of less concern to the United States government.

On May 11 Seward sent a reply via Dayton to the French Foreign Minister. Though negative, it embodied a pithy, and, in some respects, prophetic, review and restatement of American foreign policy. In his opening paragraph, he indicated polite approval of the French dispatch to St. Petersburg, but also hinted in a few choice phrases that the government of the United States did not intend to tread in any way on the toes of its Russian friends. It stated that the "enlightened and humane" character of Alexander, "so recently illustrated by the enfranchisement of a large mass of the Russian people from inherited bondage," and by "the establishment of an impartial and effective administration of justice throughout his dominions," would not permit him to ignore the appeal of the powers.[8]

Then, in a one-sentence paragraph, Seward presented his government's rejection of the suggestion that the United States make an approach to Russia. He noted with obvious tongue-in-cheek that despite the favor with which the United States regarded Napoleon's suggestion, it found "an insurmountable difficulty in the way of any active cooperation" with France, Austria, and England. To support this conclusion, Seward added two long paragraphs of historical explanation.

In the first of these, he mentioned that the then young American Republic had refused an urgent appeal for aid from revolution-torn France in spite of the existence of a mutual assistance treaty signed during the American Revolution; to this treaty,

Seward admitted, Americans owed their sovereignty and independence. The rejection of the French request was made in deference to the advice which George Washington had given in his Farewell Address. It involved a stern decision altogether contrary to emotional feelings towards France but governed by Washington's reminder that the location of America, "the characters, habits and sentiments of its constituent parts, and especially its complex yet unique and very popular Constitution" called for forbearance "at all times, and in every way, from foreign alliances, intervention and interference."[9]

The paragraph was in effect a lucid summation of a policy which had been adhered to by the American government since its establishment, but whose expression at official level had often been vague enough in the past to give European revolutionaries false illusions and hopes. It was most appropriate and shrewd on Seward's part to remind the French government of the first precedent, that of the French Revolution of 1789. This appropriateness and shrewdness were, ironically, underscored by the fact that the third Napoleon was, at the moment, trampling upon basic principles of that revolution.

The second paragraph of Seward's reply began with an admission that the first president had actually thought that a time might come when American institutions would be so well consolidated as to allow for participation in consultations with foreign states "for the common advantage of the nations." The Farewell Address was not an unchangeable, canonical writ of isolation. But Seward enumerated occasions where the American government, with the approval of the people, had avoided "seductions" into foreign projects. These included a congress of Spanish American states, the 1848 Hungarian Revolution, a joint guarantee of Cuba to Spain proposed by England and France, a "co-operative demonstration" in Mexico with England, France and Spain, and a suggested common council of republics in the Western Hemisphere. American reaction to all of the cited instances had strengthened the precedent set in Washington's day, Seward pointed out, and it certainly would not be wise to depart from this policy when the existence of a "local disturbance" prevented a portion of the American populace from giving the government its counsel.[10]

The note ended with some shallow expressions of American amity towards France. Seward was careful to note that Lincoln had hoped the French Emperor would not "see anything but respect and friendship for himself and the people of France" in his reply, and in American adherence to a policy which had been "pursued with safety, and not without advantage . . . to the interests of mankind."[11] In the entire note there was not a single phrase referring directly to the Poles, to their plight, or to their rights to freedom.

The very few American historians who have taken scholarly notice of Seward's note of May 11 tend to agree, and justifiably so, that on the basis of tradition, precedent, and immediate circumstances the Secretary of State could not have done otherwise. Further, the fact that three years later he had to resort to the Monroe Doctrine and to tell Napoleon in a less mild diplomatic note to get out of Mexico, points up the wisdom of his decisions in 1863.[12] Some historians see the French invitation to participate in the demarche as an act of spite, or as a move to embarrass the United States and retaliate for its caustic reply to Napoleon's 1862 mediation offer. Some also view it as a futile attempt to break up the "unwritten alliance" between the United States and Russia. Others consider it an attempt to focus the spotlight of European opinion on the "alliance," such opinion to include not merely that of anti-Northern conservative circles but also definitely pro-Northern and pro-Polish liberal views.[13]

Circumstantial historical evidence might substantiate any and all of these theories. However, it is evidence embodied in formal, diplomatic correspondence and in patterns of events and precedents. One might also theorize on the basis of the same evidence and see the attempted demarche as part of a crude, ill-timed, but, nevertheless, a calculated move by Napoleon to draw the Union closer to France, and, simultaneously, to alienate it completely from Great Britain. Some historians would even go to the extent of concluding that Napoleon envisaged a possibility of eventual Union recognition of the Maximilian regime in Mexico, with much improved relations. However, thus far, none of these judgments and conclusions have been based on exhaustive research into such often productive sources as the diaries and letters of contemporary French statesmen and diplomats, and the truism that the judgments of history are never final would seem to have strong application here.

Furthermore, historians who have dealt with the Seward reply have neglected to treat it in a really full light. They have not included considerations of that document's effects on both Polish and Russian morale. It seems that a few "safe" references by Seward to the legacy of Polish-American amity, perhaps just a mention of the names of Kosciuszko and Pulaski, might have buoyed up the Poles and influenced the Russians to treat them less harshly after the insurrection ended, without actually committing the Lincoln government to side with France, England, and Austria. Acknowledging that diplomacy is a matter of self-interest rather than sentiment, one might wonder nevertheless to what extent it was in the self-interest of the United States government to go to such an extreme in cultivating the friendship of an autocracy whose reciprocal feelings were never of equal measure. After all, when Gorchakov made his expressions of friendship for the Union to Bayard Taylor, he did not hesitate to indicate that the Russian government harbored no enmity towards the Southern rebels, their adherence to slavery notwithstanding.

Perhaps another truism might also be injected at this point— the truism that the proper study of history permits no "ifs" to be applied to the past. While the historian's craft tends to discourage the practice of retrospective prognostication, retroactive questioning, even in the form of rhetorical questioning, often stimulates further research which may lead to new conclusions. With this in mind, the rhetorical as well as other questions posed in the previous paragraphs will stand.

Finally, American diplomatic historians who have written about the May 11 note, have missed one of the interesting and significant denouements of the story. Copies of the note were forwarded to the United States ministers at two key listening posts. One went to Adams for possible use in discussions with members of the government in London. The other was sent to Clay in St. Petersburg. Adams made a routine acknowledgment. Partly at Seward's suggestion, Clay was to go several steps beyond that. But before taking them, he returned to his narrow view of the Polish situation.

On May 19, Clay sent his superior a dispatch concerning the notes which England, France, and some of Europe's smaller nations had addressed to Gorchakov re the Polish question. With great satisfaction, he commented that the Russian Foreign Minister's response had been "triumphant and exhaustive" and that it was so regarded by an "almost universal sentiment" among the Russians; the commercial circles, previously quite excited by fears of war over Poland, now had hopes of peace.[14] After taking a verbose "potshot" at England for her sympathies with France in the Mexican case, he brought in Poland, and, with all the air of a seer whose prophecies were being fulfilled, cited his own past opinions. He referred Seward to a dispatch he had sent him on March 19, 1862. "That letter fully expresses all I have to say upon Russian policy in Poland now," he noted confidently. The sum and substance of that dispatch was that England had agitated the Polish question to injure Russia just as Russia "was fixed in favor of the unity of the United States." The English were finding oppression in Poland under Alexander, Clay noted, while "they were quite satisfied with the liberalism of Nicholas!" And, after having continued in the same viciously Anglophobic vein through two paragraphs, he concluded that: (1) "England is full of grief over the progressive policy of Alexander in Poland, but has no tears to shed whilst a nation is destroyed by her ally France, in Mexico!" and (2) "The independence of Poland would injure Russia our friend—and the ruin of Mexico would weaken the United States." He suggested that the reasoning which governed American opposition to interference by European enemies in Mexico should dictate the course which the United States should pursue if they took action on Poland.[15]

Fortunately for the Polish cause, telegraphic communications had not yet been established between Russia and the United

States (it was one of Clay's unrealized projects to have the two nations linked by telegraph wire via Alaska). His suggestions arrived much too late to be of any influence on the State Department, and Seward's reply to the French invitation was drafted without the benefit of his dubious advice. Before Clay's copy had arrived in St. Petersburg, he had composed another dispatch in which he included the texts of addresses sent to Alexander by the "peasants" of Moscow and Smolensk and pledging their willingness to fight for him if a war developed over the Polish question. Clay pointed out that a "self-devotion and National feeling" which had "so often illustrated the history of Russia" had begun to exhibit itself in "a most marked manner," and that the notes of the European powers had aroused the whole empire sufficiently to make its enemies pause before attempting any intervention. Appended to the dispatch was a postscript, based on information from what he held to be "an intelligent, but unofficial source," which stated that the European powers had presented the Russian government with an ultimatum. He further expressed dismay that some of his countrymen might think a war between Russia and the Western powers would aid the Union. If successful in such a war, he warned, the powers would fall upon America in its "hour of distress and isolation."[16]

Clay killed the rumor of an ultimatum in his next dispatch and also reported a revealing conversation which he had had with Lord Napier. He stated that during their talk the British Minister to St. Petersburg had told him that "there was no decision on the part of the Western Powers in reference to Poland." Clay recorded other alleged admissions that Lord Napier had made to him. The British diplomat was supposed to have said that the popular feeling in England for the Poles was based upon false sympathy, and that although Alexander had not granted the Poles sufficiently liberal institutions, "it could not be denied" that they "had in all history showed themselves factious, and cruel in their foreign and domestic contests." Clay had remarked that the "Catholic element," which had caused Poland's downfall in the past, semed to be the real cause of its new unrest, and that a general war over Poland would only bring

France to the Rhine and help Catholicism in obstructing the progress of civilization. Lord Napier had allegedly responded that he was not sure "that it was the true policy of England to strengthen the Catholics [*sic*] and the 'Latin race' in Europe." [17]

Clay was back in his old vicious form. He made statements which would have heartened any fanatic Panslavist. Although Lord Napier's comments were more in the nature of headshaking elicited by Clay's leading questions rather than volunteered statements, they constituted still another revelation of the duplicity of the European powers towards Poland, as well as of their distrust of each other, and bore out the truth of many cynical American editorials.

With the leading actor thus warmed up for his role, the performance was about to begin. Clay received his copy of Seward's note to Drouyn de L'Huys on May 30. The same day, he drafted a note of enclosure to Gorchakov. As might have been expected, the note went beyond the bounds of diplomatic requirements and contained some most unnecessary embellishments. He had been instructed by Seward to communicate the contents of the note to the Russian court in an "informal way," he wrote Gorchakov, and he could think of no other way of performing "this agreeable duty" than by transmitting a "true transcript" of it. With great satisfaction he ended with the statement, "The undersigned is highly gratified to find his government thus sustaining so fully the sentiments which, indirectly in reference to Poland, he had upon the occasion of his late reception the honor to express to his Imperial Majesty." [18]

Gorchakov immediately submitted the notes to Alexander. The Czar was greatly pleased and ordered a letter signifying his satisfaction to be sent to Clay for transmittal to Seward. Gorchakov's epistle, replete with expressions of approval, amounted to no less than a declaration of friendship and came close to making at least one side's commitment to the "unwritten alliance" a *written* one. The letter was indeed good cause for expressions of painful embarrassment to appear on the countenances of those who had initiated the demarche proposal. In three very long paragraphs Gorchakov noted that Alexander was "sensibly moved" by the sentiments of confidence which the government of the United States had expressed in regard to his views and designs for "the general well-being of his Empire." Such a manifestation "must strengthen the bonds of mutual sympathy which unite the two countries," he added. He noted that the Czar had "equally appreciated the firmness with which the government of the United States maintains the principle of non-intervention, the meaning of which in these days is too often perverted." This, Gorchakov reiterated, "must increase the esteem" that Alexander had already avowed towards the American nation.[19]

The letter, which Gorchakov addressed to Clay, was not only expressive of amity but also of gratitude for an additional service rendered the Russian government by Clay. That service was spelled out in the dispatch to Seward in which Clay included the text of his note of transmittal to Gorchakov. In it, Clay reported that Gorchakov had called him for an interview the day before. He had asked the American diplomat for "the liberty" to publish Seward's reply to Drouyn de L'Huys. Without hesitation, or a necessary clearance from his superior, Clay had assented. Then, in typical fashion, he brashly justified to Seward his breach of procedure. He cockily pointed out that it was he who had decided upon its publication in Russia, and he then gave his reasons. He flattered Seward a bit by stating that his position in the note was not only just but not offensive to the Union's "principal rivals," who, on their part were acting offensively towards Russia. He felt that the intended effect upon England and France had already been achieved. Finally, he considered the moral support afforded Russia by such publication. That support was needed at once, he emphasized, and its efficiency might have been lost by a delay caused by asking for further instructions. "Above all," he went on, "I felt that it was due from us to be grateful for the past conduct of Russia towards us in our troubles by a like moral support of herself in defence of the integrity of her Empire." Clay concluded in a tone of virtual condescension to his superior. He stated that while he would try to make his actions harmonious with Seward's as to general policy, and this the Secretary had "a right" to expect, he would, in the absence of special instructions, pursue "the same frank and just conduct in state affairs" that he held to be proper in his private life.[20]

Seward acknowledged receipt of the dispatch at the end of June. In his acknowledgment there was absolutely nothing to indicate that he objected to Clay's action or resented his undue boldness. He stated: "While this government could not with propriety publish this correspondence, it could not object to its publication by either of the powers to whom it was furnished."[21] Meanwhile, Clay had already gone further. He had given Gorchakov permission to publish his own letter in the *Journal de St. Petersbourg,* and had advised Seward that "the whole correspondence" seemed to have been "most gratifying" to the Russians.[22] Again, the Secretary of State responded with a written nod of approval, deeming publication "entirely satisfactory."

Clay then began to rub salt in Polish wounds. In July he wrote Seward about the replies which Russia had given to the powers in regard to the so-called "Six-Point" note, their second attempt at a demarche. In his first paragraph he defended the logic of the replies. He applauded Gorchakov for stoutly refusing to allow even a projected European congress to discuss the Polish Insurrection and thereby intervene in Russia's internal affairs. He noted with glee that Gorchakov had skillfully gained an edge on England and France by reminding the London and Paris governments that the 1815 Treaty of Vienna, upon which they based their rights to intervene in Poland, had left the administration of the "Polish Kingdom" to the "discretion" of the Russian Emperor, and that Gorchakov had won the point on the basis of facts and logic. And then, in an addendum, Clay rubbed in more salt:

For my part, I see no reason to change my views in any respect to this contest: whether to weaken a rival in Europe—or our ally, who will, not to enter into a crusade against democracy in all the world for the benefit of the allied freebooters France and England, our interests and my sympathies are on the side of Russia—*liberal* Russia—against *reactionary,* Catholic and despotic Poland.[23]

The very same day Clay decided to give Seward the unsolicited benefit of his opinion on Mexico and to reiterate his belief that England would have welcomed a quarrel between the United States and France over that country. When he shifted his focus to Poland, however, he made a completely new analogy. He theorized that England would never condone the establishment by France of a Polish "Catholic monarchy," the reason being that only a "Greek monarchy," such as that of Russia, would side with the Protestants in any "war of religions." Therefore, he concluded, England would only temporarily support France and the Poles. She would foment trouble and keep up the fires of revolution to weaken Russia, but would never go to war. She was using Poland as a cat's-paw, concluded Clay, just as she was using the Confederacy—and she would not go to war over either. "What we have to do then," he bluntly advised Seward, "is to put down the rebellion—sustain Russia and the liberal party in Mexico—and, if need be, fight England and France in defence of Democracy and protestantism—or rather *toleration* in America."[24]

Clay reinforced his stand in two dispatches which he sent Seward in August. The first began as an acknowledgment of Seward's approval of his having allowed immediate publication of Gorchakov's letter in reply to the American note. After stating that he was awaiting the response of the powers to Russia's refusals and would "see how much further they will push their selfish interference with Russian affairs," he quoted from correspondence that had appeared in the London *Times* of July 31; this "unimpeachable testimony" from a friend of Poland and an enemy of Russia held that no measure based upon the six-point demands would ever "satisfy or even tranquilize Poland," and, also, that the Poles of the "Kingdom" had had everything short of complete independence before the insurrection. The fiery Clay put in his customary two cents by informing Seward that the three powers that had presented the demands (i.e., England, France, and Austria) were "stirring up strife from abroad, contrary to the desires of the great mass of the Polish people." He noted that they aimed to do one of two things: to gain by bloodshed, revolution, and waste of property what Russia was ready to grant peacefully, or, what she had already granted; or else, they aimed to wrest away from her territory "by treaty committed to the discretion of Russia for its government, and subsequently committed to the Russian Empire by conquest and the prestige of possession of three-fourths of a century!"[25]

After statements such as "consecration by conquest" and "prestige of possession," Clay continued by ranting:

> Here then I ask once more, why should Americans take part against an avowed friend, in behalf of the ally of avowed enemies? Why should protestant United States set up Catholocism [sic] against the tolerant Greek Church? Why should Republicans desire the overthrow of Russian liberalism to build up Polish conservatism with avowed anti-democratic institutions? For in the recent publication of Mr. Rolland a democrat, he declares that the Polish rebels hate liberalism as much as they do Russian tyranny. And still more, what right have these revolutionists to expect the support of any man of any party and of any religion, who have organized assassination into a system, as a means of establishing their Nationality?
>
> Their cause is as bad, as their methods are repugnant to the just sentiments of mankind, and violative of the laws of God: and every "progressive" the world over, should rejoice in the speedy overthrow of both.[26]

After he had freely quoted from English and French sources to substantiate his negative contentions in regard to Poland, Clay turned to a new source of justification—the Russian press. In his next dispatch, he included a translation of an article in the *Gazette de la Baltique* which stated that the insurrection had passed into the hands of the Polish aristocracy and that its "executive committee (self-styled the National Government)" sat in Paris; that its chief was Prince Vladimir Czartoryski, the son of Adam Czartoryski who had been the leader of the conservative forces in exile after the November Insurrection. The "Democratic Party" which had started the insurrection, the article indicated, had been pushed aside and had declared on several occasions that it preferred the rule of Russia to "that of the *Aristocracy and Priests*."[27]

There was a measure of truth in the *Gazette's* account. As has been indicated above, the "Whites" did, in fact, take over the insurrection for several months, and they did ignore the "Reds," who had engineered it. But even though the "Whites" placed their trust in European diplomacy and worked closely with the Paris Committee, they did not take their orders from Paris.

Clay added a few comments in his already established anti-Catholic, anti-British, pro-Czarist vein, directing them at those American editors who had hoped that the Polish Insurrection would forestall European intervention in the Civil War. In the margin he made the notation, "Folly of the American Press," and added:

> Our press may build hopes of liberal progress upon Catholic revolution, I shall not. Napoleon who in the name of freedom, overthrew the French Republic—who, in the cause of the integrity of nations, warred upon Russia,—and yet dismembered Austria, in the name of progress, which he stays by a French army in Rome,— who sets up a Catholic and Monarchial automaton in Mexico, avowedly to check the expression of Republican power,—is not the man to do any work which progressives anywhere can approve. And yet our press insanely following the lead of British journals, wars upon our natural and avowed ally the emperor of Russia, to build up the Kingdom of Poland, the friend of France: when even the Democratic Revolutionists themselves declare that sooner than be the victims of "Aristocrats and Priests," they would return, with halters around their necks, to Russian subjugation![28]

Cassius Marcellus Clay closed with a prediction which was to come true in a matter of weeks. The Russians would stand firm, he told Seward, Austria would hesitate, England would not risk a war, and France would be balked in her designs. Thus, his second series of vituperative discourses on Poland ended—he had gone far beyond the boundaries of his diplomatic calling and also very far beneath propriety and politeness. And Seward's tolerance had made him a virtual accomplice in Clay's actions.

How did the American press react to all this? The May 11 note, although it brought the Civil War and the Polish January Insurrection into the closest proximity, received amazingly little editorial attention in both Northern and Southern journals, and only after a long lapse of time. Because of the State Department's policy of not publishing diplomatic correspondence in the newspapers, the contents of the note became known late and via a circuitous route. The dispatch was printed in the New York papers during the second half of June, as a translation of a French text that had first appeared in a *Belgian* newspaper on June 8! The New York papers had had no inkling of the note's existence until information had come from St. Petersburg the week before.

A second reason for the lack of extensive editorial comment was the fact that the Northern press approved wholeheartedly of the note's strict adherence to the Monroe Doctrine. A typical editorial presentation of the text appeared in the *Daily National Intelligencer*. The complete re-translated text of the note was printed in a column captioned "Diplomatic Correspondence," and it was prefaced by two very short and altogether complimentary paragraphs. Here the comment was made that the correspondence between Drouyn de L'Huys and Seward was interesting because of its subject matter and, equally so, because of "the admirable temper on which it is conducted and the spirit of international comity which it breathes." Seward's note would "commend itself to all, being no less dictated by present considerations of public duty than by conformity to the traditional policy of the Republic."[29]

Only the *New York Spectator* made a more extensive analysis. It is noteworthy because it shows the ambivalence which must have plagued its editor. The editorial opened with a statement to the effect that the sympathies of the American people were "almost without exception on the side of Poland against *all* the Powers that despoiled her of her independence." It added that Seward's policy would "elicite an equally general approval." It applauded the logic of his reply and, particularly, its logical adherence to the Monroe Doctrine. "There are, no doubt, evils in almost every region of the globe," it contended, "which are susceptible of removal, and some of which might be modified by us, if we are to set out on a Quixotic errand of a pell-mell regeneration of the universe. But the operation would be vastly more costly than beneficial." Because of this, it agreed that the best thing America could do was to follow its own destiny on the North American continent and recommend that other nations profit by her example "wherein it is worthy of imitation."[30]

The second half of the *Spectator's* editorial hit at more significant and immediate considerations. Had Seward agreed to a demarche, it noted, he would have played into the hands of England and France, for these powers would have committed him to "a crooked line of conduct." In the wake of such a commitment, every "Tory or reactionist" newspaper in Europe would have called for the same remedy to be applied to the United States. In conclusion, it reminded its readers that the Czar had shown himself a friend of the Union since the outbreak of the Civil War. No privateers had been allowed to escape from his ports to prey on Northern commerce, no demonstrations had been made in his realm for the recognition of the Confederacy, and whenever his government had spoken, it had spoken in favor of preserving the Union. Censuring him on Poland meant censuring a friend for evils which had been inaugurated by his predecessors. The editorial equated the oppression of the Poles with the oppression of the American Negro. The former as well as the latter, it claimed, had been bequeathed by one generation to another and, therefore, "those that went before" should be held mainly responsible for the abuses and crimes that had resulted.[31]

Southern journals utilized Seward's May 11 note as ammunition for their constant barrage of insults against the North. The *Richmond Daily Whig* mentioned the note in a one-paragraph editorial entitled "The League of Despots," which called Seward presumptuous for replying at all, since he was the representative of a government that was "breaking down." It satirized the friendship between the Czar and Lincoln by saying that it was only natural that "the two greatest of living despots, each engaged in an effort to subjugate a people struggling for independence, should sympathize with and encourage each other." Its final comment was terse and biting: "Alexander II and Abraham I are a very loving and interesting pair."[32]

In another column in the same issue, a much longer editorial attacked England for her failure to intervene on behalf of the Confederacy at the invitation of France. It contrasted this failure with British attempts on behalf of Poland, and noted that in the case of the Confederacy her intercession would have been for a people "descended from her loins, speaking her language, inheriting her laws, religion and, to a large extent, institutions," whereas her intercession in Poland was volunteered for a people "foreign to her by lineage, language, interests and religion." Intervention in favor of the Confederacy would have been "on behalf of States had been acknowledged by herself nearly a century ago, to be free and independent" while the Poles had not known independence for nearly as long a time and had been recognized merely as "the liege subjects of Russia" by a treaty to which England had been a party. Its final conclusion was that all of England's actions on behalf of the Poles were prompted by "the pompous and Pecksniffian morality, the cheap and pretentious philanthropy with which she is accustomed to comfort herself and delude mankind."[33]

Even more cynical was an editorial which appeared in the *Whig* a few days later under the caption, "Poor Alexander!" While it pointed out that "the French remonstrance" had compounded Alexander's troubles with the Poles, it added that "the last of the Romanoffs" knew better than anyone else that "the last of the Napoleons" was swimming with the current of French opinion to avoid drowning in it. French opinion, commented the writer, was sincere in its sympathy toward the Poles. Frenchmen remembered the past struggles of the Polish nation and felt some guilt at the absence of aid from their own government. The name of their current ruler served to remind them of the heroic achievements of Polish soldiers who fought under the first Napoleon. However, all that Napoleon III had done was to protest. The writer felt that the protest, had it been made by Napoleon alone, would have been like a nauseous draught to Alexander but that he would have gulped it down "like a man and a philosopher." But there had been mixed into it bitter doses on the part of Austria, a partner and accomplice "in the grand act of highway robbery" which had swept Poland from the map of Europe, and of England, "the oppressor of nationalities in Ireland, in India" and wherever else it had suited her selfish interests or her commerce. Worst of all, the editorial groaned in mock pity, poor Alexander would also be exposed to "genuine Yankee vulgarity and impertinence." Seward would inform him that "the great Yankee nation, so powerful at home—(*vide* Manassas, Seven Pines, Fredericksburg, etc.)—so highly respected abroad (*vide* the Slidell-Mason affair and the European newspapers *passim*)— would not cast its powerful weight and immense moral and material influence on the side of Poland and the Continental Powers."[34]

The *Daily Richmond Examiner,* sounding equally militant, took time out from its almost exclusive preoccupation with domestic affairs to inform its readers of the situation in Poland. Its appraisal was another illustration of the feeling that the Southern cause was superior to that of Poland. After generalizing about the Confederacy's struggle for self-preservation as a factor which made for indifference and lack of interest in the struggles of other nations, it called attention to "two scenes" which "would at another time be observed, one with breathless interest, and the other with warmest sympathy." The former, the French conquest of Mexico, was noted in a single sentence. The latter, the Polish struggle, received extensive treatment. The *Examiner's* editor felt strongly that the Polish cause was "in essence" identical with the Confederate cause. Both Poland and the Confederacy, it commented, were engaged in a "battle of a nation for independence, an effort of a people to deliver themselves from foreign tyranny, to gain the power to govern itself, by its own laws and according to its own interests." In this respect the editorial noted a minor difference: the Confederacy was fighting to prevent subjugation, while the Poles were fighting to shake off a subjugation that had been of long duration.[35]

The editorial, switching from parallels to contrasts, next described Poland as a "galvanized" corpse and the Confederate States as "a family of giants, obscure only because they have never known calamity." It stated that Poland had never had a government worthy of the name while the Southern states had governments "older than the Federation which oppressed them."

Thus, while the Polish revolutionary National Government resembled the "desperate writhing of a trodden worm," the Confederacy had "stept on the Globe like a Minerva when she sprang from the brain of Jupiter." The Southerners, it went on with an obvious air of superiority, were "a race unbroken to servitude, skillful in arms, generally educated, and possessing an abundance of trained officers." This resulted in "gigantic battles, systematic campaigns, and all the glorious circumstances of historic war." Poland's struggle, on the other hand, was "only a grand guerilla fight, without plan, beginning or end."[36]

The *Examiner's* editor saw some so-called advantages accruing to the Poles. He termed Czar Alexander "a weak and vacillating monarch, with head full of theories and a sentimental heart," and the "oligarchy of the United States" more brutal and determined than were Alexander's despotic predecessors, Peter and Catherine the Great. He lamented that Poland had the help of Europe, while Europe left the South to fight alone. In his summation, he argued that the situation in the Confederate States and that in Poland paralleled each other "in nothing but their impulse"; that the South and also the Poles obeyed a human law which would not allow "two peoples, powerful and distinct, to remain under the government of one of the two." He saw only two alternatives in such a situation: extermination or endless insurrection until independence is achieved anew.[37]

The *Examiner's* editorial revealed as strong a sense of identification and as much sympathy as the Southern press would want to make explicit in the Polish question. It was a partial identification reflecting a limited sympathy. The Confederacy could by no means be considered an ally of the Poles either in letter or in spirit. The relationship was certainly not akin to the much greater warmth which the North had begun to feel toward Russia.

As the summer of 1863 reached its mid-point, stories of atrocities began to come out of Poland. Among the papers which gave them editorial space was the *North American and United States Gazette*. It prefaced them with the statement that "the conduct of the Russians continues to be of the most ferocious

kind, and utterly disgraceful to a nation pretending to be civilized." It told of "ladies and aged men being carried bound . . .
and shut up in barracks, of children being shot, of wives applying to Russia commanders on behalf of their husbands, and
being answered that the latter would certainly be put to death,
of burning and pillage everywhere, of mercy nowhere." It added:
"Had the Czar a horde of wild savages to deal with, he could
not act with greater barbarity."[38]

But in New York, the *Times* issued an editorial warning. It
stated that without information from Russian journals and without other means "of learning the Russian version of affairs," the
American press was almost entirely dependent on the London
Times and other British newspapers for its information. The *New
York Times* told its readers that the spirit prevailing in the
columns of British newspapers was largely anti-Russian, and
what was worse, "nearly all of them, and the [London] *Times*
especially, have an inveterate habit of lying without scruple
whenever their inclinations prompt." It detailed the story of a
Dr. Mackey, who was the correspondent of the *Times* in the
United States and had been sending back lies about the Civil
War. It then commented: "When we see in the London Times
letters from the special in Poland, we should at once understand
the moral level of their author . . . there is not a particle of reason
why its correspondent in Warsaw should not be presumed to be
just as mendacious as we know its correspondent in New York
to be." Strongly doubting the atrocity stories and the accounts
of insurgent victories, the *Times* advised readers to place the
stories of barbarities committed by Russian General Muraviev
in the same category as the stories of the barbarities of Union
General "Beast" Butler and Colonels Turchin and McNeill, and
also to place the stories of Polish victories in the same category
as stories of Confederate victories. Furthermore, it urged that
"Polish claims to sympathy and Polish prospects of independence
should have just the weight of the same judgments upon the
Confederate claims and prospects—and no more." This was followed by a sentence sounding like a slogan: "Hatred of Russia
and hatred of the United States shape all alike."[39]

However, the *Times'* editorial did not stop at merely warning its readers against believing the English press. It gave its own evaluation of the insurrection, dwelling at first on alleged similarities between Russia and the United States. Western Europe hated both powers, the *Times* told its readers, because of jealousy of their gigantic growth. The *Times* also told them that the Polish struggle had received an impetus from the fact that the liberal and progressive Alexander had filled nearly all administrative posts in the "Kingdom" with Poles; similarly, the South had derived its first great advantage in the Civil War from the fact that its state and local governments were also in the hands of natives.[40]

Next, for the first time in the Northern press, some odious parallels were drawn between the Polish and the Southern rebellions. The editorial expounded:

What the Polish revolutionists claim is not political amelioration, but national independence. They demand that the Russian ruler shall submit to a dismemberment of his empire. They will take nothing less. Americans who are fighting against a similar movement, cannot call in question the Emperor's right to resist. There is still another analogy between his contest and ours. We have always said that but a minority of the Southern people are at heart in favor of the rebellion. In Poland the minority is comparatively much smaller. Out of the twenty millions of Poles, not more than five or six millions are taking any part in the movement. The peasantry are almost universally opposed to it. They believe it to be a movement for the benefit of the nobles, and that their own interests really bind them to Russia, which has so decisively committed itself to the elevation of all the lower classes within its dominions. Their case, in fact, is very much like that of the "poor white trash" in our Southern States, but they are wiser in their action. The latter were drawn into a revolution designed to benefit only the great landholders, but the former have steadfastly held out against all attempts to use them for such a purpose. There has been no nobility in all Europe more utterly selfish, more completely regardless of the comfort and well-being of their vassals than that of Poland; and even up to the very time of the insurrection, they opposed all allotment of land to the peasants, like that secured to the Russian serfs by the imperial edict of emancipation. Undoubtedly there are Democrats in this revolutionary movement—men who would rejoice to throw themselves into any enterprize that would break up the present condition of Europe. But those Democrats are not numerous enough to give distinctive character to the struggle. The Polish insurrection is not, in any just sense of the term, a popular revolution—less so in fact than our own Southern rebellion. Our sympathies with it ought to spring from better knowledge of the truth than is afforded by the Russia-hating press of England.[41]

As the news of Gorchakov's reply to the Six-Point Note reached America, the atrocity stories were shelved and the balance of American opinion began to tip more in favor of Russia. The European powers, the foes of the Union, had shown diplomatic weakness. Gorchakov had shown diplomatic strength, and many Americans wondered whether the Poles perhaps had asked too much in demanding complete independence rather than autonomy. This particular line of reasoning was embodied in an editorial appearing in the *Philadelphia Inquirer*. Like Cassius Marcellus Clay, the *Inquirer's* editor praised Gorchakov for his coolness in handling the Six-Point Note. He listed the Russian minister's three counterpoints: (1) The Polish Insurrection was a movement limited to "a turbulent minority upon which all Governments would look with reproach." (2) The Insurgents did not want "liberal institutions, and a reasonable autonomy" but called for full independence. (3) The insurgents counted on foreign intervention and agitation in foreign capitals. Temporizing a bit, he admitted that in the "European imbroglio" the first American impulse would have been to side morally with Poland "*par excellence*, the most ill-treated country on the map of Europe; the dupe, the victim, the martyr of a contemptible autocracy, in which if Russia was the chief gainer, Austria and the corrupt Hapsburgs were the chief machinators." Poland's independence, were it possible, would be a realization of many Americans' childhood dreams. But, he hastened to add, at the moment there had to be an abeyance in the realization of such dreams. Napoleon III was not interested in Polish freedom; neither was Napoleon I "when he roused the Poles with his clarion voice in 1812." Both Napoleons wanted to humiliate Russia, the editor explained to his readers, and although Americans might wish for the reconstitution of Poland, they could not wish for an increase in French power or for the "loss of influence" by their "new ally Russia." Americans could still feel sanguine about Poland's freedom, he noted half reassuringly in his closing sentences, but it should be a freedom worked out in "regular steps," not by "the volcanic force of a revolution." Who would take the "regular steps"? The *Inquirer's* editor had a pat answer, embodied in somewhat poetic phrases: "The private spirit that prompted and the public spirit that urged the emancipation of Russian serfs . . ." would "day by day ameliorate the Polish condition."[42]

*   *   *   *   *

An interesting and ironic postscript to the story of the May 11 note and its repercussions may be found in the diplomatic correspondence of the Polish National Government to its Paris representative, Prince Wladyslaw Czartoryski. Item 9 in a routine dispatch from Warsaw, dated June 24, 1863, tersely noted:

Regarding foreign diplomacy, attention here was called to two items which happened to arrive from abroad almost unnoticed, namely the Spanish and American notes on our question. In our national press the subject was not even discussed. As for America, we here regard Mr. Seward's dispatch as a symptom of the Union's weakness, as an act of petty spite against the stand which the Western Powers take in favor of the Confederacy. Yet, although Mr. Seward's note is not favorable, neither is it in the least injudicious.[43]

CHAPTER VI

AIDING THE POLES:
ACTIVITIES AND FRUSTRATIONS

AT THE TIME of Cassius Marcellus Clay's second departure for St. Petersburg two interesting paragraphs of comment appeared in the *Philadelphia Inquirer*. The comment was partly revealing, partly damning, and partly damaging. Written by the *Inquirer's* special correspondent in New York, it was hidden among several nondescript items dealing with local events. The correspondent started off quite routinely with a brief report of a reception that had been given in honor of Lincoln's friend-emissary by a few individuals in the metropolis. Before he concluded his first paragraph, however, his description gave way to personal opinion. He gave as his opinion that Clay would be returning to the Russian capital under more embarrassing circumstances if New Yorkers had yielded "to popular impulses," i.e., to the demands for a public meeting at the Academy of Music that had been voiced immediately after the American press had printed the first news of the Polish Insurrection.[1]

In his next paragraph, the correspondent proceeded to elaborate on this statement. He supported his conclusions by pointing out that a pro-Polish demonstration of sympathy would have done the Poles no good and probably would have "put the Russian bear in bad humor" with Americans. Americans could not help but instinctively sympathize with Poland, he admitted, but it did not follow that they ought to go out of their way "to

122

make an enemy of a friend" when they had no friends to spare in Europe; and the surest way they could help the cause of liberty in the Old World was to concentrate all their energies on the preservation of their government in the New World.[2]

Had the correspondent chosen to terminate his comments here, his readers might have had cause to credit him with original thinking. They would have had no reason to believe that his entire disquisition, along with its cautious rationale and patriotic considerations, were not expressive of his own feelings. However, he added a closing sentence which indicated that his strongly expressed sentiments had been inspired by a conversation during the reception and that "they were cordially endorsed and responded to by Mr. Clay himself."

In spite of his allusion to sympathy for Poland as an American "instinct" and in spite of the quasi-exonerative tone of his concluding sentence, a shadow of justifiable doubt might be cast on the objectivity of the *Inquirer's* man in New York. His later correspondence referring to the Polish situation bears this out.[3] Nevertheless his comments are rather significant, since they reflect the thinking of an important segment of urban society in the North. Socially, politically, and philanthropically, the men who had feted Clay were among the most powerful and highly respected in New York. Even though no specific names were mentioned in the report, it noted that the reception had been held at the residence of a well-known personage on the then fashionable Lexington Avenue. The report is also of great interest for its making plain the fact that Clay had sanctioned or agreed to the comments made; at the same time it indicates that he had an obsequious coterie around him, far from averse to disseminating his opinions among the city's more sophisticated inhabitants.

The correspondent's comments went beyond what might have been logically anticipated—beyond the mere apathy and indifference which certainly would have been excusable in a war requiring the mobilization of charity and propaganda as well as the military. But did the same or similar considerations of expediency and the desire for Russo-American amity govern the attitudes of many other Americans? There is ample evidence to warrant a conclusion that such was the case. There is some evidence to that effect in written sources, but there is even more convincing proof in the unwritten record of silence. The former can be cited. The latter becomes apparent when the scanning of hundreds of pages of newspapers and journals confirms that there were no more than a few random columns pertaining to public meetings, protests, aid committees, and fund collections on behalf of the Poles. The apparent disinterest is further evidenced when the coverage of the activities in 1863 is compared with the abundant coverage of the activities in 1831.[4]

American journals in 1863 printed scores of items dealing with what some had termed a "Polish crusade." They told of a movement which had taken hold of the entire European continent and the British Isles as soon as the insurrection had shown signs of sustaining itself. And as previously mentioned, they printed the texts of exhortatory addresses made by Garibaldi.[5] In a single edition of the *Philadelphia Inquirer* there was not only an account of a meeting held in Glasgow which had been addressed by the exiled German socialist Karl Blind, and a meeting held in Stockholm which had been addressed by the exiled Russian anarchist Mikhail Bakunin, but also accounts of English town meetings held in Wakefield and Leicester, presided over by the town mayors, and a proposed meeting under the aegis of the London Trades Unions, which earlier had demonstrated in favor of the North. There was also a note on collections that had been taken up for the Polish insurgents in impoverished Greece.[6] Before the year reached its mid-point, the press noted that the ripple of collective sympathy had reached as far as Australia.

But these journals printed almost nothing to show that similar movements had been initiated in their own cities; nothing to indicate that a zealous spark might have been kindled anywhere in the United States or the Confederate States. The occasional, usually terse, items which they did contain togther, formed a loose narrative that seemed to end almost immediately after its weak beginning. This narrative salvaged from miscellaneous and rather obscure sources, is scanty, widely spaced in time and location, and it has a roster of characters whose names are, in the main, obviously not native American. Among the very few who helped write it was the previously mentioned New York correspondent of the *Philadelphia Inquirer;* his semi-sarcastic humor would have made his readers wary or completely indifferent to any call by Polish exiles to aid their struggling compatriots. His opening lines in a letter dated March 10 betrayed his attitude:

A meeting to sympathize with down-trodden Poland is to be held at Steuben House on Saturday evening next. Many eminent orators are announced to speak. There is some talk in the lager beer salons, by the way, about organizing a "Legion" here, to take an active part in the Rebellion, if circumstances should render it expedient.[7]

Obviously, the last sentence did not convey the idea that the proposed meeting was to be taken seriously. In his following letter, when the correspondent wrote about the meeting, his phraseology had the same air of flippancy about it. He reported that a preliminary demonstration had been held on March 14 at the Steuben House; that there had been "spirit-stirring addresses by Messrs. CEDROWSKI, KACZEWSKI, RAZEWSKI and others"; and that at the "very earnest and enthusiastic meeting" an eloquent message to the Polish National Committee had been agreed upon. "In the course of a few days," he informed his editor, "we shall have a rousing meeting at the Academy of Music for Young Poland."[8]

Aside from the sympathetic editorial endorsement given the Steuben House gathering by the *Sun,* New York newspapers devoted no space to it. But the *Sun's* approval and its hope that the gathering would devise a plan for "an adequate expression" of the sympathy felt by Americans for the Polish insurgents, were in part negatively inspired. In addition to pointing out that such an expression was a matter of honor to the people of the United States "as republicans," it admonished Americans not to lag behind the subjects of the monarchical governments of Europe in manifesting that sympathy "for a cause that seems to represent the wants and necessities of the oppressed in all the earth." Surprisingly, the *Sun* concluded that the "ardent sympathy" of the American people could "go far towards saving the Polish Revolution from falling into the desperate clutches of Lord PALMERSTON and the French and Austrian Emperors."[9]

The *Herald,* which later assumed a negative attitude in the matter of aid to the Poles, was the only New York journal that covered the Steuben Hall gathering in any detail. Next to a three-column account of an "immense meeting" held the same evening at the Academy of Music by the rabidly pro-Union Loyal League, it noted that the "resident Poles of New York and their numerous friends" also had an "interesting meeting" to express their feelings and to devise measures for "raising practical aid" and for enlisting "the generous and already awakened sympathy of the American nation." Another phrase indicated that the individuals who had called the preliminary gathering entertained some fears regarding the possible success of the contemplated mass demonstration. The writer of the article noted that they intended to call it only "when there cannot be a doubt [that] the attendance of our citizens will be of an overwhelming kind, as serviceable to Poland as creditable to the United States."[10]

The roster of speakers at the Loyal League rally included New York's Mayor Opdyke and the future Vice President of the United States, Andrew Johnson. The *Herald's* account listed no personage of comparable political stature at the Steuben House meeting. The addresses, which it printed in English, were delivered in Polish and directed to Polish exiles. The chief speaker was Roman Jaworowski, whose prominence derived from the fact that he was to be the editor of New York's first Polish-language newspaper.[11] Cedrowski (who acted as chairman of the gathering), Karczewski, and Raszewski were undoubtedly well-known among their fellow exiles, but it is doubtful whether their influence extended to significant numbers of native-born Americans. It was in such manner that the first sparks of attempted collective expression on behalf of the Polish January

Insurrection were kindled in America—much too inauspiciously —by Poles themselves.

To carry out a program of propaganda and philanthropic work, the Steuben House gathering selected a committee to be called the Polish Central Committee in the United States. All sixteen members were from the Polish community. Three were officers in the Union Army: Brigadier General Vladimir Krzyzanowski, Colonel (later Brigadier General) Joseph Karge, and Captain (later Major) Alexander Raszewski. Through them a spiritual link was forged between the Committee and the many ex-European revolutionaries who were serving with the armies of the North. The link would prove to be a durable one.[12]

The final act of the Steuben House gathering was the adoption of a message, composed by Jaworowski and addressed to the "Red" Central National Committee in Warsaw. It was, in effect, a pledge of loyal support even to the point of sending volunteers.[13]

From its headquarters at 926 Broadway, the Polish Central Committee established contacts with Polish exile groups in London and Paris. Towards the end of April it issued an appeal to the American people. The text of the appeal was printed in some of the Northern journals. A few newspapers called their readers' attention to it; but nearly all of these refrained from making any editorial comments. There were two noteworthy exceptions, the *New York Herald* and the *New York Spectator*. Interestingly, their opinions were almost complete opposites.

The sensation-inclined *Herald* took a negative stand. It printed the appeal on one page and on the next it advised its readers that giving "pecuniary aid" to the Poles would be contrary to America's position and policy. "At no time have the American people evinced much disposition to interfere in the political struggles of other communities," it generalized, and the best form of encouragement would be their own successful efforts at self-government. It admitted that on several occasions in the past collections had been taken to aid foreign revolutions, but that they had been "on a very limited scale, and not at all to be taken as expressions of the national sentiment." Furthermore, the funds had been diverted from their original purposes in a manner which had destroyed American confidence.[14]

Giving vent to nothing but a feeling of discouragement, the editorialist also skirted the full truth in his historical generalizations. If he had recalled the subscriptions which poured in for the Polish cause in 1831, he would have reconsidered his statements to the effect that such subscriptions were on a "limited scale" and that they were not to be taken as expressions of the national sentiment. On the other hand, his statement concerning the diversion of funds reflected the disillusioning effect of the petty squabbles among the exiles and the suspicion that had followed in their wake.

Lastly, the *Herald's* writer reinforced his blunt admonitions with a new consideration, and thus put an added damper on the Central Committee's appeal, while also indicating that the thinking of the *Herald* was very much in step with that of Cassius Marcellus Clay and his entourage. It would be both ungrateful and unwise, the editorialist concluded, to add "sanction to a proceeding" which, without doing the Poles any good, would certainly destroy the cordial relations between the Union and Russia.[15]

The editor of the more restrained *Spectator*, James Hall,[16] was especially impressed by the wording of the appeal. He built his editorial around the words of forgiveness directed by the Poles toward their Russian enemies; these expressions probably had been intentionally inserted by the committee in order to win over those citizens of the United States who had sympathetic inclinations towards Alexander and his government. The *Spectator's* editor began by calling the attention of his readers to the phraseology of the appeal and by advising them that it was not "the language of a feeble, nerveless race, who are afraid of danger, and who anticipating failure, would have the world attribute it to an excess of Christian sentiment."[17]

After quoting further from the appeal, Hall called the attention of his readers to areas where a "hearty sympathy" had already been manifested on behalf of the Poles—Paris, Stockholm, Madrid, Turin, Belgium, Switzerland, and Denmark, and even St. Petersburg itself where a society had been formed to "put forth a strong manifesto."[18] He also noted that the Polish exiles had called upon "the home of the exile, the land of liberty, the country in which the names of Kosciusko and Pulaski are household words" to help the victims of the "glorious war" waged in order that "Poland may once more live."[19]

Hall's concluding paragraph was a brief but sincere endorsement of the appeal. Its single sentence read: "The hands of our countrymen are now full; yet we cannot doubt that many of our citizens, whose munificence has been shown on every occasion when the claims of suffering humanity presented themselves, will share their abundance with the Polish sufferers, even though the Emperor of Russia be our friend."[20]

No one could have accused the *Spectator's* editor of being an excited idealist or a rabid Polonophile. His concluding statement proved that he, too, had given thought to some of the practical realities of the moment. It showed, in particular, that like his journalistic confrére of the *Herald*, he was fully aware of the friendship between the United States and Russia. However, this awareness did not make him as extremely cautious as the editor of the *Herald*. To the Polish Central Committee—and to the insurrectionary cause—it was unfortunate that the livelier daily *Herald* reached a much larger reading public than the sedate *Spectator*. It seemed that, as far as New York City was concerned, the committee's appeal had fallen on deaf or deafened ears. There were no reports of collections nor of subscriptions. There were no mass demonstrations or citizen's committees.

The only sign of any response by native New Yorkers to the appeal appeared in a local news item tucked away in the middle pages of the *Times*. The item noted that on May 21 a group of ladies had met at the home of "Mrs. Dr." Crane at 31 West 21st Street in order to organize an American Ladies' Committee. The group's statement of purpose clearly indicated that the functions of the committee were to be purely charitable; and, lest anyone still might have misinterpreted their intentions, the good ladies added: "We have no wish to harm Russia. She has given evidence of friendship too often to allow us to regard her with a single feeling of ill-will, but we are women, the cause of humanity is our sacred trust and through us it must ultimately prevail."[21]

Subsidiary to the Polish Central Committee in New York were Polish Committees in Cincinnati, Chicago, St. Louis, Albany, Philadelphia, Leavenworth City, and San Francisco.[22] The activities of the first six of these have not been recorded in American journals. It might well be assumed from this that they met with the same disappointments and indifference as their parent body. The activities of the San Francisco committee, however, were extensively recorded, not only by the local press but by newspapers all over the Union, and are worthy of recounting in detail.

The Poles of San Francisco held their first meeting relative to the insurrection on April 16 at the Russ House, a leading hotel. According to the San Francisco *Evening Bulletin,* the gathering was a "numerous" one. Its chairman was a prominent California surveyor, Captain Casimir Bielawski, who had also been elected president of the Polish Committee. The first address was delivered by a "Forty-Niner," Captain Rudolph Korwin Piotrowski. In it, he exhorted his compatriots to "go to work" to encourage their brethren in Poland and at the same time to show them "that the American interest was with them." The second address was delivered by Colonel James C. Zabriskie, a native son whose Polish ancestor had come to America in the seventeenth century. After discoursing briefly on the tragic chapters in Polish history, Zabriskie discussed the feasibility of American aid to the insurgents. He mentioned the argument that it would be prudent for Americans to refrain from such activity while the United States was engaged in a "tremendous struggle for national existence." This argument he answered by first acknowledging its validity, and then by noting that "the shock of arms and the tumults of the war was [sic] but little felt in California," and that "from that very circumstance" Californians should prove "more susceptible to sympathy with the Polish cause."[23]

The colonel also took into consideration the argument that Russia was a friend of the United States, and countered it quite astutely. He argued that Russia could afford to show kindness to the Union since her main intent was to promote commercial intercourse. He praised her government for having liberated the serfs, but stated that he would never cease to condemn it for the barbarities perpetrated against Poland. He then likened Russia to a hero-turned-traitor whose wooden leg was buried with full military honors but whose body was ignominiously suspended from a gibbet.

Piotrowski and Zabriskie pleaded Poland's case successfully. On May 22, the citizenry of San Francisco held a mass rally at Platt's Hall. According to the *Bulletin,* it was "fully attended" and graced by the presence of some of the city's eminent personages. The newly elected mayor, William A. Cornwall, presided. One committee was chosen to collect funds, another was elected to draft resolutions. Speeches were delivered by native Americans as well as by Polish exiles. The commander of the Union Army's Pacific Department, General George Wright, sent his best wishes, and a message of sympathy was composed and unanimously approved.[24]

Although the newspapers of San Francisco refrained from extensive editorialization, they gave both meetings wide and unequivocally sympathetic coverage. The *Bulletin's* timely publication of the Polish Central Committee's appeal to the American people on the day of the mass meeting was undoubtedly of value in assuring a large attendance.[25]

Ironically, the *Bulletin* later printed a lengthy letter of protest addressed to its editor by a Russian resident of San Francisco. The writer, whose name was not given, lamented bitterly that "shrewd" Polish exiles had managed to collect "the best talents, orators and learning" in California in an attempt to "turn away the hearts of the Americans from their best and sincerest friends." While he began by describing the Polish people as "valiant and heroic," he also termed them "very quarrelsome." He cited instances of disunity in Poland's past history and noted that such disunity was reappearing in the quarrel between Mieroslawski and Langiewicz. He accused the Polish clergy of ignorance and fanaticism, the Polish nobility of oppression of the peasantry, and England and France of hypocrisy for condemning Russia's rebellion while ignoring their own. "Ah, you Americans," he bewailed in his conclusion, "you forget that the fire not only rages in your own houses but also in your neighbor's, and still you run to put the torch to the homes of your far distant true friends." Finally, he addressed himself half apologetically to the exiles: "As to our brethren, the Poles, I can only say there is no harsh feeling in any Russian breast; but the honor of Russia demands that she should not be forced into conditions which she could not accept."[26]

Subsequent editions of the *Bulletin* carried no rebuttals to the Russian letter writer's arguments. However, they gave sufficient indication that such arguments were much less effective than the appeals of the Polish exiles and their supporters. As evidence of this there are several lists of subscribers and subscriptions to a Polish aid fund, a brief report of the Polish Committee of San Francisco, and also a letter of acknowledgment from Europe. The report, printed in the *Bulletin's* September 4 edition, contained a laudatory editorial preface stating that the Polish fund was "steadily growing towards respectable dimensions." It boasted that Californians had been able to take care of the feeding and clothing of Union troops while at the same time they employed "a portion of their superabundant vigor and wealth in encouraging those who are struggling to achieve liberty." It also announced that $6,000 had already been received by "Poland's friends in France" and that another $2,000 was aboard a steamer heading for the east coast.[27]

The report noted that the second installment of funds also was to be remitted to the Polish Revolutionary Committee in Paris (of the $2,000 total, $750 had been received from Victoria, British Columbia), and that the Paris Committee had acknowledged receipt of the first installment. The report was signed by Edward Lazard, who was the Chairman of the Polish Committee of San Francisco and a partner in Lazard Frères, the international banking firm that transmitted the funds to their European destination, and by the Committee's Secretary, Colonel Zabriskie. The full text of the Paris Committee's acknowledgment, written by its President, Ksawery Galezowski, was printed in translation in the *Bulletin* in late September. Indicating the gratitude of the recipients, it pointed out that the sympathy of American citizens was "precious" to the Polish cause. This statement appeared on the same page as a very brief item which portended an event that was to draw this sympathy away from Poland to the gain of her adversaries. The item noted that several units of a Russian naval squadron were on their way to San Francisco.[28]

Over and above the "respectable dimensions" of $8,000, the San Francisco Polish Committee, together with a subsidiary committee in Sacramento headed by Senator Newton Booth, collected no more than $785. The total amount was not impressive in itself. Proportionately, however, it represented more than one half of the overall total of $16,000.16 collected throughout the United States by all eight Polish Committees.[29] Moreover, its activities did not fade out with the diminution of its collections. On the contrary, the following year its efforts were to reach another peak, but of a different kind.

On January 22, 1864, at exactly 1:00 A.M., a high mass with special prayers for Poland was celebrated in St. Mary's Cathedral. In the evening, about 200 persons attended a dinner at the Russ House; Captain Bielawski, the master of ceremonies, introduced speakers representing the city's Hungarian, German, Irish, and Italian nationality groups. He also introduced the eloquent Senator Booth. On the following day, a Saturday, special prayers were said for the Poles in the Jewish synagogue.[30] Thus, the inhabitants of city at the Golden Gate had been reminded—and had themselves remembered—that Poland's struggle for independence was continuing into its second year. And the initiative for arranging the day-long series of commemorative exercises, undoubtedly the most impressive manifestation of American sympathy on behalf of Poland since the Boston commemoration of 1831, had been taken by the still active Polish Committee.

The staunchest supporters in America of the Polish insurrectionary cause were European immigrants who were themselves veterans of various liberal revolutions and insurrections. Some had had direct ties with the men who led the January Insurrection; some had fought by their side in the earlier revolutionary movements. Foremost among those who belonged to the latter category were the numerous German "Forty-Eighters." Union Major General Carl Schurz, who was one of the leading "Forty-Eighters," had been a comrade-in-arms of insurgent leader General Mieroslawski during the ill-fated Baden uprisings of 1848.[31] In addition, he was a personal friend and brother Mason of his subordinate, Brigadier General Krzyzanowski of the Polish Central Committee.[32] Krzyzanowski was the organizer and commanding officer of a brigade of mostly German volunteers. Schurz's compatriot, Major General Franz Sigel, who was also a veteran of the Baden uprisings, spoke out frankly on behalf of the Polish cause on several occasions. He reminded American audiences of Poland's desperate situation under Russian rule and opposed America's entering into any "alliance" with Czarist despotism. He even made several such statements in campaign addresses delivered in New York, Ohio, and Pennsylvania in support of administration-backed candidates.[33]

A clarion call for donations to the Polish revolutionaries came from the editors of America's foreign-language newspapers. Unlike their cautious native-born counterparts, the immigrant, and often exiled, journalists pulled out all stops in their editorials dealing with the insurrection. To them, it was a clear-cut struggle between republicanism and despotism, cordial American-Russian relations notwithstanding. Oswald Ottendorfer, the editor of the German-language New-Yorker Staats-Zeitung, took every opportunity to lash out at Prussian as well as Russian despotism in Poland. For his sympathetic stand, he received a letter of appreciation from Henryk Kalussowski, President of the Washington Polish Committee and Association of Friends of Poland. Appropriately, he printed it in his paper's edition, of July 4, together with an editorial on joint participation by Germans and Poles in various European revolutions.[34]

The French-language Courrier des États-Unis, also published in New York, not only devoted many columns of space to emotion-stirring reports from its own Warsaw correspondent, and to editorials in support of the insurrectionary struggle, but it also printed lengthy epistles from its Paris correspondent, Gaillardet, which echoed some of the bitter phrases which the French press had used about Americans for their failure in not participating in the expressions of collective sympathy for Poland.[35] The tone of the correspondence became so sarcastic that only its careful allusions to "foreign sources" prevented the *Courrier* from being shut down by military authorities and from sharing the fate of several of the "Copperhead" journals.

But the staunchest of the staunch supporters of the Polish cause in America in the year 1863 were the Irish. The unique story as to how their support came about is chronicled in the pages of the New York *Irish-American*.

The story began in Poland itself, with an almost chance visit by the Irish nationalist leader William Smith O'Brien. O'Brien had made a journey to Constantinople at the beginning of 1863 and in April he was en route back to Ireland. While in Vienna, however, he decided to make a detour into Poland in order "to ascertain what is the true character of the Polish insurrection, and by what means those who sympathize with the cause of Ireland can most effectively assist the gallant nation which is contending for its liberty with a heroism that excites and deserves universal admiration."[36] Traveling via Cracow, he stopped at various centers of the insurrection, and even planned to visit a distant relative in Lithuania, whose ancestor, O'Brien-De Lassy, had fought in the Napoleonic campaigns.

From first-hand observations that he made during his brief stay in Poland, Smith O'Brien became fully convinced that the insurrection was the struggle of a people for its national existence. He came to that positive conclusion, he wrote later, after questioning in Cracow, Warsaw, Grodno, Wilno, and other areas "a large number of persons who belong to that portion of society which naturally loves order as well as freedom."[37]

In his chronicle the Irish leader countered the arguments to the effect that the insurrectionary movement was unpopular with the peasants and the Jews, and that it was led by the clergy. He saw all classes of society embracing the movement, "from the wealthiest nobleman to the humblest artisan." The minority of peasants who did turn against it, he felt, were impelled by Russian promises of plunder. As for the clergy, Smith O'Brien gave them a very clean bill of health, especially for preaching that to die for liberty is "an act which is acceptable to the Creator."[38]

Smith O'Brien also viewed the insurrection as "a last resource of despair" against the most extreme kind of tyranny. He commented that the insurrection had won wide sympathy, "equally intense on the part of those who represent the most antagonistic principles of public policy," and noted that nearly the same language in respect to Poland was employed by the "Conservative noblemen of Protestant England" as by France's "Ultramontane champions of Catholicity." He attacked European diplomacy and pointed an accusing finger at cabinet ministers who professed to be friendly to Poland but had made decisions that had been "serviceable" to Russia rather than to Poland, inasmuch as such decisions had often barred or impeded other forms of action that might have been taken on behalf of the Polish cause. Finally, he singled out the British Foreign Minister, Earl Russell, who had "sent a lecture" to the Russian government but at the same time had declared that under no circumstances would England take up arms in support of Poland.

What did the Poles themselves want? In answer to that question, William Smith O'Brien related that during his visit he had heard "on the part of the timid and the feeble, prayers for the armed intervention of France and of England." However, "on the part of the bold and resolute" he had heard a cry for arms so that they could fight their own battles, and for a policy of "real neutrality" to be carried out by Austria and Prussia, both of which had been seizing arms shipments and imprisoning volunteers and potential volunteers, and were thus merely playing at neutrality.[39]

The Irish leader's main hope was that the requests of the fighting Poles would be met with all-out aid from the governments of Europe and that such aid should include the Circassians and the Finns, who were also seeking freedom from Russian rule. He fully realized that such a policy would be considered too hazardous by the governments of Europe. Therefore, he proposed an alternative policy which would secure for the Polish National Government all the rights of a belligerent government—all the rights which England and France had extended to the American Confederacy, he added. Making further references to the Civil War, he noted acidly that the neutral British government allowed shipments of weapons and passage of volunteers to both sides in that struggle but it did not take a stand against the policies of Austria and Prussia which were so partial to the Russian side in the Polish struggle.

Smith O'Brien felt that his alternative was a feasible one on the grounds that the public opinion of Europe was strong enough to effect realization of a "perfect neutrality" even without war. Intimations could be made to Austria to the effect that if she were to continue her one-sided policy vis-à-vis Poland, the Hungarians and the Venetians would be encouraged to "take up arms in vindication of their own national rights," and the "madman" who wore the Prussian crown could be made to understand that he might soon be deemed by foreign nations, as well as his own subjects, to be unworthy to govern a free nation.

He also expostulated on a second alternative which might be employed if the governments of Europe did not move to adopt any measures in favor of the Poles. Alluding to Greek history, he pointed out that the struggle for independence of that country against the far greater might of Turkey had been won without the backing of any European government and it had been achieved by a mere handful of men encouraged by "Phil Hellenes" such as Lord Byron. He asked whether there were no English gentlemen who would "fling themselves into the forests of Lithuania" in imitation of the "Phil Hellenes." Referring to Irish history, he noted that in one week the people of Dublin had raised ten thousand pounds to support an Irish brigade to be sent to defend the Pope against Italian revolutionaries, and that throughout "impoverished Ireland" over one hundred thousand pounds had been contributed for "that doubtful enterprise."[40] He believed that an equally successful result would have been readily achieved in London provided the individuals who had convened meetings of sympathy on behalf of Poland had issued appeals for financial aid instead of appeals for diplomatic notes. He reserved his fiery closing words for the people of the United States:

America, too—shall America, once the advocate of universal liberty—shall America do nothing for the cause of Poland? I will not believe that the generous friends of liberty, who welcomed me to the States and to Canada, are insensible to the sufferings of the Poles. If my voice could be greeted by them as it was greeted in 1859, it would exclaim—"Now, now is the time to save Poland! Not an hour is to be lost! When the snows of winter shall arrive the forests will be no longer tenable, and the noble defenders of their country must be prepared to suffer death or exile if their work be not accomplished before the end of October; and even though the struggle be renewed from year to year, and from generation to generation, still incalculable suffering would be avoided if Europe and America would, by armed and diplomatic intervention, or by the magnanimous effort of heroic men, rush to the rescue of the gallant nation which is now suffering the martyrdom of despair, and restore to it, once and forever, its complete independence."[41]

William Smith O'Brien's comments and observations on Poland were made in a letter of May 31 written in Königsberg, Prussia, to a Monsieur Ducpetiaux in Brussels. He also enclosed his first subscription of ten pounds to the Paris Polish Committee. A postscript indicated that the letters had not been mailed until June 3, after his arrival in Berlin and he there had heard, and had received with extreme skepticism, the news that the great powers of Europe had undertaken to send a second series of protest notes to the Russian government. The letter was printed in its entirety in the July 4 edition of the *Irish-American.* Although it contained good first-hand information on the situation in Poland, no other newspaper in New York reprinted or summarized its contents. Why? It might be pertinent to note that in July of 1863 the popularity of the New York Irish waned to its lowest point, as the city was being convulsed by bloody

anti-draft riots in which most of the rioters were disgruntled
Irish immigrants.

Members of the Polish Central Committee did read the letter.
They had it translated into Polish and read at the committee's
July 5 meeting. In gratitude, they addressed a note to Smith
O'Brien and asked the *Irish-American* to print it. The paper's
editor not only complied with the request but also prefaced
the letter with an editorial which equated the Polish cause with
the cause of Ireland and was simultaneously an attack on England ("Betrayed by England, they [the Poles] are not deceived
by her specious affection of love and liberty, and see in her
helpless victims only the counterpart of their own enslaved
condition"). The editor also prodded his readers by noting that
the Poles had a unity which the Irish still lacked ("But more
fortunate than our unhappy race, they [the Poles] are united—
noble and peasant, priest and layman. . .").[42]

More than two months later the *Irish-American* printed Smith
O'Brien's acknowledgment to the Central Polish Committee. He
again expressed his disillusionment with European diplomacy.
He remarked that when he had been in Poland, he had earnestly
exhorted all those whom his voice had reached not to place
their confidence in foreign diplomacy but to rely on their own
bravery, and to seek assistance "from the sympathies of foreign
nations, rather than from the aid of foreign *governments.*" Again
he cited Greece as an example, but this time as an example of
what might happen if the European powers would decide to
intercede at the last moment on Poland's behalf, and then act
as her protectors and benefactors. He believed that, like Greece,
Poland would then be confined within the narrowest territorial
limits possible, and that, also like Greece, she would be perpet-
ually subjected to interference in her internal affairs.[43]

Apologetically, Smith O'Brien stated that impoverished and
overtaxed Ireland could give the struggling Poles "little except
sympathy," but he hoped that the Central Committee would
derive some assurance from the knowledge that in Ireland there
was "more unity of opinion in favor of Poland than upon any
other political question." He used the final paragraph of his letter

to lash out against American apathy, and to exhort his compatriots throughout the United States, especially in New York.
He did so in the following eloquent language:

I trust, also, that our fellow-countrymen who are settled in America will cooperate in aid of the Poles with all who love national
freedom. I find it difficult to believe that native Americans, who
were formerly the devoted friends of liberty—that the men who
welcomed Kossuth to America with so much enthusiasm—are now
indifferent to the fate of Poland. However this may be, we have a
right to expect that the Irish inhabitants of America will not be
wanting in the duty which they owe to the cause of human freedom. We earnestly hope that the Apostolic benediction of the re-
vered Archbishop of New York (Dr. Hughes), the glowing oratory
of General Meagher, and the senatorial eloquence of such men as
Shields, O'Conor, Brady and O'Gorman will be heard at the other
side of the Atlantic in championship of the rights of Poland. The
time has arrived for generous exertion in America. It has too long
been believed—I trust without foundation—that Russian tyranny finds
apologists and defenders amongst the Democrats, and Republicans,
and the expatriated Irish of America.[44]

But on the same page the *Irish-American* printed two other
items which provided very strong evidence that both time and
sympathy were running out for Poland. Below Smith O'Brien's
letter and calmly captioned "The Disposition of Russia Towards
the Poles," translated extracts from the Cracow *Czas* (Times)
told of vengeful atrocities perpetuated against suspected insurgents by "Hangman" Muraviev, the governor of Lithuania, who,
"in order to make the anniversary of the coronation of the Czar
more brilliant," had a scaffold erected in the square in Wilno.
The editorial column contained a long commentary, entitled
"The Russians in America," which castigated those "gracious"
New Yorkers who were engaged in whitewashing the Russian
government's "coal-black" character. It lashed out in particular
against the sponsors of receptions honoring officers of visiting
Russian warships; it claimed that such sponsors had lost sight
of the despotic power which the officers represented and did
not stop to think that this power reached its lowest moral level

when barbarously murdering Polish men, women, and children.
"We shudder to think," the commentary moaned, "that American
citizens should stoop so low as to welcome its representatives
upon the mere suggestion of an unscrupulous press that the
possible alliance of such a despotic power may be necessary to
our national safety."

Taking a special line of attack against the *New York Herald,*
the commentary called attention to that paper's editorial of
October 7 and labeled as mendacious its statements that the
best the Poles could do was to submit to Alexander, who would
"grant them all they desire." Putting up a staunch argument in
rebuttal of this contention, the *Irish-American* expressed utmost
irritation at the *Herald's* statement that "The future of the great
Russian empire will be marked by the same peculiarities which
shall distinguish the fortunes of the American Republic." The
Irish-American noted that the Poles, unlike the Confederates,
had "*peaceably* and *respectfully*" asked the Czar for their rights
before they had resorted to insurrection. But this had been too
generous of them, since the Russians, Austrians, and Prussians
had the same title to Poland that the English had to Ireland, or
that pirates had to stolen goods or convicts to the city prisons.

Harking back a few centuries, the *Irish-American* noted that
the Poles by their steadfast and heroic resistance had saved
Western Europe from being overrun by Moslem invaders from
the East, and for this alone Christians everywhere owed them a
debt of gratitude. Further, the paper hinted that the Poles were
still a Christian bulwark against the barbarian infiltration of
Europe, and that "if we do not feel disposed now to aid them,
we should, at least, do them justice by not misrepresenting them."
The article closed with an appeal to all Irishmen in the United
States whose similar fate of past oppression made them sympathetic to the Polish cause, not only to respond to William
Smith O'Brien's call but also to emulate the example of the Poles
in the struggle they waged against England.[45]

As will be seen in the next chapter, the *Irish-American* editorial was merely a voice crying in a wilderness of Russophilia.
But, it was not a voice which was altogether unheeded. Through-

out the American Union, Irishmen responded to it and looked upon William Smith O'Brien's call as a mandate. Donations were sent to the office of the *Irish-American* to be forwarded to the Central Polish Committee. At the congress of the newly organized Fenian Brotherhood, which was held in November in Chicago, a special resolution of sympathy was passed unanimously. It contained a statement to the effect that the Polish struggle should serve as a precedent for the Brotherhood's future liberation of Ireland from English rule.[46]

The grand culmination of Irish sympathy in America was to occur on the evening of November 30, an evening when "the elements of a Russian Winter seemed to have conspired to defeat the effort made to benefit the victims of Russian tyranny."[47] A mass meeting to commemorate the anniversary of the outbreak of the November Insurrection was held in New York's Cooper Union under the auspices of the Central Polish Committee. As in the case of the San Francisco meeting, representatives of various nationality groups attended and addressed the assemblage. However, the Irish strongly predominated. Seated on the platform were members of the Knights of St. Patrick and the Irish Catholic Library Association, officers of the Union Army's Irish Brigade and its predominantly Irish Phoenix Brigade. In addition to the Polish national anthem and the Polish air "Third of May," the band struck up "The Harp of Tara" and "St. Patrick's Day." A flag bearing the inscription "Independence or Death!" was presented "through the hands of a well-persecuted rebel, Mr. John D. Hughes and his lady" as a symbolic gift from Ireland to Poland, and was accepted by the newly commissioned American representative of the Polish National Government, Henryk Kalussowski.

Several members of the city's Irish community made brief remarks. As the *Irish-American* put it, John M. Harrington "handled the slavish adulators of Russia severely." Captain William Lyons of the Knights of St. Patrick alluded eloquently to the identity of the Polish and Irish cause. John O'Mahoney, newly elected "Head Centre" of the Fenian Brotherhood promised that his organization would work for Poland as hard as it did for Ireland. Attorney Richard O'Gorman delivered the main address, containing a long enumeration of Poland's contributions to mankind and of the wrongs perpetrated against the Polish people by the powers of Europe. Noting carefully that he could not venture to speak for any citizens of American birth, he nevertheless lamented the fact that no American with the eloquence of a Daniel Webster had come forth in 1863 to plead the cause of Poland. "But for Ireland," he added, "for her children scattered all over this continent—for them and in their behalf I venture to speak to-night." And, on behalf of Irish immigrants "in the North and the South, in the East and in the West" he expressed the hope that "God speed the White Eagle of Poland wherever it soars; may victory light on the banner of Sobieski wherever it waves in the breeze."[48]

The Central Polish Committee at the Cooper Union meeting issued a second appeal to Americans, an address "to the Land of the Free and the Home of the Brave." It was filled with words denoting desperation and frustration. One paragraph contained a lightly veiled condemnation of the negative response made by the United States government to the demarche invitation. It complained that nations that had not been involved in "the robbery and murder of Poland" were "basely viewing" her struggle with indifference, and that in some of them "even the costless expression of 'sympathy' with the unfortunate Poles" was being denied.[49]

Letters from well-wishers were also read during the Cooper Union meeting. There was a letter from General Sigel, and there were two others which indicated that the Polish cause had found sympathy with at least two native Americans known to be supporters of seemingly hopeless causes and ardent crusaders for human rights. Both were Protestant churchmen and abolitionists, and both were active workers on behalf of the Union cause as well. Their names, Gerrit Smith and William Curtis Noyes, are well-known in American social history. But, as far as can be determined from available written sources, one of the most active supporters of the Polish cause in 1831, Samuel Gridley Howe, used neither his voice nor his pen to endorse the gathering, even though its initial purpose was to commemorate the 1830 November Insurrection. Howe had become a close friend of the renegade Count Gurowski and might have been influenced by him to alter his formerly pro-Polish views.[50]

The pleas voiced in the address, the eloquent remarks made by the orators, and the comments contained in the letters read at the Cooper Union meeting were all fruitless. They did not bring about any sudden change of heart in the American public nor in the American press. On the contrary, in the case of the press, they elicited some unfavorable and even uncharitable comments. Such a reaction, however, must be viewed in context and within a fuller perspective. The context will be discussed in the next chapter.

✿   ✿   ✿   ✿   ✿

As a postscript, but not an irrelevant one, the story of American activities and attempted activities on behalf of the Polish insurrectionary cause in 1863 one should discuss the effects and reactions of these activities in Poland among Polish exiles in Europe. Most of the source material for such a discussion is available only in widely scattered depositories in Europe. But that there were ramifications and reactions abroad is more than hinted at in several sources available in American repositories.

There is some material dealing with Henryk Kalussowski, who has been mentioned in this chapter as Secretary of the Central Polish Committee, as President of the Washington Polish Committee and Association of Friends of Poland, and as American Delegate of the Polish National Government; by one exiled writer he has been termed the "soul" of the movement among the Poles in the United States to aid their fighting brethren.[51]

As Secretary of the Central Polish Committee, Kalussowski established contact with the Committee of the Polish Emigration (*Komitet Emigracji Polskiej*) in Paris. In its reply to his first letter, the Paris group complained that a rival committee, "hastily improvised" under Ksawery Branicki, was attempting to seize control over all exile organizations; the group maintained that it alone represented the will of the majority of Poles abroad and emphasized that it would act as a central agency for them until they would come under the direct orders of the "definitely existing but invisible" Polish National Government. It listed the standard requirements to be fulfilled by all Polish committees and agencies in exile (collecting funds to pay transportation costs for volunteers, caring for widows and orphans of volunteers fallen in battle, influencing the opinion of people already well-disposed to the Polish cause, and circulating the London journal *Glos Wolny* (The Free Voice); it also took special and pessimistic cognizance of the situation existing in America and, noting that "the civil and fratricidal strife amidst which you live confronts us only with impossibilities,"[52] advised the Central Polish Committee to judge for itself as to the possibility of raising funds.

On July 30, 1863, the Paris committee of the Polish Emigration, on instructions from the National Government in Poland, appointed Kalussowski its representative in the United States and requested him to arouse the sympathy of American citizens and to raise subscriptions throughout the United States. The document was in the nature of an order, and in subsequent dispatches the Central Polish Committee gave as his title "Delegate and Collector" (*delegowany i poborca*).[53]

There is a *lacuna* in the subsequent correspondence, but two letters sent late in 1863 from Paris would indicate that Henryk Kalussowski was making attempts to secure United States political recognition of the Polish National Government. The first letter, addressed to "Citizen Kalussowski in Washington," and signed by Ksawery Galezowski, stated that the Paris committee could not confer on him diplomatic functions, but that its chairman would "make a full representation to the National Government," and would, without doubt, secure a nomination for him as its agent in America.[54]

The second letter, dated December 5, 1863, again thanked Kalussowski for his dedication, and after discussing the difficulty in obtaining arms for the insurgents ("the Austrians confiscate two-thirds of all shipments") it asked him whether he thought some of the bonds which the National Government intended to float for a loan could be issued in the United States.

Further, the letter assured Kalussowski that his nomination would definitely come.[55]

On February 12, 1864, the Polish National Government did finally appoint Henryk Kalussowski as its political agent in the United States. The announcement of the appointment was transmitted by the Paris Committee; it also informed him that he was to be the Government's agent for the entire United States *except* California, where "Citizen Mayer had obtained a separate appointment." Since there was some ambiguity (the Polish National Government had appointed him agent in New York, while the Paris Committee advised him that he was to be agent in Washington), Prince Adam Sapieha, the Polish Commissioner Plenipotentiary in England and France, interceded and secured for Kalussowski a new document designating him Commissioner Plenipotentiary in the whole United States. The document was dated June 25, 1864![56]

The United States Government never recognized Kalussowski's much belated status as a Polish diplomat. However, the Polish Republic which came into existence after World War I listed him in the yearbook of its Foreign Office as having been the first Polish emissary to America.[57]

Thus, from the little material presently available, there is a vague indication that Polish official and semi-official circles did not have any great expectations of American financial aid for their cause even though they could have used such aid. There are also clear indications that the curse of factionalism hampered their own activities and that slowness and confusion in communications further prevented any possible "lobbying" for American support. Ironically, there is nothing in the sources to indicate that the Polish National Government manifested any concern over the seemingly inordinate American friendship for Russia.

The Polish exile press, on the other hand, did give space to several sharp barbs of criticism of the United States. In its summary of the activities carried out in America on behalf of the insurrection, the *Glos Wolny* lamented that besides the "exclusive preoccupation" of Americans with their Civil War, their "expansionist aims" and hatred of England and France "required a cultivation of friendly relations with expansionist and despotic Moscow and prevented them from showing any kind of inclination to Poland in her struggle for freedom and independence." Only some women, "repelled . . . by the alliance with barbarians who tortured and degraded their sisters," maintained goodwill and admiration for Polish heroism. The paper mentioned the name of Mrs. Martha Walker Cook, "a translator of the poetry of the Polish bards." After also noting the aid given by other immigrant groups, the summary concluded that the Poles in America had actually achieved much by collecting a few thousand dollars amid all obstacles and in spite of indifference and opposition on the part of native Americans.[58]

CHAPTER VII

THE SAD DÉNOUEMENT:
THE VISIT OF THE RUSSIAN "FLEET"

"The New Alliance Cemented"—"Russia and the United States Fraternizing"—"An Enthusiastic Popular Demonstration"— "The Russian Cross Mingling Its Folds With the Stars and Stripes."[1] These headlines, and similar ones, appearing in New York newspapers during September, October and November of 1863, proclaimed the arrival and extended stay of a "fleet" of Russian warships. Without prior publicity the vessels had begun anchoring in New York harbor on September 11.

The eventful visit of the Russian "fleet" is a lesser known aspect of American Civil War history; it rates at least one sentence in most general present-day works dealing with the war, and in recent years it has been the subject of several scholarly and popular articles.[2] There is no longer any speculation as to the motive and purpose behind the visit. The Polish Insurrection motivated it, and strategy was the main purpose behind it. After having turned down three series of protest notes on Poland, the Russian government feared that a scheming and frustrated Napoleon, perhaps in alliance with England, would resort to a general European war in order to save the failing insurrection, to "liberate" Poland, and, more importantly, to take what he could in the way of territory and prestige in the aftermath of such a war. Recalling a bitter experience in the Crimean War, Russian strategists decided to move warships out of the Baltic where they might again be bottled up by the French and English navies. The plan was to anchor them in friendly warm-water ports. If hostilities had broken out, the ships would have been sent to prey upon British and French merchant shipping in emulation of what Confederate privateers were then doing to Union shipping.[3]

This, in brief, is how impartial and dispassionate present-day historians interpret the Russian action; this view is based mainly on official and indisputable evidence, primary sources uncovered in Russian archives prior to or shortly after World War I. In 1863, however, all orders and communications regarding the fleet movement were secret and known only to a few high-ranking Russians and to no Americans. Placed alongside the myriad exciting events of the Civil War, the Russian naval visit seems insignificant and it cannot be said to have placed the Polish January Insurrection and the Civil War in a closer relationship to each other. But if one were able to conjure up past atmosphere and tension along with facts, it would certainly not be so. The very much concerned Americans who reacted to the visit in various ways did not know, as would future historians, that the Civil War had already reached its turning point and they were still most anxious about its outcome. There was still widespread anxiety about the possibility of a final offensive by Confederate armies and there were rumors of possible raids on coastal cities by Confederate rams being built in English shipyards. There was also renewed apprehension of a last-minute intervention by France and England. And American readers depended for virtually all of their information on newspapers whose editorials were frequently based on hearsay embodying much wishful thinking. In view of all this, the magnitude and the meaning of the visit of a half-dozen Russian war vessels would inevitably be inflated in many minds, and it was greeted with irrational enthusiasm. Any mention of Poland, even accounts of recent atrocities committed against her people by "Hangman" Muraviev, the new Governor General of Lithuania, by Count Theodore Berg, the new Viceroy, and any other super-local Czarist lieutenants, caused a conflict in the minds and consciences of many liberal and humanitarian Americans. How was this conflict to be resolved? Could the events in Poland be explained away or just buried in the back of one's mind? Some of the answers may be found in the newspapers of the day, since their editors experienced this conflict in their own minds.

The number of Northern newspaper editorials touching upon the Polish question was to reach a peak while the Russian vessels were anchored in New York, in October of 1863. A survey of nine New York dailies made by Arthur and Marion Coleman, has shown that forty editorials were printed in that month on the subject of the visit of the Russian vessels. Most of them included some reference to Poland. Only one of the journals, the *Times,* initially refrained from making any editorial comment whatsoever on the visit, and only one, the *Journal of Commerce,* was consistently anti-Russian and pro-Polish. As the Colemans have aptly noted, "the rest of the New York daily press burst into a chorus of welcome for the Russians with the *Herald* cheering the loudest and seeing in this visit the most amazing consequences, even to an alliance between the United States and Russia against France and England."[4]

The first few editorials were filled with optimistic speculation about the purpose of the visit. Towards mid-September, the *Sun* in highly laudatory phrases expressed great pleasure at the way New York City was greeting the Russian naval personnel, as "representatives of the Russian government, the only European power that has maintained a hearty sympathy with the United States during our present troubles." It also made a suggestion that they be tendered an official entertainment which should be "both elegant and economical."[5]

A week later the *Sun* began to speculate about the motives behind the visit. It concluded that the vessels had crossed the Atlantic in order to closely observe French activities in Mexico and in the Gulf of Mexico. It added hopefully that such an activity could ultimately prove of benefit to the Union because "if France should enter into war with us as an ally of the rebels, Russia might act as a counter weight in the scales."[6] The same day, the *Post* hailed the arrival of the Russian "fleet" as "evidence of the friendly feeling of the Czar and the people of Russia at a moment when the other governments of Europe have been in accord, of feeling at least, with a desperate band of traitors and rebels seeking to destroy our Union and nationality."[7]

The following day, the *Herald* added a loud editorial voice to the growing chorus of welcome. After noting that the city was preparing to fete the Russian visitors, the sensation-minded James Gordon Bennet, wrote in glowing terms: "We have ever liked the Russians. In the face of their great Empire we see a reflection of our own march to power; they have the same vast extent of country, the same immense population and display a portion of our great activity and enterprise."[8] In his closing paragraph, he, too, theorized that Russia was anticipating trouble with Napoleon, and made this comment: "Should France and Russia go to war, the Czar would find then as now a refuge for his vessels in our harbors and our hearty sympathy for his success in the struggle with a nation which has forfeited, through the treachery of its ruler, our good will and alliance."[9] The fact that such a "war" would have been over Poland was completely overlooked! The same day, both the popular pro-administration *Sun* and the anti-administration *World* also printed words of welcome addressed to the Russian visitors.[10]

Within a few days the editor of the *Herald* ventured another guess about the purpose behind the visit. After some journalistic headscratching, he vaguely concluded: "Whether the unusual rendezvous of Russian war vessels in our waters has or has not a political significance is a question it is not necessary to discuss here. Even though it may not have been so intended, it will probably have a political effect."[11] The next day, he added: "France and England will stop short in their evidences of ill will when they see Russia making overt show of her friendship."[12] And two days later, he warned both France and England that it now depended on them whether the United States would make a move to cement its friendship with Russia by a *formal* alliance or not.[13]

Written in a milder vein, an editorial in the *Sun* included a practical commercial consideration which must have been of interest to New York's business-minded element. It stated that whatever the purpose of the visit, it should be remembered that the Russian Czar had always been a good "customer" of the United States and he had never lent "a quasi-countenance to the rebellion by declaring the disaffected people belligerents."[14]

The last day of September had been set aside for New York's official reception for the Russian visitors, but it was also the day when the news came that Gorchakov had turned down the third and final series of protest notes on Poland. The *Sun* segregated the two items editorially. In one editorial, "The Russian Reception," it expressed a hope that the city's reception would "be in every way worthy of an event that is intended to strengthen the social and political ties that unite the most powerful empires in the world . . . empires that are destined to overshadow all others."[15] In another, entitled "The Bold Attitude of Russia," it complimented Gorchakov on his firm stand and his shrewdness. "Russia has gained what she wanted by the delay," it stated, "which leaves her at liberty to pursue a winter campaign in Poland with the knowledge that France can not interfere before spring." The *Sun's* editor then boldly made the assumption that the warships in New York harbor were "nothing more nor less than a menace against France, and cannot fail to be so regarded by the astute French Emperor. They may not indicate an alliance offensive and defensive, between the United States and Russia, but they were no doubt intended as a threat against the French arms in Mexico."[16]

The municipal reception occasioned more platitudinous editorializing about Russo-American friendship and the "alliance." The Board of Aldermen passed a fervid resolution, and Mayor George Opdyke delivered a message of appreciation of "Russian steadfastness and fidelity to international obligations as contradistinguished from the course which certain other European powers have seen fit to take during our domestic troubles."[17] All this was well reported and, undoubtedly, well received.

The day after New York City had arranged a parade for the Russians, the *Commercial Advertiser*, whose editor had stood virtually alone in endorsing the appeal of the Polish Central Committee, gave in and shyly boarded the welcoming bandwagon. He interpreted the warm reception given by the city fathers as an expression of gratitude to the Czar for his having been friendly to the Northern cause, and the visit of the vessels as an indication of international friendship which, as he rightly surmised, might leave them free to attack English and French shipping in case of war over Poland.[18]

The other conservative business daily, the *Journal of Commerce,* was the only newspaper that did not share in the general editorial joy. In an editorial captioned "Courtesies to Foreigners" its editor inquired bitterly: "Why display to the autocrat of all the Russians our republican sympathies while the tri-color and the cross of St. George flutter unnoticed?" He saw a need for an appreciation of "kindness in season" because of Russia's friendliness to the Union, and "a certain affinity of interest" between the two nations in the Pacific." However, he denied that there were any common features in their rebellions. The American rebellion, he stated, was "a disaffection among citizens against a government of their own creation," while in Poland "a distinct nationality" was in rebellion to restore its "ancient rights." Certainly, there was little "community of interest between the United States and Russia, compared with the United States and Western Europe," and, therefore, he concluded, "we must be careful to treat all alike."[19]

The arguments set forth by the *Journal* seem calm and logical to the present-day observer. Ought not the much-vaunted Monroe Doctrine, whose recent invocation by Seward had inspired unanimous editorial cheers in the North, also apply to a possible "alliance" with Russia? And wasn't Russia's Polish "rebellion" different from the American rebellion? At the time the *Journal* was not only ignored but also viewed with suspicion and disfavor, for its domestic leanings were anti-administration and pro-slavery.[20]

A few days after the official reception for the Russians, the more popular and usually cautious *Post* hesitated editorially and criticized the over-exuberance displayed by its sister journals, the *Herald* and the *Sun.* It warned that foreigners might conclude that these papers were also applauding Russia's oppressive government and its tyrannical excesses against the Poles.[21] In a matter of weeks, its fears were to be realized. French and English journals seized upon the opportunity to heap scorn on the United States and on its press. In a subsequent editorial entitled "The Logic of Malice" the *Post* noted that the London *Times* had written that "the resemblance between the United States and the Russian Empire have not only been remarked by every one who has thought on the present and probable future state of the world, but they have created a sympathy between the two powers which is becoming stronger under the influence of calamity, disappointed ambition, and the rebukes of the civilized world." Half apologetically and half accusingly it complained that the London *Times* was making mere international courtesy appear as "complete political reciprocation, and the desire for a more intimate and living alliance."[22]

Criticism of the United States came not only from European journals, such as the *Times*, which could readily be accused of being pro-Southern in the first place. What was much worse, it often came from liberal individuals who had sympathized with the Union throughout the Civil War. For example, Henry Ward Beecher, the Union's unofficial "goodwill ambassador" in England, was at one time questioned from the floor during an address made to a pro-Union mass meeting. As may be judged from the following transcript of his remarks, he managed to assuage his audience with a mixture of humor and equivocation.

A gentleman asks me to say a word about the Russians in New York harbor. As this is a little private confidential meeting—(Laughter)—I will tell you the fact about them. (Laughter) The fact is this—it is a little piece of coquetry. (Laughter) Don't you know that when a woman thinks her suitor is not quite attentive enough, she takes another beau, and flirts with him in the face of the old one? (Laughter) New York is flirting with Russia, but she has got her eye on England. (Cheers) Well, I hear men say this is a piece of national folly that is not becoming on the part of people reputed wise, and in such solemn and important circumstances. It is said that when Russia is now engaged in supressing the liberty of Poland it is an indecent thing for America to flirt with her. I think so too.

(Loud cheers) Now you know what we felt when you were flirting with Mr. Mason at your Lord Mayor's banquet. (Cheers)[23]

But Beecher soon became exasperated with the Russian visit because of its effects on his mission. At another meeting, he bluntly denounced as "monstrous" the "flirtations of America with powdered and whiskered foreigners."[24]

Charles Sumner, the Chairman of the Senate Foreign Relations Committee, took a realistic view of American-Russian relations, especially in regard to "common interests." On September 10, a day before the first Russian vessel entered New York harbor, he delivered a major address on United States foreign policy at Cooper Institute. In it he spoke out against the interventionist ambitions of the Western European powers, but commented that "in Poland, although there has been no declaration of neutrality, the intervention has been unarmed . . . and, so far as it has yet proceeded, it is, at least in Poland on the side of liberal institutions." He dismissed Russian amity with the statement that "we have but one friend—Switzerland—in Europe."[25]

When the entire "fleet" had anchored in New York harbor, Sumner felt obvious disgust. Almost correctly guessing the true purpose of its visit and as ever levelheaded about international relations, he wrote his friend, the English liberal leader John Bright, a letter in which he stated that the vessels were there to keep from being "sealed up at Cronstadt." From New York, he pointed out, they could harass the French at Vera Cruz. Digressing, he wrote a few words in praise of Alexander, ("The emperor of Russia has done well in emancipating the serfs, and I doubt not himself and his empire are both elevated by the act and better prepared for good things"). Then he added: "But I am not a Russian; and I believe yet in Western civilization. But England and France must retrace their steps."[26]

The comments and observations in Sumner's address, which took up almost an entire page in most Northern journals and elicited miscellaneous editorial praise, were completely ignored amid the pro-Russian hysteria. Adam Gurowski, the renegade

Polish count, was among the loudest in the chorus praising Gorchakov and the visit of the Russian "fleet." In the second volume of his *Diary*, which was soon to go to press, he wrote that the Gorchakov notes were masterpieces of "bold and decided exposition and argument."[27] He joyfully commented: "The Russian fleet evokes an unparalleled enthusiasm in New York and all over the country. *Attrapez* treacherous England and France! The Russian Emperor, the Russian Statesman Gortschakoff, and the whole Russian people held steadfastly and nobly to the North, to the cause of right and freedom. Diplomatic bickerings here could not destroy the genuine sympathies between the two nations."[28]

Thus the one Pole who most effectively might have used his contacts in the Lincoln government to secure some official sympathy for his compatriots, helped instead to reinforce the idea of "alliance," an idea that undoubtedly first had been broached by his erstwhile friend, Cassius Marcellus Clay.[29] Meanwhile, the commander of the "fleet," the English-speaking Admiral Lessovsky, dropped cryptic hints about his "sealed orders" without alluding to their contents. He did nothing to halt or correct the references to the "fleet's" saving mission made by naively enthusiastic speakers at the receptions where he was the guest of honor.

The "alliance" idea was most elaborately expounded by *Harper's Weekly* in an article whose opening sentence read: "Times have changed greatly since Washington had warned his countrymen against entangling foreign alliances." It enumerated many alleged "common interests" between the United States and Russia, the two nations of the future "in the agonies of a terrible transition." Pointing out parallels such as abolition of slavery and serfdom, Alexander's struggles with the boyars and the Union's struggle against slave owners mutinying over loss of their property, and noting the greatness of size and of population of the two countries, the article also devoted a paragraph to an unusual "common interest" which justified the visit of the Russian vessels:

At present time Russia and the United States occupy remarkably similar positions. A portion of the subjects of the Russian empire, residing in Poland, have attempted to secede and set up an independent national existence, just as our Southern slaveowners have tried to secede from the Union and set up a slave Confederacy; and the Czar, like the government of the Union, has undertaken to put down the insurrection by force of arms. In that undertaking, which every government is bound to make under penalty of national suicide, Russia, like the United States, has been thwarted and annoyed by the interference of France and England. The Czar, like Mr. Lincoln, nevertheless, perseveres in his purpose; and being perfectly in earnest and determined, has sent a fleet into our waters in order that, if war should occur, British and French commerce should not escape as cheaply as they did in the Crimean contest.[30]

In formulating its radical proposal for the "alliance" and seeking "common interests" to justify it, the popular *Harper's Weekly* altered the facts about the Polish Insurrection to such an extent that they were completely unrecognizable. If fully accepted by believing readers, the misinformation and half-truths provided them with an easy way to erase Poland from their consciences. Even though this extreme form of wishing away uncomfortable truths was not followed by the active Northern press, even at the height of the pro-Russian hysteria, other types of rationalization were resorted to, more especially after the receipt of the news that Gorchakov had rejected the last protest notes from the European powers.

The New York journals expressed various degrees of editorial pleasure at Gorchakov's diplomatic triumph and his humiliation of France and England. The statements made by the *Herald* were the strongest and in fervor equaled its praise of the Russian visitors. Early in October it printed an editorial under the self-explanatory caption, "Russia a Winner on the Political Chessboard," which concluded: "The world will ask what excuse Napoleon has for carrying out his pretended mission of humanity on the American continent when in Europe he dares not intervene on behalf of the unfortunate Poles."[31] And in the editorial which was to be so roundly attacked by the *Irish-American* it made the following bellicose comparison:

There is another view to be taken of the present attitude assumed by Russia and this most interests us. Suppose that France should succeed by her machinations in inducing England or Austria to make common cause with her against Russia. The Czar in that case can find an ally in this government, and a most powerful one we assert. The attitude assumed by France against Russia is paralleled by her attitude towards this government. She finds both undergoing internal troubles and she seizes the moment to dictate to and insult them. Like Russia, we are struggling with a rebellion; like her, we find the sympathies of France and England all on the side of the revolted. Russia has scorned the intrigues of her enemies. We have done the same. And the world beholds the great empire and the great republic drawn together at this moment by the most natural sympathy. What could the Western Powers accomplish against us combined? We, like Russia, have a million of troops. We have five hundred vessels of war. We can increase our navy until it shall assume such formidable proportions as would terrify the world. . . . Should the Russian empire and the American republic form an offensive and defensive alliance they would necessarily preponderate and rule the world.[32]

Other New York journals also felt that the next event in the European arena would be a general war. The *Tribune* took cognizance of the belligerent tone of the English press and concluded that the Polish Question would become "the great European complication."[33] And the *Sun* printed an editorial entitled "Signs of a General European War" which gave a backhanded compliment to Czar Alexander for being a victor in the game of diplomacy. Alexander had won time, it commented—"all the time he wanted—for the prosecution of his remorseless policy in Poland." It predicted that there would be no war over Poland before the winter snows, and this would give him even more time.

The *Tribune* went on to predict that the diplomatically beaten Napoleon would secretly initiate a movement for a general European recognition of the Poles as belligerents, and that he would pour supplies and money into Poland to check Russia until he could step in with more effectual aid in the spring. Pointing out that in New York harbor there were other foreign vessels besides those of Russia, it concluded that they gave New Yorkers an illustration of "the troublous condition of Europe— and the mutual jealousy, armed neutrality and treacherous diplomacy of the old world Kings and Emperors."[34]

The thorough *Times*, which continued to refrain from making any direct comments on the visit of the "fleet" and which was never favorably inclined towards the Polish Insurrection, on October 11 summarized the changing situation in an editorial entitled "The Russian Ultimatum—The Polish Insurrection." It commenced by simultaneously approving the Gorchakov replies and criticizing the Polish Insurrection. Alexander's speech in 1863 before the Diet of the Grand Duchy of Finland wherein he had granted the Finns autonomy within the empire, was to the *Times'* editorial writer a sign that he would have been ready to do likewise for the Poles. He blamed England and France for ruining the chances of such a concession being made. The Western powers, he commented, had "roused the war party" in the Russian government. They acted as if the entire Polish nation were in arms when only the aristocracy and "the democracy of the towns" were involved. He concluded that the vast majority of peasants were "not only quiescent, but even devoted to Russia —devoted to her because she had raised them from the degradation of serfs to the dignity of freedom, and had secured to them possession of the soil, as well as personal liberty."

Besides questioning the extent of the popularity of support behind the Polish struggle, the editorial writer proceeded to strengthen his position by criticizing the Poles' unorthodox military tactics. "The very mode of warfare adopted by the insurgents," he asserted, "demonstrates that the great body of the people are not engaged in the insurrection." The guerrilla warfare to which the insurgents resorted in his opinion was an admission of numerical weakness and lack of support from the civilian populace. He stated that neither the Americans in their

Revolutionary War nor the Poles in their 1830 Insurrection had found it necessary to resort to such tactics.

Saving a last word of praise for Russia, the *Times* condemned the Western powers for their foolishness in backing a weak cause, and the Poles, in turn, for expecting too much from the powers. It dismissed as "great fuss" the editorials in European journals which had prognosticated Napoleon's impending recognition of the Polish National Government following the publication of that Government's appeal to Prince Czartoryski in the official *Moniteur*. It could not see "that astute knave" recognizing a government "which has no military force at its disposal . . . and which fears even to show itself in the light of day" when he had failed to recognize the Confederate Government which maintained great armies in the field and which had "a public, though not a legitimate existence." At any rate, the *Times'* writer concluded, Napoleon would never fight Russia without England's and Austria's aid, and as he could obtain no such assurance, the Poles would "be left to their fate" while Alexander's firmness would regain for Russia her former prestige as a great power.[35]

This rather negative analysis in the *Times* of the nature and extent of the January Insurrection greatly facilitated the minimization of Poland's plight in American minds at a critical moment. The analysis oversimplified the fact that peasants had not lent their support, and it failed to take cognizance of the fact that many of the peasants who had been "devoted" to Russia were either non-Polish Ruthenians or had been swayed by Slavophile demagogues. It did not take into consideration the fact that in 1830 there had been a Polish army because there had been a technically autonomous Polish "Kingdom." The editorial also discounted the activities of Berg and Muraviev as well as the tortures, mass deportations and repressions which were already taking place in Poland. Above all, it ignored the fact that Alexander's emancipation of the serfs had not extended to Poland.

A few days later the *Times* printed an editorial entitled "A

New Phase of the Polish Question." It began with a quotation from an address by Earl Russell. The British Foreign Secretary had stated that since Russia had not lived up to the conditions of the Treaty of Vienna in regard to Poland, she had lost her "rights of title" to that "Kingdom." The *Times* noted several other instances in which the treaty had been violated—the return of a Bonaparte to the French throne, the disappearance of the Republic of Cracow in 1846, the creation of a free Belgium out of Dutch territory in 1831, the annexation of Lombardy and the Two Sicilies to Italy in 1861—and then preemptorily concluded that Russell "might as well in fact have declaimed about the virtue of a harlot, as about the sanctity of the Treaty of Vienna." It also stated that the French government-controlled press loudly applauded Russell's declaration, and that it clamored for a "formal manifesto" by the Western European nations "announcing" that the articles of the treaty which had guaranteed Russia "her Polish provinces" were to be "void and of no effect." The *Times* added a dash of sarcasm: "if this is the only punishment which the Governments of the Western Powers dare venture to inflict on Russia for her disregard of these articles, it will be more to their honor to leave matters as they are."[36]

The *Times* editorial writer finally observed that the defeat of the Western powers in the diplomatic arena was inevitable because their spokesman "had entered the lists, apparently unacquainted with the real nature of the question at issue." The Western diplomats, he pointed out, had initially demanded "the restoration of certain privileges to a fragment of ancient Poland, at a time when the Poles themselves were in arms to battle for the independence of the original kingdom in its integrity, and denouncing all idea of compromise."[37] This observation was essentially correct. The Polish National Government had not only carried the struggle to Lithuania and other areas outside the "Kingdom," but had also committed itself to a maximal goal based on Poland's pre-partition history and past boundaries rather than on a minimal policy based either on ethnical considerations or on the Treaty of Vienna. Undoubtedly, this factor, which many Americans had viewed as a symptom of Polish unreasonableness, worked very much to the detriment of the Polish cause in the United States.

Most of the other New York journals were so greatly pleased at the British pusillanimity and French duplicity exhibited in the betrayal of the Poles that they refrained from discussing the legitimacy or illegitimacy, the reasonableness or impracticality of the Polish claims. Towards mid-October they fully capitalized on the betrayal by making odious comparisons between Britain's favorable treatment of the Confederacy and her nonrecognition of the Polish National Government. The *Herald*, for one, was willing to forgive France, since that country was "in the power of an ambitious monarch, who must, to keep his hold upon the throne, pander to the thirst of his people for military glory." However, it could not do the same for England, because she had not only armed raiders to prey upon Union commerce and furnished money to the rebels but she had "sought to destroy a kindred people from the basest of all motives; jealousy."[38]

Horace Greeley's *Tribune* echoed these sentiments the following day when commenting on an appeal in the Cracow journal *Czas* (Time) to the British and French governments to recognize Poland as a belligerent nation, as had been done in the case of the American Confederates. The editorial began with a biting rhetorical question, "Why not?" and continued, "They so recognized the Rebel Slaveholders before they had mustered an army or fought a battle." Compared with Poland, "whose Kings have been recognized by those of France and England centuries ago," the Confederacy was, to the *Tribune*, "a Jonah's gourd which has no past and no future."[39]

A few days later the *Tribune* again attacked England. In an article entitled "Foreign Policy of England," it discussed the British abandonment of the Poles in the same light as alleged British treachery towards the Union.[40] The *Herald* linked the cautious policy of France and England towards Russia with the fact that the warmth of Russo-American friendship had been greatest at about the time that Gorchakov had replied to the last protest notes.[41] A week later it ran another editorial which, in effect, thanked the Russians for having indirectly removed a danger to the United States, the reference being to the seizure by the British government of the rams built in British shipyards for the Confederacy.[42] In its enthusiasm it neglected to give any credit to a strong protest note delivered earlier by United States Minister Charles Francis Adams, or to notice a possible "warming" in the relations between England and the Union.

As the Northern editors were making their analyses, continually castigating the Western powers for their betrayal of the Poles while gradually realizing that there would be no general war in Europe and no intervention in America, prominent citizens of New York, numbering at least 171 and including members of such families as the Roosevelts, Jeromes, Hewitts, Coopers, and Fishes, formed a Russian Ball Committee and completed plans for a ball in honor of the Russian officers.[43] The gala event took place on November 5 at the Academy of Music and Irving Hall. It was held on a scale which had never been equaled and was never to be surpassed.[44] And, of course, the press reacted. But, in surprising contrast to the laudatory statements which had filled its pages only a few weeks before, the reaction was almost entirely unfavorable.

The *World* stated that enough had already been done to entertain the visitors and hinted that they should be sent merrily on their way out of New York. "Now let them have their ball!" were the closing words, seemingly uttered in disgust.[45] The *Herald*, the erstwhile leader of the chorus singing the praises of the Russians, expressed the same thought.[46] After their calm admonitions had gone unheeded, and in the wake of the ball, their comments, as well as the comments of their sister journals, were to include much sobering criticism.

The morning after the ball the *World* gave vent to rather strong feelings in an editorial entitled "The Russian Festivities." Its opening remarks dealt with the generally bad taste of New Yorkers in overdoing their welcome, whether it be to the "hideous little Japanese Tommy," to Charles Dickens, to Kossuth, to the Prince of Wales—or to the Russians. It added that the various kinds of attention given the Russians had been "both disproportionate and misplaced if they could possibly be intended as a demonstration in the face of Europe of friendship to the Russian nation. . . ." "Most assuredly we do not intend to say to Europe that we regard our contest with the South as resembling that of Russia against Poland!" it emphasized further on. It pointed out that the Union was fighting to prevent the dismemberment of a nation, while in Poland a nation was fighting to throw off the shackles of dismemberment. It waxed eloquent as it pointed out that "the partition and appropriation of Poland was the greatest crime in modern history" and expressed the hope that "the day be far distant when Americans especially shall cease to revere the name of Kosciuszko!" It concluded that New Yorkers were merely making "one of those thoughtless and shallow demonstrations "more for morbid self-gratification" than to honor their foreign guests or to express their sentiments.[47]

That morning's edition of the *Journal of Commerce* was not as restrained as the *World*. In utter disgust, the editor reminded his readers that while many people "occupied themselves" at the Academy of Music "with music and dancing in honor of the Russians, there were men and women and children perishing in the dungeons or under the sharp hand of despotism in Poland, because they had dreams of liberty." He philosophized in a pessimistic vein: "So the world rolls. While the sun shines on one side it is dark on the other. We hope that the people who were guilty of the folly of getting up last night's affair will now permit the Russian bear to gnaw his paws in peace."[48]

That evening, the *Post* printed a curt editorial which expressed no less disgust. However, its main concern was not the Poles in Russian dungeons but rather the Union soldiers dying on battlefields while their compatriots dined and danced with "gold braided" foreigners.[49]

The *Herald* refrained from commenting on the ball for almost a week and then printed several paragraphs highly charged with Russophobia. After "a few sensible words to those who have made themselves so farcically ridiculous during the recent performances," it let loose with the following verbal assault:

We have discovered the truth of Napoleon's observation, "Scratch a Russian and you find a Tatar." We have always shown more enthusiasm than common sense in our hospitality to foreigners—and they, in turn, have always gone home to knife us. So, upon the arrival of the Russian fleet we were seized with a Russian mania. We indulged in banquets, speeches, we even went so far as to compare Alexander with Lincoln. And then the ball! A failure as we had predicted it would be. And what has this gained us? Nothing! We had the Tsar's sympathy before, in a diplomatic way, and that, after all, is really of little value to us. Russia sends her navy here to keep it safe in the event of a war with France, but we doubt if she would send it here if we needed it to aid us in fighting England. Her navy in fact is not worth the sending. One of our Ironsides could blow it out of the water with all the barbarians aboard, in a couple of hours. How else can Russian sympathy avail us? What assistance is her barbarian legislation or her barbarian sympathy to a people able to take care of themselves. If she has any sympathy to spare let her expend it upon the Poles, who have groaned for half a century under her iron yoke, and have been deprived of all their natural and national rights except the right of being sent to Siberia. For free America to become cheek by jowl with such a despotism is contrary to all the traditions, all the sentiments, all the principles of this republic. We may have forgotten this during our recent excitement. Let us remember it now.[50]

The *Herald* also denied that there was any similarity between the Polish and Southern "rebellions," and it also pointed to the differences separating the government of the United States from that of Russia. It categorized the American rebellion as "the attempt of a few ambitious politicians to destroy the government in order to retain power," and the Polish rebellion as "the struggle of a brave people for the right of self-government of which they have been robbed."[51]

A few days later, the *Herald* launched an even stronger editorial attack against Russia. Editor James Gordon Bennett ran the entire gamut from Russophobia to Polonophilia and a virtual Francophilia as he discussed "Napoleon's Views Upon the Polish Question." In his most startling conclusion he declared that Americans neither desired nor demanded an alliance with Russia, and, furthermore, "Nowhere more than in this country will Napoleon meet with encouragement when he commences his campaign against the Russians." American sympathizers were always on the side of "the unhappy Poles," he affirmed, and Americans abhorred the atrocities which had been committed by the Russians to subdue them. "We have seen enough of the Russians lately to more than satisfy us that these barbarians cannot be sympathetic to us," he concluded. New Yorkers had made "a violent effort" to treat the Russian visitors "with distinction," but, "owing to their barbarism the affair assumed the proportions of a stupendous joke. Barbarians they are and barbarians they will remain for some time to come."[52]

What had motivated Gordon Bennett to make this complete about-face in a period of less than a month? Had he been influenced by newly arrived stories of the atrocities which Berg, Muraviev, and their underlings were committing against the Poles? Or, did he suffer sudden pangs of conscience? Actually, the motivation was not that profound. It was to be revealed by one of the Russian officers in a report to Admiral Lessovsky. Without prior notification, the wife of the *Herald's* editor had visited one of the Russian frigates at the same time that a group of schoolchildren were on board. She took offense at not having been given preferential treatment, and, as the reporting officer put it to his superior, "we Russians, who had previously been treated by the *Herald* as friends, became 'barbarians.'" [53] Thus, the wrath of one woman did more for the Polish cause in Civil War America than the reasoning and writing of many men. Loyal *Herald* readers, who had been led to believe the worst about the Polish Insurrection, were now guided along a completely different path.

A personal reason for an editorial policy vis-à-vis the Russians' visit was not limited to the *Herald*. The "post-ball" issues of the *Tribune* offered no editorial comment on the event. Why had such comment been withheld and why was this popular journal not heard amid the new chorus of remorse and complaint? Most likely it was because Editor Horace Greeley was one of the members of the committee which had organized the controversial affair![54]

On November 21 the Russian visitors left New York and headed for Washington. Within a fortnight of their departure, the New York Poles had their evening. This event also was given some advance publicity by the New York press. Exactly one month before it occurred, the *Sun* announced it in its "Local News" column. It stated that the Poles resident in the city had been "deeply chagrined" by the "flattering reception" tendered the Russian naval officers, and that they regarded "with apprehension and dislike" the growing closeness between the Union and Russia. Then it added: "With them, friendship for Russia is synonymous with enmity to Poland," and stated that the purpose of the event, which was to be held at the Cooper Institute on November 30 in ostensible commemoration of the November Insurrection, was to "check" the Russo-American alliance "by presenting startling facts" on the January Insurrection.[55]

The *Journal of Commerce,* still raging at the gala ball, suggested "now let the people of America call a free meeting of free men to express American sympathy with Poland." With editorial tongue-in-cheek it also stated: "Russia has treated us well and we thank her. But if her kind treatment implies that we are to keep silence on her great national crimes, we can spare her embraces and friendship."[56]

As it turned out, however, neither New York's journalists nor citizenry were to be entirely won over to the Polish side. The Cooper Institute meeting, as has already been noted, was, at best, an immigrant-exile manifestation. Generally, the press treated it with indifferent silence or curt editorials, despite the fact that appearing on the list of its honorary vice presidents were the names of William Cullen Bryant, James Gordon Bennett, and the *Sun's* owner, Moses Beach.[57] Among the many brief press notices there was one noteworthy exception. The *Commercial Advertiser* printed an editorial, "Sympathy with Poland," which gave adequate indication of the ambivalence which still existed in the minds of many New Yorkers. It began on a high note of sympathy for the Poles. First, it noted that it was part of the nature of Americans to side with oppressed nationalities. The American people had sympathized with French republicans, with the Italians, and with the Hungarians. Russia's friendship notwithstanding, the Polish nation, which was "pouring forth its heart's blood like water," deserved not only the same consideration as the others but it deserved more, since Kosciuszko, "one of its brightest names," had aided Americans in their hour of trial, their revolution. The "crime of partition" committed against Poland, the editorial maintained, gave Poland still another "peculiar claim" to American sympathy, for, as Gerrit Smith had written to the meeting's secretary, "If Poland may be torn in pieces so may this nation, and so, at last, there shall be no sacredness in nationality to forbid the designs or repel the approaches of anarchy or piracy."[58]

In the next paragraph the *Commercial Advertiser's* editor wavered. He warned against "wholesale denunciations" of Russia. He cautioned Americans not to forget the wise reforms that Alexander had inaugurated in Russia; while condemning the harsh and cruel policies which he permitted his deputies to carry out in Poland, they should not overlook "the extenuating fact" that Alexander "in common with the rest of Europe" believed that the Polish Insurrection had been instigated by agents of Napoleon. "It is well known," the editor asserted, "that French revolutionary agents were very active in Poland for months preceding the outbreak of hostilities, and that the insurgents look to France for material aid and moral countenance." He also hinted that the Polish insurgents had not accepted Alexander's proffered amnesty because of French pressure on them to continue fighting.[59]

After noting General Sigel's letter to the meeting, the editor again gave consideration to the Polish position. "We do not defend the barbarities of the Russian soldier nor the exercise of despotic tyranny over a brave people," he told his readers, "but indiscriminating censure is as bad as indiscriminating praise." He expressed regret that the general had shown himself "intemperate" by making people think that Russia was the only power guilty of oppression in Poland. Securing Poland's freedom from Russian rule would merely constitute a partial realization of her independence, he reminded his readers, noting that "Prussia and Austria would also have to disgorge their portion of their prey . . . and these powers should come in for their proper share of the odium now cast entirely upon Russia."[60]

To further buttress the Russian position, the *Commercial Advertiser's* editor dwelt on Napoleon's role in the insurrection and warned that if he should never be able to control it completely, the insurrection would become "an instrument for pulling down a rival power, but not for building up an independent nation." But, having gone as far as he could in trying to convince his readers of the unpleasantly close relation between the Polish insurgents and the hypocritical French emperor, he again reminded them that the Polish revolutionary cause was "right" and worthy of success. He complimented O'Gorman, the main speaker at the meeting, for having expressed "the true American feeling" with his statement that on the basis of its past glories and recent suffering Poland deserved her freedom. Yet he disapproved vehemently of the Irish orator's closing remarks wherein he had labeled Russia "Asiatic" and had urged that she expand eastward rather than into civilized Western Europe. Then, the writer took occasion to hint that O'Gorman's domestic sympathies had "a decidedly Southern tendency."[61]

Quoting extensively from a translation of Roman Jaworowski's speech, the *Commercial Advertiser's* editor excused the anti-Russian remarks of his Polish colleague. After all, a Pole could not be expected to display the same sentiments toward Russia as an American, and besides, Jaworowski had included a condemnation of the other partitioning powers and the timidity of Western Europe as well. He ended up at dead center of ambivalence:

The cause of Poland is indeed the cause of oppressed humanity throughout the world. America would gladly welcome back the lost nation to her place among the great peoples of Europe; but at the same time she prays that her independence may redound not to the injury but the glory of our best friend among the powers of Europe.[62]

The association of the Cooper Institute meeting with the Copperheads, which was only hinted at in the *Commercial Advertiser* editorial, was less subtly handled by a writer with whom we have become familiar. Before the end of October, when the editorial page of the *Philadelphia Inquirer* had hailed the New York receptions as having "at once municipal, national and international" significance and as giving "a special honor to Russia as our moral ally in the present great crisis,"[63] its New York correspondent commented that there was reason to believe that "Secession [ists] here, anxious to counteract the favorable impression made upon our Russian visitors, by the popular reception given to them by the American people, are doing their best to stir up the Polish residents to some sort of an opposition demonstration." The effect of the demonstration, he hastened to add, would be to "kill off the *entente cordiale* between the two nations." He felt that if the Poles were wise they would realize that they were falling into a trap "which has been so artfully set for them." They would surely have the intelligence to understand that no American approved of Russia's policy towards Poland any more than Russia approved of America's democratic form of government or of her republican institutions. Yet, it was a fact that England and France were sympathizing with avowed enemies of the Union, and that keeping on friendly terms with the only power in Europe which England and France feared detracted nothing from the Union's position as a friend of freedom.[64]

The Polish Central Committee did not let the correspondent's remarks go unanswered. On November 13, the *Inquirer* printed a letter embodying this answer. After a sarcastic "thanks" to the correspondent for his advice, it tore his logic apart. The letter began by declaring that its members were *"as loyal and as dutiful citizens of the United States as the President himself."* It reminded the *Inquirer's* editor that some of them had served and distinguished themselves in the war to *preserve* the Union; that commemoration of the November Insurrection, a regular annual event among the Poles in New York, dated back to that insurrection's very first anniversary, and, therefore, his correspondent was utterly wrong in thinking that any *"unusual effort"* had been made to celebrate it in 1863, with or without the prompting of "Secession sympathizers."

In the second half of the letter the accusations were skilfully made to boomerang. "We believe," it stated, "that his [the correspondent's] own statement will make those Russians who are here feel that they are only tools of policy, and that all *said* and *done* is not meant at all. And we doubt if the commemoration of the anniversary of the Polish Revolution will have as good an effect on them, as the knowledge the Russians have that they are only big little creatures, *petted* to suit the convenience of some people." The letter closed with a challenge: If the *Inquirer's* editor had the courage to print it, he would "confer a favor" on the Poles living in the United States.[65]

The editor did have the courage to print the committee's letter, but it had no appreciable effect on the thinking of his New York correspondent. Eight days later there was another letter from New York denouncing the meeting. He said that its "animus" could be gathered from a leading editorial in a journal "which was recently the organ of Archbishop Hughes." The pertinent paragraph of that editorial had merely stated that "a splendid opportunity" was being offered to "redeem" New York from "the odium and disgrace which have been inflicted upon it by the miserable toadies who have been paying court to the servants of the Russian Czar for the last three or four weeks." But, to the correspondent of the *Inquirer* it read "very much like a cunning Secesh sympathizing dodge" designed to "neutralize the advantages accruing" from the manifestations of Russo-American amity in the city. In his concluding sentences the correspondent reverted to ideas he had expressed the previous April. The best way to "give a practical turn" to American sympathy for "struggling Poland," he reiterated, was to preserve liberty in America and save "the great Republic" which was "the hope" of nations. If Alexander could be made to "incidentally" help in the preservation of the American Union, he ended in a realistic tone, "he is for once, doing excellent service in a good cause, whether he knows it or not."[66] Unfortunately, the finale of the correspondent's letter did not remove the imputations which he had made initially. And they were to be strengthened when Northern journals reprinted editorials from the major

Southern newspapers in which endorsement of the Polish Insurrection was coupled with deprecation of the Lincoln government.
The fact that a few of the most vocal supporters of the Polish
cause in the North were, indeed, known Southern sympathizers,
further weakened the arguments and the pleas of the Polish
Central Committee.[67]

South of the Mason-Dixon line, the Russian visit drew many
editorial potshots but very few healthy broadsides. The Confederate press tended to look upon both the visit and the rumors
of an "alliance" with more than a grain of skeptical salt. A day
before the first Russian vessel docked in New York, the *Richmond
Whig* had postulated that Napoleon would abandon Poland for
Mexico and that he would not incur the risk of war in enforcing
his policy. It held that the French Emperor's main object was to
"assuage the revolutionary spirit in Poland, and obviate the
periodical outbreaks, so dangerous to the peace of Europe, which
that spirit leads to." The editorial was certainly not pro-Polish
in text or tone. In its conclusion it expressed the hope that after
a "peaceful adjustment" of the Polish Question, Napoleon would
be in a position to enter into an alliance with the Confederacy
and that England would finally extend full recognition. The
editorialist also complained that Cassius Marcellus Clay was
still hard at work "throwing every obstacle" in the way of both
the settlement of the Polish Question and the recognition of the
Confederate government.[68]

The Richmond *Dispatch* was more vehement than its sister
journal. It placed the stories of Russian atrocities in Poland next
to stories of alleged Union atrocities in New Orleans and other
areas occupied by Federal troops. On September 16 it printed
an extensive catalogue of parallels and titled it "Alexander II
and Abraham I." "Alexander, with all the pomp and circumstance
of boundless power, is but a splendid semi-barbarian after all,"
the editorial began; "Abraham has had no time to become civilized, having spent the best part of his life among the flat-
boatmen or splitting rails and drinking whiskey on shore." Alexander, it continued, had instructed Muraviev to incite peasants
against landowners, while Lincoln had issued a proclamation

informing Negroes that landowners were their natural enemies. Muraviev issued arms to the peasants; Lincoln's officers were ordered to form Negro battalions and regiments. Muraviev persecuted the Catholic clergy; Lincoln did likewise through "Beast" Butler. Alexander had ordered the leader of the Polish rebels to be shot; Lincoln had ordered Jefferson Davis and General Lee to be hanged if captured. Both Alexander and Lincoln had ordered retaliatory action against the families of rebels; their troops tortured prisoners, raped women, shot hostages, desecrated churches. . . . The *Dispatch's* list took up several columns. It was climaxed by an equally emotional discussion of a possible formalization of the liaison between "Alexander and Abraham" in the wake of the visit of the Russian "fleet." The two were so naturally sympathetic to each other, it remarked, that they *should* form "a 'Holy Alliance' against civilization." Yet, it doubted whether they actually would do so. Cockily, the editor concluded by laughing off the effects of such a possibility. Alexander, he predicted, could only "contract to loan" Lincoln "a few Muscovites to bolster up his failing fortunes," and this would be good because it surely would bring France into the Civil War.[69]

Richmond's *Daily Examiner* strongly doubted that an alliance would result from the "fleet's" visit. It identified Poland's cause with that of the Confederacy and stated that the two rebellions provided Russia and the United States with "an additional bond of Union." One of these states, if noted, was "striving to crush the embryo independence of a free-born race," while the other was struggling "to repress the efforts of a gallant people who shake the yoke to which long years of injustice and oppression have failed to render them submissive." [70]

At first the *Richmond Whig* referred to the Russian officers as "gentlemen" who "have the reputation of being a well-bred class" and, therefore, concluded that they would have no difficulty in detecting "Yankee snobbishness and vulgarity" and would be amused by the entertainment arranged for them.[71] But a few days later it made a turnabout and commented that "The Muscovite barbarian, and the semi-civilized representative of Western vulgarity and boorishness might well be pigging together—to use one of John Randolph's figures of speech—in the same truckle bed." It linked the visit of the vessels to events in Mexico rather than in Poland, calling it a "show of strength" to intimidate Napoleon into abandoning his satellite empire.[72]

In a temporary wartime office in Atlanta, Georgia, the *Memphis Appeal* also published a lengthy editorial dealing with the rumored American-Russian alliance. Even though some of its hypotheses were farfetched it makes for interesting reading and makes one wonder how it was accepted by its Southern readers. It began by noting that there was general sympathy for Russia in the North because of the rumored alliance. It also mentioned a few "special points of sympathy" between the two governments. It contended that while Alexander's government had used emancipation to break the "patriarchical power" of the Russian nobility and Lincoln's had used it to break "that more than oligarchical doctrine of States rights," both men would end up with a stronger control over the people. Then, it suddenly introduced a novel thought: Might not the Polish revolt itself have been "a secret instigation" of the United States government, "intended to involve the Western Powers in an imbroglio with Russia, in order to draw their attention from cisatlantic affairs and give itself opportunity of making an ally of the Czar."[73]

The visit to the Russian vessels by Mrs. Lincoln in October was not mentioned in Northern journals. In the South, however, the toasts given the first lady by the Russian officers occasioned more editorial sarcasm, and Richmond's *Daily Examiner* led off with an editorial, "Common Bonds," which began:

The Czar emancipates the serfs from their bondage of centuries and puts forth the strength of his empire to enslave the Poles. LINCOLN proclaims freedom to the African, and strives at the same time to subjugate free-born Americans. In this striking coincidence a similarity of character and feeling is denoted, which accounts for their close friendship, heretofore suspected, and now clearly displayed to the mingled admiration and awe of the world by MRS. LINCOLN's toddy.[74]

The *Examiner* also stated that Mrs. Lincoln occupied "a sort of frontier and dubious position" and that it was difficult to say in what way the Poles would be affected by the news of her visit. It concluded: "They are but a small and unimportant fraction of the population of the world, and like the people of the Southern Confederacy, it is of little consequence what their opinions or feelings [are] on any subject."[75]

The *Memphis Appeal* agreed with this identification of causes in a discussion of Russia's possible imperialistic designs on "Southern Europe" (i.e., the Balkans), such designs, in the editor's opinion, overshadowing her designs on Poland. Making another fantastic hypothesis, the *Appeal* suggested that "by joint connivance" Russia and the United States might choose Poland as a Patroclus to be sacrificed for both. If France could be made to take its stand on Poland's side, it reasoned, she would not only be diverted from Mexico and the Civil War in America, but also from the Balkan area in Europe. The two "allies" would then be enabled to expand their imperialistic hold into the respective vacuums. That the "Moving" *Appeal* was not in the least sympathetically inclined towards Poland was evidenced in a single sentence appended to the editorial: "As for Poland, the Sarmatia, the political dream land of poets and patriots, we think if she could have a good, strong wholesome government—which she never yet has had—one which would elevate plebeians and depress patricians, she would cease to be a political nuisance, and her partition would be her salvation."[76]

All in all, the visit of the Russian "fleet" did little to make the South feel any greater affinity to the Polish cause. The temporary "equalization" of the two struggles in the Confederate press soon gave way to restatements of the opinion that the South suffered more, that its government and people were superior in various ways, and that the Poles were getting more consideration from England and France.[77] There was to be no spiritual Polish-Confederate "alliance" as a counterweight to the near *entente* between the Union and Russia.

Not long after the arrival of the Russian vessels in New York, another "fleet," consisting of units of Russia's Pacific squadron commanded by Admiral Popov, steamed into the harbor of San

Francisco. Its purpose was also connected with the Polish Insurrection and the probability of a European war developing over it. (Popov feared that in the event of such a war his vessels would be attacked by the more powerful units of the British Navy operating in Chinese waters.)[78] In the eastern United States, the event seemed to give support to the rumors of an "alliance" and served to increase the already existing enthusiasm. But in San Francisco, the Russians were greeted with some coolness. Two dances were tendered by private citizens for the officers, but there was no official reception or gala ball. Unlike their fellow Americans in New York, few San Franciscans visited the ships.[79] What is most significant, the leading journals of the city refrained from including lengthy editorial encomiums in emulation of their New York counterparts, but generally confined mention of the event to social trivia and anecdotal material about Russia. The only extensive editorial appeared in the *Bulletin*. Entitled "Amity and Alliance," it reflected much hard thinking at a time when opinion in the East had given in to extremes of emotionalism. With a bit of tongue-in-cheek it reviewed the differences between Russia and America ("they have slightly differing styles of civilization. . . . Religiously they look at the same cross from somewhat different standpoints. . . . Their languages are a mutual puzzle. . . . Her eagle has two heads, ours naturally but one"). More seriously it noted that progress was the "one impulse" uniting both ("Russia has awaked to progress—America is embodied progress"). Both were "busy unshackling their slaves," it further noted, and both were "repenting an old sin." Among causes "of a less enduring nature" which put both powers "in report," the *Bulletin* editorial mentioned the tensions with Britain and France, and then it concluded at midpoint that "Under all circumstances . . . it would have been an unnatural restraint of brotherly feeling, if, when Russian representatives come to our ports, Jonathan had not put on his swallowtailed coat and done his very best to make them welcome."

"Russia is a comely maiden of noble dowry," the editorialist allegorized in the opening line of the second half of the article, "but she belongs to a quarrelsome family—the family of European nations. She cannot do a noble thing but that her sisters are jealous of her and plotting to spite her. She cannot blunder in her policy but that her cruel sisters spring to avenge the wrong." And, into such a family Jonathan was not old enough to marry, and he never would be. Finally, in a sobering vein, the editor called attention to a portion of a speech that General Sigel had made in West Virginia; in it he had warned that a diplomatic alliance with Russia would lose America moral support and sympathy from her old friends in Europe, the "liberty-loving masses of England, France, Germany, Poland, Hungary." Finally, the editor reminded them that amidst the thundering of salutes, the music, and the revels with the Russians they should recall the "noble sentences" of Washington's Farewell Address, which began with the words "Observe good faith and justice towards all nations; cultivate peace and harmony with all."[80]

HISTORIOGRAPHICAL NOTE

References which deal either directly or at greater length with the visit of the Russian "fleet" include:

E. A. Adamov, "Russia and the United States at the Time of the Civil War," *Journal of Modern History,* Vol. II, No. 4, December, 1930, pp. 568-602, which minimizes the seriousness to Russia of the Polish Insurrection; Thomas A. Bailey, "The Russian Fleet Myth Re-Examined," *Mississippi Valley Historical Review,* Vol. XXXVIII, No. 1, June, 1951, pp. 81-90, a survey of over seventy newspapers which leans to the conclusion that Americans were deceived as to the true motives of the visit; Marshall B. Davidson, "A Royal Welcome for the Russian Navy," *American Heritage,* Vol. XI, No. 4, June, 1960, pp. 32-43, which gives colorful details of the visit but dismisses the insurrection in one sentence; Edward W. Ellsworth, "Sea Birds of Muscovy in New England," *The New England Quarterly,* Vol. XXXIII, No. 1, March, 1960, pp. 3-18, which discusses the 1864 visit to Boston and makes interesting observations in regard to conflicts Bostonians might have had between their feelings for the Poles and their friendship for the Russians; Benjamin F. Gilbert, "Welcome to the Czar's Fleet, An Incident of Civil War Days in San Francisco," *California Historical Society Quarterly Review,* Vol.

XXVI, No. 1, March, 1947, pp. 13-19, further cited in this chapter; Frank A. Golder, "Russian Fleet During the Civil War," *American Historical Review*, Vol. XX, No. 4, July, 1915, pp. 801-802, the pioneer work which did not utilize journalistic sources and as a result maximized the belief that Americans were completely unaware of the true motive for the visit; Robin D. S. Higham, "The Russian Fleet on the Eastern Seaboard, 1863-1864," *The American Neptune*, Vol. XX, No. 1, pp. 49-61, which brings in a discussion of the Polish Insurrection as a motive and will be further cited in Chapter VIII of this study; William E. Nagengast, "The Visit of the Russian Fleet to the United States. Were Americans Deceived?" *Russian Review*, Vol. VIII, No. 1, January, 1949, pp. 46-55, an incomplete survey of the American press which concludes that Americans were not deceived but touches lightly on the question of Poland; Earl S. Pomeroy, "The Visit of the Russian Fleet in 1863," *New York State History*, Vol. XXIV, No. 3, October, 1943, pp. 512-17, which touches very lightly on the insurrection as a motive.

Besides Tarsaidze, *op. cit.*, a pro-Czarist slant is taken by Pitirim A. Sorokin, *Russia and the United States* (New York: E. P. Dutton and Co., 1944), and the more recent Victor Alexandrov, *L'Ours et la baleine: L'Histoire des relations extraordinaires Russo-Americaines* (Paris: Librairie Stock, 1958).

USSR, the Soviet English-language magazine, in its July 1961 edition, which was devoted to the Kennedy-Khrushchev Vienna meeting (pp. 54-55) recounted the visit but made no mention of its motive However, M. Malkin, *Grazhdanskaya voina v. S. Sh. A. i tsarskaya Rossiya* (The Civil War in the U.S.A. and Czarist Russia), Moscow-Leningrad, 1939, discusses it at length and with much sympathy toward the Poles.

Noteworthy not only because of its discussion of the visit but also because of its separate treatment of the influence of the Emancipation Decree and the Polish Insurrection in Civil War America is Erwin Hoelzle, *Russland und Amerika, Aufbruch und begegnung zweier Weltmächte* (Munich: Verlag R. Oldenbourg, 1953), pp. 194-202; pp. 203-207.

In 1961 the Polish Book-Shop in Paris published a thirty-page monograph *Powstanie polskie w.r. 1863 i Stany Zjednoczone* (The Polish Insurrection of 1863 and the United States) by Juliusz Szygowski which reviews the visit from a Polish point of view. It is based mainly on secondary American sources.

CHAPTER VIII

1864:

AFTERTHOUGHTS AND REASSESSMENTS

AS FAR AS the American press was concerned, the morale-raising effect of the visit of the Russian "fleet" had just about spent itself by the end of 1863. There were no new editorials on "alliance" and no paeans extolling the friendship between the two "empires." In December the visitors left New York and were formally and properly received in Washington. The official banquet for the officers was attended by six senators and fifty-three congressmen. House Speaker Schuyler Colfax voiced appreciation for the "words of cheer and sympathy" which the Czar had earlier expressed, and greetings from the President were brought by Secretary Seward. (Lincoln was indisposed with a mild attack of smallpox.) For a few days there was a rumor that Admiral David Farragut had given the toast, "Russia: May her friends be ours." However, this was firmly denied by the Washington journals all of which restricted their comment to a detailed coverage of the visit without speculating on its meaning.[1]

But perhaps the ailing Lincoln had the visit in mind when he wrote Bayard Taylor a note on Christmas Day. In it, he stated: "I think a good lecture or two on Serfs, Serfdom and Emancipation in Russia would be both interesting and valuable. Could not you get up such a thing?"[2] Three days later the chargé d'affaires turned lecturer and "expert" on Russia replied that his own "short" experience had satisfied him that no country (except,

179

perhaps, the United States) had been as misrepresented as Russia. He begged out of "Serfs, Serfdom and Emancipation . . ." because he felt that it was too late to prepare a new series, but he offered "Russia and Her People," a lecture which he had already given "in some thirty different cities,"[3] and which contained a statement to the effect that the Polish people regarded the rule of Czar Alexander II as better than that of Nicholas I, and that "the attempted revolution" in Poland was "the result of a greater enjoyment of liberty taken advantage of by priests and petty nobles to carry out a plot originating in Paris, in which the peasantry had no sympathy."[4] Thus, like his quarrelsome ex-superior in St. Petersburg, Bayard Taylor personally had contributed much to the weakening of sympathy for Poland among knowledgeable Americans, and he was going to contribute even more.

By the end of 1863 there was evident a timid renaissance of Northern editorial sympathy for the insurrection itself. This renewed sympathy was reinforced by occasional mention of the increasing cruelties perpetrated by the Berg-Muraviev reign of terror. The Southern press continued to capitalize on atrocity stories from Poland. It still used them largely in order to draw parallels with actual or alleged atrocities committed in the South by the advancing Yankee armies. The same stories had been carried in detail in the news columns of some Northern journals even while their editorial columns had welcomed the Russian visitors, extolled American-Russian friendship, and advocated an American-Russian "alliance." For example: A reader of the New York *Herald* who read James Gordon Bennett's editorial entitled "The Russian Empire and the American Republic Against Western Powers" could turn a few pages and read a lengthy and factual account of Russian repressions and atrocities, its caption being "Death Roll of the Patriots of Poland."[5] And, in the issue which included Gordon Bennett's endorsement of the grand ball for the Russian visitors, he could also read an account entitled "Russian Confiscation and Its Results," which dealt with property seizures, imprisonment and mass shipment to Siberia of individuals who were not even involved in the insurrectionary movement. That issue also contained an article about the wanton destruction of the Zamoyski Palace in Warsaw and other items which indicated that a deliberate cultural extermination was in progress.[6] Unfortunately, during October and most of November, the *Herald* and other popular Northern journals had refrained from making any comment on the atrocity stories. Aside from being preoccupied with the Russian visitors and with speculations about the international situation, these journals kept editorially silent on the matter because of a fear of broadcasting some possible exaggerations and propaganda having originated with those violent anti-Russian journals in England and France that were known to be sources of most of the atrocity stories. But, as soon as the "fleet" weighed anchor, some of this "latent" material was moved to the editorial pages and there was more easily singled out for attention and sympathy.

The *Commercial Advertiser* led the way with an accusing article entitled "Russian Policy in Poland." In it the editor reminded his readers that the cruelties perpetrated in Poland were carried out "in the name and by the authority of the Czar."[7] He then noted that the *Schlesische Zeitung,* which as a German journal, in contradistinction to English and French papers, would be unlikely to exaggerate atrocity stories, had detailed some of the "specific expedients" the Russians were using to extort confessions. The *Herald,* now anti-Russian to a superlative degree, speculated about Napoleon's never-to-be-realized European Congress and asserted: "In any war between France and Russia, having for its object the redemption of Poland, Napoleon may depend on our good will. Russia will never have our sympathy while she continues to treat the Poles so barbarously."[8]

The *Journal of Commerce* also mentioned the atrocities in Poland in its discussion of the contemplated European Congress, and also took occasion to castigate England for her inactivity. "Why should England be disturbed at the wail of Poland?" inquired its editor sarcastically. "That cry comes to her and finds her in peace and prosperity; why should she disturb her profound calm because murder and outrage and wrongs are done in Warsaw?"[9] To this, the *Sun* added another accusation: ". . . is she not depopulating Ireland as ruthlessly as Russia is depopulating Poland?"[10]

Finally, the Philadelphia *Inquirer* added its editorial voice to the bitter upsurge. Its pro-Czarist platitudes of October were cast aside as it told its readers that if the Russians continued their policy the Polish people would soon be exterminated and the country would be depopulated. It pointed out that Russian officers had employed inexcusable methods for the purpose of overwhelming Polish resistance "ever since the revolution commenced," even though the insurgents had fought according to rules of civilized warfare. "The Muscovites," it warned, "by their wholesale expatriations of the people of quiet villages, their hangings, shootings, rackings and burnings, place themselves in a contrast so marked and disgraced that it may be fatal to their cause." It took strong exception to the word "pacification" which Czarist authorities used to justify their action, pointing out that "It is that pacification which changes cities into smoking embers and busy streets into solitudes. It is a pacification that bids fair to leave the Czar neither insurgents nor subjects." Finally, it reached a point of disillusionment:

The Czar, by the emancipation of his Russian serfs, appeared to be warm-hearted and just, but, unfortunately, the manner in which he treats his Polish serfs makes him now appear precisely the opposite. His policy may suit himself and be precisely the thing for effectually silencing the Poles, but he should calculate what effect it has on the minds of National lookers-on.[11]

The *Inquirer's* editorial was brief and mild in comparison with one that occupied several columns of space in the *Boston Post*, a journal which had applauded the visit and also the invitation extended the visitors by Boston's city fathers. In late December the *Post*, under the caption "Poland; Russian Atrocities," printed four very long and damning paragraphs. In the first paragraph, containing a historical review of the wrongs which Russia had heaped upon her Polish subjects, the editor complained that the Poles had been continuously cheated and fooled by promises that had been made only to be broken; that the broken promises of England and France to aid the Poles were as bad as the broken promises of the Russian government to give them self-government. The editorial included a *mea culpa*: "The uniform friendliness of Russia for the United States, doubly acceptable to us in our extremity, lulled us into peace while human nature itself was being outraged. And we went so far as to feast and flatter the naval representatives of a Power even then steeped to the lips in the blood of Patriot Poles. Our flattery of the Russian navy was so much endorsement of the cruelty of their master." There was also an expression of repentance: "The American press is at last beginning to awake to its high mission of exposing oppression and injustice throughout the world, and vindicating the cause of oppressed nationalities wherever struck down under the armed heel of tyrants."[12]

The second paragraph of the *Post's* editorial poured anathemas on the Western Powers and predicted that Napoleon's vaunted European Congress "will be delayed until Poland is deluged with blood, and either the field, the gibbet or Siberia has claimed the bravest champions of Polish liberty." The editor also enumerated the Russian atrocities. In the prison in Wilno, he noted, there were over 100 female state prisoners, ranging from a girl of fourteen to a matron of 69, besides the 2,600 male prisoners. He noted that there were two Muravievs "entrusted with the work of extermination in Lithuania"—"two as black-hearted miscreants as ever disgraced this world since Caligula or Nero." The younger one, who was Governor of the Kowno area, outdid his father by having ordered the burning of half a dozen villages.[13]

In the third paragraph the *Post's* editor gave full vent to his indignation. His cry for public opinion to rally and show its opposition to Alexander's despotism rang with an eloquence which would have been worthy of his liberal-humanitarian predecessors of 1831 who had inflamed American opinion against Alexander's tyrannical father, Nicholas. "There is something on earth," he concluded "greater than arbitrary or despotic power. The lightning has its power, and the whirlwind has its power, and the earthquake has its power; but there is something among men more capable of shaking despotic thrones than lightning, whirlwind or earthquake—and that is the excited and aroused indigations of this whole civilized world."[14]

The names of about a dozen new Polish heroes were listed in the opening sentences of the editorial's concluding paragraph. The editor had mispelled several of them, but he must have convinced his readers that the January Insurrection was not an unpopular harassment action but a genuine struggle for independence which was still in progress. His comments on nationality and nationalism are timely even today. "A wronged and subdued people," he said, must become "a flaming furnace of discord and perpetual unrest. . . sad history will be repeated until nations learn that justice to nations and to races is the highest wisdom."[15]

Late in 1863, the danger of intervention in the Civil War had passed as British and French statesmen turned to new problems on the European scene, including the problem of the territory of Schleswig-Holstein which Prussia demanded from Denmark. The tide had also turned sharply on the American war fronts as General Grant assumed command of the Union armies and led them deep into Confederate territory. From then on Americans were able to spare more sympathy for Poland and were apt to be receptive to sentiments such as those expressed by the *Boston Post*'s editor. The stage was set for 1864, the epilogue year in the story of the Polish January Insurrection and Civil War America.

Hopes of intervention had also passed as far as the Poles were concerned. The "Whites" gave way once again to the "Reds." Romuald Traugutt, son of an impoverished landowner, and a former officer in the Czarist army, assumed the dictatorship of the Polish National Government and vowed that he would carry on without outside aid and with the support of the peasants. He sent out agents to stir up the peasantry, some of whom had already been fighting stubbornly since the middle of 1863. But Alexander II had already initiated a counterplan. As early as the summer of 1863 he had sent Nicholas Milutin to Warsaw to formulate a program of agrarian reform, the objective being to stifle further insurrectionary activity on the part of the landowners in the "Kingdom." The grand culmination of the program was a series of imperial decrees issued March 2, 1864; the decrees finally proclaimed the emancipation of the serfs in the "Kingdom" and included benefits which were more generous than those which had been granted the Russian serfs three years before.[16]

The situation having somewhat improved, the Russian government ordered Admiral Lessovsky to sail his "fleet" home. After some private sightseeing he and his officers responded to an invitation to visit Boston which had been extended to them during their New York stay. A banquet and reception was held in that city in early June, but there was none of the fanfare that had marked the New York receptions. The journals of the "Hub of the Universe" reported the proceedings without comments about the political import of the visit and with no testimonials to American-Russian friendship.[17]

The celebrated poet Oliver Wendell Holmes opened the Boston reception by reading his poem "Sea Birds of Muscovy," which embodied the thought that Russia "was our friend when the world was our foe."[18] Mayor Thomas Lincoln delivered a brief address which contrasted with the address of New York's Mayor Opdyke in that it actually discarded the idea that the "fleet" had arrived to save the Union; he said *inter alia*: "The Russians did not bring arms or munitions of war. They brought more than these, the kindly sentiment of brotherhood." As an afterthought on arms and munitions, he added that "these we did not need for with our might we are bound to put down this Rebellion."[19] Admiral Lessovsky no longer hinted at sealed orders. He pleased his liberal-minded New England audience with a brief discourse on the results of the emancipation of the serfs.[20]

Poland was not mentioned until almost the final moments of the Boston reception. The principal and concluding address was delivered by Edward Everett, who had no peer as an orator. The old Brahmin ran true to form. His address was long, flowery, and replete with praise for Russia. Everett was almost finished, when he paused, and digressed to make a remark which he had almost passed over. He reminded his audience that when its "respected guests" had been in New York, "that portion of the English press which thinks the day lost, when it has not found some thing to abuse, or some person to villify in the United States, was profoundly grieved at the honors paid to Russian officers—it showed such a want of sympathy for the poor oppressed Poles, on the part of the pretended friends of liberty" With the admonition that "Censurious people . . . ought to have good memories," Everett stated that he was old enough to remember "the acclamations of joy which burst forth in England when the armies of the First Napoleon, or rather the wretched fragments of his armies, were driven from Russia." In an added flourish, he noted: "There was a thrill of popular excitement which has never since been equalled. From every roaring cannon, from every pealing organ, from every human tongue, throughout the British Empire, arose one jubilant chorus of triumph."[21]

Citing the English historian Sir Archibald Alison, Everett then reminded everyone present that Poland had furnished Napoleon with 85,000 men for his Russian campaign, and "that army over whose calamitous defeat all England was in raptures, was literally one-fifth to one-fourth Polish." He noted that England had then allied herself with Russia, even though the world was fifty-one years nearer the partition of Poland, and "the memory of that transaction was proportionally fresher in the minds of men." If the English had had no qualms about entering into a formal alliance with one of Poland's despoilers at that time, he concluded in what seemed a logical afterthought, and, furthermore, if they had had no qualms after the partitions when they entered into "the most intimate relations, political or personal" with all three despoilers, then Americans could certainly be "forgiven" years later for following their example.[22]

Undoubtedly, Everett's afterthought betrayed some feelings of guilt. It took the moral courage and frankness so characteristic of the venerable statesman to discuss Poland in such a manner in the presence of the Russian guests. His main line of reasoning, however, reflected no great credit on his reputation. It was, rather, a line that had been employed by European national leaders of Machiavellian leanings whenever they had joined hands with tyrants who had overwhelmed nations and nationalities. Everett's concluding remarks detracted even further from his liberal reputation. Disregarding the fact that Czarist underlings were already implementing a policy of total suppression of all facets of Polish culture, he maintained that he still had faith in Alexander. He concluded that no one presumed or desired a restoration of "the ancient kingdom" of Poland, by the Czar or by his brother sovereigns, for this "would simply be the restoration of the worst government in Christendom." He was utterly confident that Alexander would do all in his power "to improve the condition, promote the welfare, and elevate the character of his Polish subjects."[23]

The day after Everett delivered his address, the editorial silence in Boston was oppressive. It was broken by what could have been considered no more than a whisper from the *Pilot*, a journal which bore the triple stigma of being Irish, Catholic, and anti-abolitionist. "We are frequently reminded that history repeats itself," it said in prefacing its report of another reception for Admiral Lessovsky held at Faneuil Hall, "we are quite sure that it sometimes contradicts itself." This contradiction, it explained, stemmed from the fact that the same hall had been the site in 1831 of an emotionally charged gathering on behalf of the Polish fighters in the November Insurrection, at which time two banners had been dedicated on behalf of Boston's youth to be sent to Poland. At that time the hall had rung with odes and addresses extolling Polish heroism and damning Russian tyranny. And, Edward Everett had been among the most active members of the so-called American-Polish Committee which had sponsored the dedication.

The *Pilot's* editorial writer stated that he, "simply as a citizen" regarding the Russians "simply as guests," had no objections to the city of his "love and admiration" sustaining "its character for open-handed, open-hearted receptions of strangers within its gates." However, at the same time, he felt morally obligated to refresh the minds of his readers in the matter of some bitter realities. "Does anyone with the light of history and the lamp of experience," he questioned with eloquent bluntness, "believe that the Cossack would have sympathized with us had not selfish policy dictated the course?" He replied that Russia had "no more regard for Republican America than haughty and heartless England" had for Turkey during the Crimean War, or that "treacherous France" had for England despite their "alliance" against Russia on the Polish question. Poland, he finally noted, was "still prostrate . . . still enslaved," and, if the fiery indignation of Bostonians directed against Czarist tyranny had been justified in 1831 it was no less so in 1864, since the principle on which it was based and the cause which had precipitated it still existed.[24]

It is almost a certainty that Edward Everett, Oliver Wendell Holmes, and the other leaders of Boston society did not cock attentive ears to this small editorial voice, for there is nothing in the sources to indicate that they had any further thoughts on what they had said at the Lessovsky reception.

Before the Russian "fleet" finally returned home, it took aboard a deserter, a Pole named Aleksander Milewski. Early in 1864, Milewski had jumped ship and had enlisted in the Union Army. Immediately, he became the subject of an extensive and urgent correspondence. On orders issued by Secretary of War Edwin M. Stanton, Major General Benjamin F. ("Beast") Butler, then Commanding General of the Military Department of Virginia and North Carolina, initiated action to "hunt him up." He was found serving with a New York artillery regiment in Virginia; he was subsequently sent to Washington, turned over to the Military Governor, delivered to the Russian Minister, Baron Edouard Stoeckl, court-martialed while the "fleet" was still in harbor, and hanged from a yardarm.[25]

The Milewski incident both angered and frightened Polish exiles in the United States. On April 27 the Polish Central Committee issued a call for a petition to the United States Congress. The document was drawn up, read at a mass meeting of Poles held in New York's Pythagoras Hall on June 12, and then circulated for signatures. It summarized their case in detail and argued that there was no legal basis in any existing treaty for the extradition of persons by the United States to Russia. It asked Congress to take steps to protect the exiles from outrage and thus assure them the freedom to fight or perish, live or labor, for the government to which they had committed their lives and their hopes. It expressed the feeling that if members of Congress acted to prevent a recurrence of the Milewski incident they would restore some of the honor which their country had lost when he was permited to be turned over to the Russian authorities.[26]

The Poles' petition was sent to Senator Reverdy Johnson of Maryland. Johnson forwarded it to Vice President Andrew Johnson (the President of the Senate) with the following note, which, as can be seen, skirted all mention of the Polish Insurrection:

I have had sent to me, with a request that I should present it to the Senate, a memorial signed by some six or seven hundred natives of Poland, most and perhaps all of whom are represented to have been refugees from that kingdom. They state (whether correctly or not I do not know) that although there is no statute or treaty upon the subject, many of their countrymen who have been enlisted into the Army and Navy of the United States, have escaped from what they call the thralldom of Russia, have been delivered up to agents of the Russian government by the naval and military authorities, acting as they suppose under the authority of the Executive. They ask that the matter may be inquired into, and relief, if relief can be had, in the future provided by Congress. It is not necessary, Mr. President, to say anything for the purpose of enlisting the sympathy of the American people or the American Senate in behalf of the men of Poland. The services of her sons during the war of the Revolution have always been held in so high an esteem that they have received, as they were entitled to receive, the national gratitude. I move the reference of the memorial to the Committee on Foreign Relations.[27]

A few days later Johnson informed Kalussowski that when the senators had questioned Seward on the matter, he did admit that one Pole had been extradited on the basis of an 1832 Russo-American treaty. Kalussowski then retorted that the treaty had expired seven years after its signing and had never been renewed. Johnson promised to resubmit the petition.[28]

The Polish exiles also protested through demonstrations, in which they were joined by other nationality groups. In New York, the dedication of the first Czech banner to fly in the New World became the occasion for a joint Czech-Polish demonstration against the "ignominious extradition." Several hundred individuals marched to City Hall, and Editor Jaworowski addressed the following words to the new Mayor, C. Godfrey Gunther:

We wish, Sir, to serve this Republic as peaceful and useful citizens, asking in return protection and the privilege of benefiting from the freedom, which was denied us in our homeland. . . . We ask for protection because we have already had occasion to sorrow at the turning over of one of our compatriots, who trusting in the protection of your flag, cast off the hated and oppressive yoke of Moscow, enlisted in your ranks, fought alongside your own [men] until finally he was returned by the government of the United States on the demand of that power, and has long since repented for the crime of loving freedom. [29]

Gunther, whose predecessor had welcomed the Russian "fleet" the previous year, remarked that the appearance together of the banners of the two Slav peoples could well serve as an example for the joining together of the two flags then flying over the moral combat on American soil. He regretted that the group was mourning the seizure of one of its compatriots and assured it that it would never have occasion to mourn such a misfortune again.[30]

The *Echo z Polski* urged the Poles and the Czechs to unite in a single organization so as to constitute a solid bloc whose voice could not be ignored by the American government. The *Echo* had already urged that such an organization support political candidates friendly to the Polish cause and had even endorsed General Frémont as an opposition candidate to Abraham Lincoln in the 1864 election.[31]

On October 29 Seward wrote a final reply to Jaworowski on the Milewski incident. Citing paragraph twelve of the 1832 treaty, he noted that it stated that although the treaty was originally in force for a period of seven years, its continuance was to be *understood* as long as the contracting parties did not give notice of its termination. The paragraph clearly provided for mutual extradition of runaway seamen. To the text of the Seward letter which he printed in the *Echo*, Jaworowski added a note to the effect that it remained to be seen whether a "Slavic Alliance" could so influence public opinion as to hasten an abrogation of the treaty. But there is nothing to indicate that any joint Polish-Czech action materialized.[32]

The year 1864 marked a new high point of Russophilia on the part of some representatives of American Protestantism. These individuals became especially vocal as the ratio of Catholics in the United States grew with the influx of German and Irish immigrants. They gave vent to their resentment by siding with any group or even any nation which stood firmly against Catholicism. To them Orthodox Russia became an imaginary religious ally even though its church was state-supported and its clergy classified Protestants as heretics.[33] As shown in some of his diplomatic correspondence, Cassius Marcellus Clay was a member of this group. Its foremost representatives on the domestic scene were two clergymen, Charles F. Boynton and Joshua Leavitt.

Boynton, a Presbyterian turned Congregationalist, and an abolitionist, whose friendly interest in Russia dated back to the 1850s, had propounded a theory that all of the moral ills and evils that beset mankind were traceable to papal machinations. In his first book, *The Russian Empire: Its Resources, Government and Policy*, he maintained that in suppressing the Polish November Insurrection, Nicholas I was "merely defending his home from the intrigues of a spy, the Pope." At one point he suggested that all Roman Catholics should be deported from America. At the time of the Crimean War Boynton warned that a victory of the Allies over Russia would be a "popish victory,"and that if it occurred, all Protestant missionary activity would be destroyed.[34]

In 1864 he published *English and French Neutrality and the Anglo-French Alliance in their Relations to the United States and Russia*. Despite its scholarly-sounding title, the volume was mainly a collection of religious polemics favoring the Czarist regime. As might well have been expected in view of the Reverend Boynton's past record, Poland became a prime target of his verbal attacks in this book. In one chapter he harked back to Nicholas I and stated that the much maligned Czar deserved rehabilitation because he had taken repressive action not against the Polish people but rather against "Jesuitism" which had threatened his government with subversion from Western European bases.[35] He waxed especially eloquent as he reiterated, with many anti-Catholic flourishes, some of the standard arguments against Polish independence. First, he complained that France was preventing Russia from giving freedom to "the downtrodden East" and that France did not allow "the national banner of the Greek Church" to take the place of the Crescent on the towers of St. Sophia [in Constantinople]." Then, he accused "Louis Napoleon and his Jesuits" of attempting to encircle Russia with a "French Catholic outpost" in Poland, this attempt being similar to the one made in Mexico in proximity to the United States.[36]

Boynton, who had a congregation in Cincinnati when he wrote the book, was later transferred to Washington and became Chaplain of the House of Representatives as well as lecturer at the United States Naval Academy. Within two years, he republished the book twice under different titles, but with only slight modifications in the text. To some Americans, of his generation and later, his theories on Russia and on the Polish Insurrection were to be the last word.[37]

Joshua Leavitt's background, like his reasoning, was very similar to Boynton's. He was also a Congregational minister, an ardent abolitionist, and a violent anti-Catholic.[38] His contribution was a long article entitled "Poland" in the New Englander Magazine and Yale Review. Its twenty pages contained absolutely nothing that would seem favorable or complimentary to Poland or the Poles. He began with a brief review of Poland's past history and noted immediately that although toleration of Protestants prevailed in the past its extent "depended upon the temper of the reigning king, who was always a Romanist." He passed rapidly over what he termed "two hundred years of persecution and oppression" and came to the conclusion that

"Poland had become the make-bate of Europe, and the neighboring nations at length relieved themselves of a nuisance by dividing among themselves a territory which its inhabitants were unable either to defend or to govern."[39]

Noting with some self-confidence that his view of Poland was very different from that generally presented to Americans by French and English writers, Leavitt maintained that "the extinction of Poland was as truly a gain to the cause of civilization as the extinction of Algiers, over which no one ever thinks of uttering a lamentation."[40] He asked his readers to reflect on how much of what they knew about Poland "rested purely on a poetical basis, and, in fact may be summed up in a single well-known line: 'And Freedom shrieked as Kosciusko fell!' " [41] His purpose, he stated, was to "appeal from sympathy to reason, from the judgment of Poetry to that of History."[42] He enumerated the various acts of persecution allegedly perpetrated against Protestants and members of the Orthodox faith by the aristocracy, bishops, Jesuits and a "Priest's party" which, he claimed, had controlled Polish kings until the partitioning powers followed "that great law of self-preservation, which all nations in their turn have been compelled to obey."[43]

Leavitt further dismissed the 1831 Insurrection as a conspiracy controlled and mismanaged by the Polish nobles and upper classes whose "clamors for independence sprung not from an earnest longing for the function of self-government, but merely from an uneasy desire to be freed from the checks and restraints which all real governments are obliged to enforce upon their subjects." He excused the fact that Nicholas I had adopted a policy of assimilation "with a strong hand and often a vindictiveness with the statement that "the madness of these demi-savages" could not have been "repressed by any gentle processes."[44]

Poland was extinct . . . the Poles of history and poetry, and romance, were exclusively an aristocracy . . . England sympathized with Poland because she "furnished excitement without calling for action" . . . France retained her "Polish Committee" because it provided sensation and a threat of "an explosion in the heart of Europe" . . . Rome saw the advantage of using

Poland as "a point of living contact" against the Greek Church . . . Poland was not a "nationality" because she had never had definite boundaries. Such scattered premises formed a nexus between Leavitt's review of Poland's past and his consideration of more contemporary events. Finally, on the eighteenth page, he got down to a discourse on the January Insurrection.

Leavitt theorized that the roots of the insurrection extended back to pre-Crimean War days—to a refusal by Nicholas I to "recognize Polish priests and nuns as the subjects of Rome." He stated that the insurrection had been fomented by the Pope in the guise of a struggle for independence with the aid of his protector, Louis Napoleon.[45] To substantiate his contention, he noted that "In the early days of the outbreak, the most ardent manifestations of interest in behalf of Poland in America came from Bishop Hughes and the Roman Catholic press."[46] Russia's determination to settle her domestic difficulties "without any foreign diplomatic pressure," he maintained, "is to the continent of Europe what the Monroe Doctrine is to America, a Declaration of National Freedom from Foreign Interference, in which England and Austria have virtually acquiesced by declining the insidious proposal for a General Congress of Nations."[47] On this idea was based a strange and incongruous vision of Russia being pitted against Prussia: "We shall not be surprised to see Russia vindicate it on the plains of Holstein, should the present iniquitous attempt of the Frankfort Diet to dismember the kingdom of Denmark be madly persisted in."[48]

European intervention in Poland's struggle not having materialized, Leavitt theorized, "the grand conspiracy" in Rome had fallen back upon "the *dernier* resort of the Middle Ages by inflaming popular superstitition preparatory to a general crusade in behalf of the oppressed faithful of Poland."[49] Again he used the American Catholic press to prove his point:

A leading Romanist paper in this country informs us, with great solemnity, that "the Pope, *as head of Christendom*, has offered up prayers to Heaven for the freedom of Poland." And it argues inevitable success, by the consideration that "If God is the Protector of nations, who should represent them to him, but his vicar on earth?"[50]

But his further citations from that newspaper, the Philadelphia *Herald and Visitor*, contained nothing about a crusade. Like the *Irish-American* and *The Pilot*, it had compared the cause of Poland with that of Ireland, and had made prophetic statements that heaven's wrath would be vented on both Russia and Britain. Moreover, like its sister Catholic newspapers, it had even complained that the Pope had not offered special prayers for Ireland as he had for Poland! The mentioning of Britain in the citations moved Leavitt to lament that her aristocracy was making her "a most serviceable auxiliary of Popery."[50]

The finale of Leavitt's polemic cast was written in the form of an "appeal" in the name of "our common humanity, and of that common Christanity which is acknowledged alike in Europe and America, by Greek, and Catholic, and Protestant," to the Poles "to cease contending against the inevitable." In his view, they were suffering for the sins their fathers committed against their fellow Christians. "You cannot resist the Russian power," he warned, "and there is no human aid that can reach you." France was too far off, and "the poor old Pope" was so helpless that his existence depended on "French bayonets." He advised the Poles that they should submit immediately to Russian rule on the best terms they could get or else face extermination, a fate not unlike that of those American Indians who had resisted the White Man. Of course, he foresaw a bright future for the Poles if they would submit—freedom for serfs, land for laborers, schools for children, a Bible for every family, newspapers, trade, roads, "telegraphs," and a peace and prosperity which would "roll in" upon them "with a tide and permanence, such as Sarmatia never knew through all its turbulent history."[52]

This "appeal" might well have been uttered by a fanatic Panslavist or an agent of the Czarist government. There was no mention in it of Berg or Muraviev or of the excesses being committed under their auspices. Joshua Leavitt would most likely have incorporated them into his twisted imagery as avenging angels.

It might be questioned, from the convenient vantage point of the present, whether it is worthwhile to recapitulate Leavitt's article in such detail. Today's sophisticated Americans would undoubtedly consider him an insignificant extremist. But such was not the case in 1864. The war had not alleviated any of the tensions between native born Protestants and "foreigners" of the first or second generation. In the newspapers there were still occasional advertisements for help wanted which specified "Protestant only." Local prejudices undoubtedly aided in creation of a bias towards an entire nation, often spoken of as "Catholic Poland." In its time the *New Englander Magazine and Yale Review* was considered a very fine publication, its topics and opinions being discussed in the highest social circles, including those with influence in the government. And while the effects of Leavitt's article cannot be gauged or even guessed at, the reprint in the Harvard University Library from which the above extracts were taken, bears the inscription: "1864, Nov. 20 Gift of Hon. Chas. Sumner (H.C. [Harvard College] 1831)."

Ironically, the first published work to present the Polish side of the story was also written by a Protestant minister. He was Michael B. Czechowski, a nephew of Leon Czechowski who had been a leader of the Polish exiles in Western Europe following the November Insurrection. Michael Czechowski had been a Catholic priest; but after some traveling and soul-searching, he was converated to a fundamentalist variety of Protestantism and became a missionary to the French, the Indians, and other settlers in northern New York State, Vermont, and Canada. He recorded his conversion in 1862 in a sensational exposé entitled *Thrilling and Instructive Developments! An Experience of Fifteen Years as a Roman Catholic Clergyman and Priest.* The following year Czechowski moved to Brooklyn, New York, and there published the fifty-eight-page monograph *Poland: Sketch of Her History.*

Most of the historical sketch was devoted to early Polish history. Not surprisingly, its thesis was that monks and foreign priests and the involvement of its kings in external and internal religious crusades had "changed this once happy country into the abode of fanaticism, bigotry and anarchy."[53] Between its ninth and twenty-sixth pages Czechowski inserted a translation of a pamphlet originally written by Jan Nepomucen Janowski, erstwhile editor of the Warsaw *Gazeta Narodowa* (National Gazette) and later a leader of liberally-inclined exiles in Paris. The pamphlet, prosaically entitled *Treatment of the Jews and Laws Concerning Them*, contained sordid accounts of brutalities allegedly perpetrated against Poland's Jews before and after the unsuccessful attempt to introduce the Protestant Reformation there. In several instances Czechowski—or Janowski, perhaps— took considerable liberty with historical facts (e.g., that Julius Caesar had reproached Catholics who stole Jewish children in order to baptize them.[54]). "All intelligent persons are aware that the GREAT REFORMATION broke the chains of darkness and superstition," Czechowski added on his own to Janowski's words, "and enabled people to better understanding their true dignity."[55]

Czechowski did not agree with Clay, Boynton, and Leavitt in regard to serfdom in Poland. He took very strong issue with the prevalent faith among Americans in Alexander II's liberalism. "I consider it my duty as a Polander," he wrote, "to make this subject as clear as possible, and tear off the mask of this so-called 'great benefactor of the age.'"[56] He cited examples of Polish noblemen, especially Protestant noblemen, who had freed their serfs. He quoted that portion of the Polish Constitution of May 3, 1791, which released serfs from their feudal obligations, and he reminded his readers that one of the aims of the 1794 Insurrection led by Kosciuszko had been to release the serfs from the same obligations. He also pointed out that the suppression of that uprising by the Russian General Suvarov had set in motion a reaction to any progress. Czechowski pointed out that the leaders of the November Insurrection, many of whom had emigrated after its failure, had also favored peasant reform. He singled out a "committee of five," including Janowski and Adam Gurowski, as being in the vanguard of the democratic movements in exile.[57]

Czechowski attributed Alexander's liberality to the fact that his defeat in the Crimean War and his "enormous debt to the

Rothschilds" had made him "tremble for his power."[58] He devoted
very little space to the January Insurrection itself, but noted
in his conclusion:

. . . Torrents of blood are already flowing, and God only can foresee
what will be the end of the struggle. May he be merciful to my poor
oppressed country, that her people may have the opportunity to
prepare themselves for the true service of God, and His everlasting
Kingdom. And may you, also, dear readers give the Czar his due
and Poland her honor and your sympathy.[56]

In a scathing review, the *Echo z Polski* labeled Czechowski's
work absolutely slanted and anti-Catholic, and declared that the
only reason it had even decided to call its readers' attention to it
was the appeal in its conclusion.[60]

Czechowski was considered *persona non grata* by the leadership of the New York Polish exile community. In a letter to
Janowski, he placed sole blame for his plight on Henryk
Kalussowski whom he saw as a complete opportunist. He
expressed his feelings as follows: "Kalussowski is a Mason, an
Italian *Carbonaro*, a Jesuit, a Republican, a Democrat, a Com-
munist and everything! . . . Where there is money, there is
Kalussowski." His barbs were also directed at Jaworowski, whom
he termed "a good Jesuit." He informed Janowski that he had
had several public debates with Jaworowski in which he had
taken the affirmative side against Jaworowski's arguments that
the Polish Democratic Society, a liberal exile faction which Janowski had helped organize in the 1830s, had lost the trust of
Europe and of Poland especially. Czechowski added that Kalussowski had sprung to Jaworowski's defense calling one of the
Society's founders an alcoholic and another a man turned insane.

Czechowski lamented that even though he tried to present a
calm rebuttal and to uphold the Society's—and Janowski's—honor,
Kalussowski had ridiculed him and made the audience turn
against him. "The [Polish Central] Committee was chosen in an
ugly manner," he noted in afterthought, "and [it] is made up
almost exclusively of Poznan shoemakers because they have a
bit of money—or of tavern-keepers."[61]

In a subsequent letter to Janowski, Czechowski suggested that

Kalussowski had opposed his work because he had written a similar book and had planned to give it to the printers the very day *Poland, Sketch of Her History* came out.[62] In the meantime Janowski had written to Kalussowski. The Polish agent, complaining that he had been "scolded," replied in his own defense. He claimed that Czechowski by his accusations had aided Bayard Taylor "at the worst possible moment," and that Polish Jews in the United States, who shakily supported the Polish cause, saw in his pamphlet a warning to be heeded and had "stepped aside." He stated that he personally respected Czechowski, but nevertheless would not refrain from saying that Czechowski had done him harm through his pamphlet.[63]

In spring of 1864 Czechowski left the United States for France and Switzerland. Two years later he wrote another letter to Janowski. He took credit for having secured the support of the undecided Jewish element for the January Insurrection; he also maintained that *Poland, Sketch of Her History* had been written to convince the Jews that it was not the Polish government but its foes, "under a nationalistic cloak," who were the cause of their troubles.[64] But the fact that the two Jewish members of the Polish Central Committee, Markson and Horwitz, both resigned a week after the review was printed in the *Echo,* might not have been for the "professional reasons" indicated in the paper.[65]

Belatedly, in August of 1864, Martha Walker Cook's *Continental Monthly* printed an article almost equal in length to Leavitt's polemic, one which might have readily served as a counter polemic, even though it actually had been written as a reply to a very critical article in *The New Nation* of May 7, 1864. It bore the same title, "Tardy Truths," as the article to which it replied. Its author was Henryk Kalussowski.

Kalussowski opened his defense of the Polish cause with an indictment of Émile de Girardin, editor of the French pro-Czarist journal *La Presse,* on which *The New Nation's* "Tardy Truths" had drawn for its material; he also indicted a M. Fouquet, a purported "ex-commandant" of Polish insurgents and the self-styled "eyewitness" who had written the report for *La Presse.*[66]

In addition, he criticized Western "experts" on Poland as "individuals who never were in Poland beyond a few hours spent in Warsaw, who never saw anything of the Polish countryside except from a train, who never understood a word of Polish or any other Slavic language, including Russian." Such individuals, Kalussowski continued, might have been entertained for a few hours by government officials or by cautious patriots. They were usually in a hurry to see St. Petersburg and the elephant in its zoo. Once in "Rossia," they learned their Polish history in the Kremlin, in the salon of some former prince, or, at best, from the Panslavist historian Koydanoff.[67]

Kalussowski next undertook a point-by-point refutation of Fouquet's allegations as well as those that had been made in American newspapers. In reply to the first allegation—that the Polish insurgents counted solely on foreign aid—he stated that Fouquet through ill-will or ignorance had forgotten the appeals made directly to the people in the National Government's two manifestos. Nevertheless, "the interest of various Governments, and the sense of justice among nations, gave the Poles a right to expect foreign aid," and such aid "would neither be rejected nor treated with indifference."[68]

Fouquet had charged that the National Government had rejected the services of seven thousand Parisian volunteer workmen lest they introduce liberal thoughts and a proletarian movement into Poland. Kalussowski laughed this off but could not help feeling bitter as a result of the Frenchman's imputations and his variations on the theme that Poland's leadership consisted exclusively of conservative landowners. "Does the author indeed think that Poland has had no Liberalists similar to Voltaire, La Mennais, Victor Hugo, L. Blanc, Mazzini or Hertzen?" he asked. He continued with a listing of eminent Polish liberals, going as far back in time as the sixteenth century and ending with more recent leaders such as Joachim Lelewel, Maurycy Mochnacki, and Ludwik Mieroslawski. Unfortunately, Kalussowski did not point out their various contributions, and American readers remained puzzled by all the Polish names. His lament that the Poles were at a disadvantage because they spoke and wrote in a tongue "unknown to the noble philanthrop-ists in the West" was justified but not as helpful as a few biographical sketches would have been.

To Fouquet's allegation that he had found no activity in Cracow, and to the allegations that Poles in Austrian Poland did not support the insurrection, Kalussowski replied that even before Austrian authorities had declared an official state of seige, the commander of the Austrian forces, Pouilly de Mensdorf, "as a personal friend of the czar," had given twenty thousand officers and men "discretionary and greatly enlarged powers," while "as many policemen and spies, with . . . increasing covetousness for rewards, promotions and orders," kept surveillance of Cracow alone.[69]

Next, Kalussowski made a direct rejoinder to the American journalists who, especially at the time of the visit of the Russian "fleet," had questioned the motives behind the insurrection, had likened it to the Southern rebellion, and had also found new inspiration in Fouquet's remarks that the Poles lacked zeal and faith in their convictions. These were calumnies, he urged vehemently; the Pole "fought for everything most dear to the heart of men, for every right which he can justly claim, for independence, national existence, the right to use his own lan-guage, for the integrity of his own country." The Southern states, he pointed out, "had all these in full possession, nay, even the right to pass the law binding the North."[70]

Kalussowski made a detailed reply to those who praised the Czar's newly issued Polish Emancipation Decrees. "The Czar gave in 1864," he noted, "what had already been given by the Poles themselves in 1863; less the soil, which indeed never belonged to him, but for which he exacts payment." He discussed the confiscations which accompanied the decrees, and a sub-sequent disturbance in the marketing of agricultural produce, the immediate cause having been the fact that goods had to be sold in distant areas and new purchasers could not easily be found. He argued that the January 22 Manifesto of the Polish National Government had equalized gain and loss by first eman-cipating the serfs, then allowing them to keep the profits from the lands on which they lived, and, finally, allowing them to purchase land directly from the owners. He explained that the vaunted Russian Emancipation of the Serfs had been initiated "by an ukase of no very decided purport, followed by many others of like uncertain character, according with the varying views of those by whom they were dictated, by the partisans of emancipation or by those standing in opposition to it." He put the grand total of such supplementary decrees at a minimum of 500,000![71]

Midway in his article Kalussowski challenged the widespread belief that the insurrection was not supported by the peasants. Prefacing his argument with a verbal assault on "the popular lecturer" and the New York editors, he queried: "If these assertions are true, who then filled the ranks of the Polish insurgents? Who furnished food to those who lived for months in the depths of forests, the haunts of mountain gorges? How was it possible that without the connivance of the peasants . . . insurgents should pass to and fro, or lie hidden in woods and fields?" He was puzzled that Fouquet could "authoritatively" state that the insurgents included some Hungarian refugees, about ten Frenchmen, and some "lesser nobles" in search of "shelter and fortune." It was "a marvellous shelter indeed," he replied, "to reward the greed of the ambitious—exile, death, and torture!" He then presented his statistics: Of seven hundred patriots hanged by the Russian authorities less than half were Catholic; "many" were Jews, Protestants, and even "Russo-Greeks." They came from various classes. Among forty thousand deportees to Siberia, there were nearly five thousand Jews, ten thousand peasants (here he added a parenthetical "known"), and from four to six thousand "of Greek and other creeds." Kalussowski also claimed that hundreds of Polish villages had been burned to the ground "by an excited and hired rabble of Muscovite Muzhiks." He laughed away the contention of those Western "observers" who could naively believe that the thousands of huts which went up in flames belonged to rich Polish landlords.[72]

Next, Kalussowski calmly parried the argument that the Polish Insurrection was controlled by the Catholic clergy, this

being a mainstay, of course, of Boynton's and Leavitt's contentions. He mentioned three rabbis who were active in the insurrectionary movement, as well as five Protestant leaders. He even
included the names of three Moslem leaders. Every one of these
religious leaders, he observed, had "a right to be a faithful son
of his fatherland and race." It just happened that in Poland most
often the Catholic priest stood opposed to the Russian "pope,"
and if the latter were a patriot, why not the former? He explained
that there was an Anglo-Saxon partiality to the Russian Orthodox
faith ever since Czar Nicholas I had visited England and "certain
ignorant or designing persons" had designated as Protestant the
creed of which he was the head. In an aside he tried to make
his readers realize that the church in Russia was so integrated
into the despotic system that the Czar could keep it as disciplined
as his army, and that "an offending pope" could be sent with
the rank of private to a remote regiment.[73]

Next, Kalussowski presented new details on the repressions
in Poland. There were more specific instances. Items were called
to the attention of readers to produce a sordid picture of auto-
cratic rule. (E.g., the use of the lash and whip on women, which,
Kalussowski acidly commented, "certain correspondents and
lecturers, with other gentlemen" would deny "because the American people cannot countenance such barbarism.")[74] He followed
up with a combined appeal and accusation aimed directly at his
American journalist colleagues: "For the sake of common humanity, say not that men placed in such situations have, in spite
of their glorious history, no rights, no claim on human sympathy, no cause to sacrifice life even when it has become a
haunting horror!"[75]

Kalussowski reserved the final paragraph of his article for a
dire prophecy about a possible breakdown of the resistance
offered by future generations of Poles under Russian rule, and
the implications this might have for the security of Western
Europe. He stated:

We of this generation are grown fixedly into our ancient habits
of thought, and now can make no change; but our successors, per-

chance, may possibly be reduced to undersign the manifesto of
Russian Liberalism, published about a year ago in Moscow, and in
return for false promises and deceptions, consent to make common
cause against Germany and the whole of Western Europe. What
American liberty would gain by such an eventuality, it is not for us,
nor for to-day, to say. [76]

The somber prose of Kalussowski's "Tardy Truths" was in
accord with Joshua Leavitt's *desideratum*. It was an appeal from
poetry to history, but a belated one. If an article like it had
appeared in 1863 it might have had at least a partially sobering
effect on some Americans who were intoxicated with Czar
Alexander's "liberalism" and the visit of the Russian "fleet."
Would earlier publication have been a possibility? Going back
to Kalussowski's introduction, we may accept the following
statement as an explanation: "Poland has no reason to fear the
truth. On the contrary, the difficulty has been to find means to
set it forth, avenues to the public intelligence and sense of justice
whereby those might be reached who forget the Latin saying:
Audi et alteram partem."[77] From this accusation it would seem
that the Poles in the United States had wanted to present their
side of the story but had actually been denied the opportunity.
Only further investigation, if such is even possible, may indicate
whether his accusation merits affirmation or denial. It was
reiterated, with more bitterness in *Echo z Polski* and the exile
press of Western Europe. That the "popular lecturer" of Kalussowski's article was Bayard Taylor, that the visit of the Russian
vessels and the Protestant-Orthodox rapprochement was also
noted, and added to the bitterness, may be gathered from the
following paragraphs:

The times of warm sympathy on the part of Americans are gone.
The fashion of adoring liberal Moscow and the Czar spread from the
journals to the nation. Lecturing literary men, whose hands were
clasped by Gorchakov, such as Bayard Taylor, travelled from village
to village, from city to city, arguing that the Polish Insurrection was
a matter of fanaticism and the Czartoryski party.

Not long afterwards, the Russian fleet appeared and gold, which
perhaps our brethren in Siberia mined, was spilled forth . . . then

loud celebrations and a cordial approach of Protestants towards the Schismatics. Heaven and earth were moved to suppress sympathy and to confound opinion.[78]

These paragraphs appeared in the influential *Glos Wolny* and were later reprinted in a volume entitled *Rachunki z roku 1867* (Accounts from the year 1867) by the exile writer Józef Ignacy Kraszewski, who used the pseudonym "Boleslawita." They were widely read by Poles inside Poland, at that time and in years to come. Their author also was Henryk Kalussowski.

Besides the bitterness which it elicited in the Polish exile press, the Northern Russophilia was to be a partial reason for a substantial group of Polish volunteers almost joining the forces of the South during the final desperate months of the Civil War. In August, 1864 four Polish representatives appeared in Richmond after having successfully run the Northern blockade. They presented a letter to the "Government and people of the Confederate States" in which they declared that Polish exiles and ex-insurgents in Western Europe desired to fight for the Southern "revolution" as Kosciuszko and Pulaski had fought in the first American revolution. In return, they asked for a grant of land which then would be a "colony" in which they could perpetuate their own institutions and customs.[79] Caspar Tochman met them and wrote to Jefferson Davis asking that their request be granted. In his note he also said that the Polish Democratic Societies in France and England had finally gotten a "clearer view" and were beginning to see the correctness of the reasoning behind his reply to their resolution of censure.[80]

Told by Davis that the Confederate government did not have the power to allocate state lands, the delegation was disappointed but still felt that several thousands of its compatriots would come if they were provided transportation, given individual land grants by the states, plus a right to form their own units and elect their own officers. The skeptical Judah Benjamin was instructed by executive order to remit 50,000 pounds from a secret fund to the Confederate Treasury Agent in England for the purpose of defraying travel expenses of the potential volunteers. Soon, a scheme was worked out whereby an infringe-

ment of international law would be avoided by having the men
debark at the Mexican port of Matamoras in the guise of colon-
ists. Their enlistment was to be recorded by an agent in Mexico
who would then send them on to another agent in Texas.[81]

Again xenophobia reared its head in the Confederacy. A
source obviously hostile to both Davis and foreigners attacked
him for entering into a secret compact with Poles to supply his
government with 20,000 to 30,000 troops. The scheme was publicized in the *Charleston Courier*,[8] and reported to Seward by
M. A. Jackson, the United States Consul in Halifax, Nova Scotia.
Seward thereupon sent instructions to European diplomatic representatives to exercise vigilance.[83]

The responses to Seward's instructions were of a reassuring
nature. From London, Charles Francis Adams advised the Secretary that British papers had already mentioned the plan, but
that he personally ignored it because the Confederacy was in
no position to finance it. He added with certainty: "It is not
likely that a few insurgent Poles who have been driven from
their country by the failure of the late insurrection, may be
tempted individually to try their chance in America by the offer
of a free passage and subsequent employment. But I think they
would much more cheerfully enlist on those terms under the
standard of the United States than with the rebels."[84]

From Vienna, J. Lothrop Motley, who was keeping Seward
posted on the state of seige which the Austrian authorities had
declared in their part of Poland, reported: ". . . so far as Austrian
Poland is concerned, the state of siege in that country still exists,
and it would be extremely difficult for any recruits for this Polish
confederate army to cross the frontier in any direction, except
with permission of the government, which assuredly would not
be given."[85]

Thus, the nebulous plan for a "Polish intervention" in the
American Civil War, like the more feasible plans for Western
European intervention in that war and in the Polish Insurrection,
never materialized. And when the Polish journals in exile finally
heard of it, they adopted a "pox upon both your houses" attitude.
They considered the four-man "delegation" opportunists who

would have traded Polish lives for land. The Southern cause was strongly condemned as the cause of slavery. Yet, in the same editorials there were also harshly worded reminders that the North had befriended Poland's oppressors.[86]

* * * * * * *

In August, 1864 Czarist authorities captured and hanged Romuald Traugutt and other leaders of the Polish National Government. The hangings took place within the walls of Warsaw's grim Citadel. Except for a few scattered bands which continued fighting until the spring of 1865, the January Insurrection had come to its tragic end. The American press scarcely took notice.[87] Two months later Cassius Marcellus Clay, with his usual air of self-assurance, drafted a dispatch to Seward in which he wrote as follows:

I enclose you a brochure . . . in which Lord Napier the British Embassador uses this language in reference to Poland:

"If that crisis has passed away without disastrous results, . . . it has been, no doubt, mainly owing to His Majesty's Ministers, who did not permit their resolutions, in a matter of general and paramount interest, to be influenced by the spectacle of partial and transitory wiles."

Here then is an explicit acknowledgment, that the evils of Poland under Russian rule, "were partial, and transitory"; just the ground which I have taken all the time, in reference to this unhappy rebellion in Poland. But the question then very justly arises, if the evils of Poland even when now absorbed into Russia are partial and transitory: what must be the grave responsibility of England and France in encouraging the Polish "reactionists" to plunge into a bloody and cruel rebellion to redress such "partial and transitory evils?"

I must do Lord Napier the justice, however, to say that his course here was in accordance with this view of the question: and it is thought that his wise counsel has much to do in averting a war between the Allied Powers and Russia.

This speech, however, of the English Embassador is worthy of presentation—in as much as it is evidence, coming certainly from not very friendly sources— that the course pursued by the United States, in reference to this delicate question, will stand fully justified in history.[88]

Justified in history? From a diplomatic standpoint—yes. In regard to Poland the United States did adhere scrupulously to the principles of its Monroe Doctrine. The Union government avoided interference in any way in an affair which was Europe's, just as it had, a very short time before, warned against Europe's interference in any way in an affair which was its own. From a logical standpoint—also yes. Like the Civil War, the January Insurrection has stirred much controversy and stimulated much debate among historians. As in the case of the Civil War, a general consensus to emerge from such a debate is that the insurrection was heroic but ill-advised. The activities in the subsequent period of "organic work," carried on by "Positivists" dedicated to reconstruction via education, industrialization, and general rebuilding under foreign occupation, proved of more benefit to the Poles than insurrections and dependence on foreign aid or sympathy.

However, from the standpoint of principle, a standpoint paramount in a democracy, the question of justification must be answered in the negative. The story of the Polish January Insurrection and Civil War America as recounted in these chapters and as concluded in this epilogue, is a story of emotion which often prevailed over compassion, of wishful thinking which often prevailed over sympathetic considerations, of local biases and prejudices which often prevailed over moral considerations. It is a story of unfortunate circumstances making for a situation in which Poland's well-wishers in Europe and, occasionally on the American scene, were also the Union's foes, while Poland's enemies and oppressors were the Union's alleged friends. Whatever might be the diplomatic and logical justifications, whatever might be the flaws in Poland's history, whatever might be the faults of Polish exiles, Americans, in the heat of battle and swayed by aroused emotions, wishful thinking, and wishful hoping, did forget some of the cardinal principles on which their own national existence was predicated. In such a situation, comfort was given to tyranny, and cynicism was sown in the minds of those who looked to the great republic in the New World for inspiration and sympathy.

APPENDIX A

SECRETARY OF STATE
WILLIAM H. SEWARD'S
NOTE ON POLAND

Department of State,
Washington, May 11, 1863

No. 342.

Sir: Mr. Mercier has read to me, and at my request has left with me, a copy of an instruction under the date of the 23d of April last, which he has received from Mr. Drouyn de l'Huys, and which relates to exciting and interesting events in Poland that are now engaging the serious attention of the principal States in Western Europe.

Mr. Mercier has, at the same time, favored me with a copy of an instruction relating to the same events which has been transmitted by Mr. Drouyn de l'Huys to the ambassador of France at St. Petersburgh.

We learn from the first of these papers that the proceeding which has thus been adopted at Paris with a view to the exercise of a moral influence with the Emperor of Russia, has received the approbation and concurrence of the court of Vienna and the cabinet at London, and that the Emperor of the French, justly appreciating at one and the same time our historical sympathy with the Poles, and our ancient friendship with Russia, would be gratified with a co-operation in that important proceeding by the government of the United States.

Having taken the instructions of the President, I am now to communicate our views upon the subject, for the information of Mr. Drouyn de l'Huys.

This government is profoundly and agreeably impressed with the consideration which the Emperor has manifested towards the United States by inviting their concurrence in a proceeding having for its object the double interests of public order and humanity. Nor is it less favorably impressed with the sentiments and the prudential considerations which the Emperor has in so becoming a manner

209

expressed to the court of St. Petersburgh. They are such only as appeal to the just emotions and best sympathies of mankind. The enlightened and humane character of the Emperor of Russia, so recently illustrated by the enfranchisement of a large mass of the Russian people from inherited bondage, and the establishment of an impartial and effective administration of justice, throughout his dominions, warrant a belief that the appeal will be received and responded to by him with all the favor that is consistent with the general welfare of the great state over which he presides with such eminent wisdom and moderation.

Notwithstanding, however, the favor with which we thus regard the suggestion of the Emperor of the French, this government finds an insurmountable difficulty in the way of any active co-operation with the governments of France, Austria, and Great Britain, to which it is thus invited.

Founding our institutions upon the basis of the rights of man, the builders of our republic came all at once to be regarded as political reformers, and it soon became manifest that revolutionists in every country hailed them in that character, and looked to the United States for effective sympathy, if not active support and patronage. Our invaluable Constitution had hardly been established when it became necessary for the government of the United States to consider to what extent we could, with propriety, safety, and beneficience, intervene either by alliance or concerted action with friendly powers or otherwise, in the political affairs of foreign states. An urgent appeal for such aid and sympathy was made in behalf of France, and the appeal was sanctioned and enforced by the treaty then existing of mutual alliance and defence, a treaty without which it may even now be confessed, to the honor of France, our own sovereignty and independence could not have been so early secured. So deeply did this appeal touch the heart of the American people, that only the deference they cherished to the counsels of the Father of our Country, who then was at the fulness of his unapproachable moral greatness, reconciled them to the stern decision that, in view of the location of this republic, the characters, habits, and sentiments of its constituent parts, and especially its complex yet unique and very popular Constitution, the American people must be content to recommend the cause of human progress by the wisdom with which they should exercise the powers of self-government, forbearing at all times, and in every way, from foreign alliances, intervention and interference.

It is true that Washington thought a time might come when, our institutions being firmly consolidated and working with complete success, we might safely and perhaps beneficially take part in the consultations held by foreign states for the common advantage of the nations. Since that period occasions have frequently happened which presented seductions to a departure from what, superficially viewed, seemed a course of isolation and indifference. It is scarcely necessary to recur to them. One was an invitation to a congress of newly emancipated Spanish American states; another was an urgent appeal to aid Hungary in a revolution aiming at the restoration of her ancient and illustrious independence; another, the project of a joint guarantee of Cuba to Spain in concurrence with France and Great Britain; and more recently, an invitation to a co-operative demonstration with Spain, France, and Great Britain in Mexico; and, later, still, suggestions by some of the Spanish American states for a common council of the republican states situated upon the American continent. These suggestions were successively disallowed by the government, and its decision was approved in each case by the deliberate judgment of the American people. Our policy of non-intervention, straight, absolute, and peculiar as it may seem to other nations, has thus become a traditional one, which could not be abandoned without the most urgent occasion amounting to a manifest necessity. Certainly it could not be wisely departed from at this moment, when the existence of a local, although we trust only a transient disturbance, deprives the government of the counsel of a portion of the American people, to whom so wide a departure from the settled policy of the country must in any case be deeply interesting.

The President will not allow himself to think for a single moment that the Emperor of the French will see anything but respect and friendship for himself and the people of France, with good wishes for the preservation of peace and order, and the progress of humanity in Europe, in the adherence of the United States on this occasion to the policy which they have thus far pursued with safety, and not without advantage, as they think, to the interests of mankind.

I am, sir, your obedient servant,

WILLIAM H. SEWARD

William L. Dayton, Esq., &c., &c., &c.

(From United States Department of State, Instructions, France, Seward to Dayton.)

ADDRESS OF THE CENTRAL
POLISH COMMITTEE

Americans! Poland is again in arms, and her battle-cry startles the world—"Give us a country or death, O God!" is sounding through every heart; nor can the sabre of the Cossack nor the musket of the Russian silence the holy chant. In the very face of death it breathes from the rosy lips of our devoted women, and thrills through the quavering accents of our children. The white eagles of Poland are again upon the gale! over fields so often hallowed by the blood of the brave, again they lead to victory; and God himself, in the perfect justice of our cause, is pledged for our success! Long crushed and tortured, Poland yet dares; frequently and ruthlessly betrayed, she is still true to herself and her high hopes; broken into fragments, limb torn from limb, yet her very name blotted from the roll of nations, and with the iron heel of the oppressor on her dauntless heart, she yet lives in a unity of being so close and entire that she is at last baffling the multitudinous powers of her enemies and rousing herself like a giant for the final combat.

What is the secret of this marvelous unity, this tenacity of life and purpose? Love of country; enthusiastic love, which never slumbers or wearies, whether in the frozen wilds of Siberia or the dungeons of the Russians, and is never soothed into forgetfulness even among the dwellers in the happy climes where Freedom makes her home, and man may live as virtue and duty dictate. Strange love of Poland which enables the tender daughters of her soil to relinquish all luxury, to live in constant privation, in life-long anguish, often to arm or die for her sweet sake; enables even children to endure torture and exile in her cause; while men of all ranks and ages rush into the very jaws of death without one thought of self in their strong souls. "God bless and deliver Poland!" the last words sounding through their firm lips! Americans, is not this feeling in itself almost sufficient to ensure victory for a cause so sacred that neither time, anguish or death have power to chill the holy enthusiasm enkindled by it?

Our countrymen are again in arms—not for conquest, spoil or revolution, but for Reorganization, Order, Religion, Toleration; that they may live and breathe as it alone behooves men to act and live —as freemen! The ancient rights of Poland have never been relinquished, her indisputable claim to nationality has never been abdicated; "the kings of the earth have risen up against her"; despots have combined to blot her glorious name from the face of the earth. But they have failed utterly, and ninety years of continuous oppression have not yet sufficed to efface it from the heart of one even among the last of her children! Poland grows no traitors on her bloody soil, and her men, women and children are as ready to die for her now as when her cruel dismemberment began.

No, "Poland is not dead," but writhes in the agonies of a new birth. The determination that she shall be free extends through all ranks and classes. Her white eagles again float in triumph over fields well known to glory; the tocsin, tolled by the anointed hands of her priests and bishops, again sounds from her time-worn cathedrals; her heart is on fire through the whole length and breadth of the soil so loved and so often drenched in gore. The flames which the Russians vainly sought to stifle when they surrounded Langiewicz almost under the very walls of Cracow, blaze now from north to south, encircling Warsaw, the center of Russian despotism, extending along the whole frontier of Russian Poland into Courland and Livonia, along the coast of the Baltic to the shores of Riga. Yes, the sacred ground, watered by the tears of noble women and the blood of patriots, is indeed on fire; the flames spread in every direction, all selfishness is consumed in the vivid glow, and every heart is ready to heave its last sob for the country of its ardent devotion.

The sons of Poland now fearlessly appeal to the sympathy of this great nation; they ask for aid in a cause which can never be buried in defeat or sunk in forgetfulness, for the conscience of the civilized world is now aroused; the universal sense of justice pants to relieve the injured victim, the long-martyred nation calls for moral support—for that overwhelming strength which will nerve her arm when she feels the vast heart of all free people throb pulse for pulse with her own, that the outrages committed against her are seen to be outrages against humanity itself, and that the prayers of all just men who know what freedom is are raised in her behalf to that God of Eternal Mercy who wills that "all men shall be free." What use now to dwell upon the agonies so long endured by Poland? Every one knows that no faith has ever been kept with her, no promises made but to be broken, no treaties signed but to be rescinded.

Wrong upon wrong has been heaped upon her; humiliation upon humiliation; the very language in which her children first learn to lisp the word "mother" they have sought to cancel in her patriot soul! Her unarmed populace have been fired upon in their own capital, when at their simple devotions, when their dauntless virgins bared their snowy bosoms to the cold sharp steel of their ruthless enemy, and the tenderest mothers held up their innocent children to the shot and shell of the infuriated Russians. This is no place to enumerate the glories of Poland; they illuminate the pages of human history; nor is this the place for the names of her sages, poets and patriots. Many of her heroes stand indelibly graved upon the tablets of her own bright national history, and live laurel-crowned in the memory of a grateful people. Kosciusko and Pulaski! are they not household words among Americans?

Europe smiles upon our cause. A meeting was called in Paris, in order to express sympathy, on March 22d, in Stockholm on the 24th, in Switzerland on the 23d, in Belgium, Madrid and Turin, during the same month. Denmark has also expressed her interest for us in our present struggle, and even in St. Petersburgh they have not been silent. A "Territory and Liberty" Society, long known as in existence there, has issued a circular commencing thus: "The time has come when you should act in union with the Poles, to assure them those rights which Muscovite Czars have usurped." Thus all countries save the home of the exile, the Land of the Free, have given up assurances of ardent and beneficial sympathy; and our hearts are saddened by the fact that as yet no demonstration has been made in our favor. But this apparent apathy cannot last.

Men and brethren! we ask aid from hearts that have been rocked in the cradle of Liberty, suckled at the breast of Freedom, and bred in the school of human rights! we ask aid, not to enable us to wreak vengeance upon our oppressors; aid, not for conquest or glory, but aid for our struggling and noble country! and succour for our anguished widows and orphans. The cry of the Legions of Dombrowski is again upon the air—"Jeszcze Polska nie zginela!"—"No, Poland is not dead!" and while there is a God in heaven she will not die! In the full confidence in that sacred brotherhood now stirring at the heart of all nations; in that widespread determination that all oppression must cease, we call upon you to acknowledge our claims. Few in number, our cause is mighty and appeals to all who feel. The Christ of Nations, bound hand and foot, is stirring in her tomb, and the day of her resurrection has already dawned.

Upon the very first day the Polish Committee met, they declared in the very moment when the holy struggle begins that "all the sons of Poland, without distinction of faith or race, descent or station, are free and equal citizens of the country. We also wish to address a few lines to the Muscovite nation. Our traditional motto being the freedom and brotherhood of nations, we pardon you even the murder of our Fatherland, the blood of Praga and Oszmian, the outrages in the streets of Warsaw, and the tortures in the cells of the citadels. We pardon you because you, too, are miserable and weary; because the dead bodies of your children are rocked on the gallows of the Czar, and your prophets freeze in the snows of Siberia," etc. Such is the language of our Committee.

Equal rights to all and forgiveness to our enemies! People of the Union, first in the upward path of freedom, consider our just and sacred claims. The feeling of the French and English people is unmistakably in our favor; even Austria hesitates, and would fain be generous. We ask aid for the victims in this glorious warfare—aid, that Poland may once more live, that her long crucifixion may cease, that she may once more emerge into the bright sunshine of national independence, the strengthening cause of constitutional liberty. Rally in her noble cause, and her millions shall greet you from across the sea; the warm tide of gratitude shall surge your souls with the bliss of well-doing; and the Brotherhood of the world shall have made its first great step in the new path now opening for fraternal advance of ever-progressive humanity!

Dr. Mackiewicz	X. Karczewski
Jaworowski	J. Markson
J. Gacek	J. Pychowski
Kalussowski	W. Piotrowski
Col. Krzyzanowski	Dr. med. Horwitz
Col. Karge	W. Kochanowski
Major Raszewski	W. Biskupski
Major Hlasko	J. Wisniowski

Capt. Maluski

CENTRAL POLISH COMMITTEE IN THE UNITED STATES

(From the New York *Herald,* April 29, 1863.)

ADDRESS OF THE POLISH COMMITTEE
TO THE LAND OF THE FREE
AND THE HOME OF THE BRAVE

Freemen! The origin of the Polish question, and the cause of the uprising of the Polish people, must of course be sought in that series of unprincipled aggressions—on many accounts perhaps the most remarkable in the whole course of modern history—*the partition of Poland.*

Nearly a century has elapsed since Russia, Prussia and Austria, taking advantage of a civil war which they had secretly fomented, violently seized the Polish territory as a common spoil, and partitioned it among themselves.

Roused to a sense of injuries, the Poles made several fruitless attempts to free themselves of the oppressive foreign yoke. After the most spirited resistance under the brave Kosciuszko, they were overpowered, and their country was then finally dismembered. During that desperate struggle, thousands, aye, millions of the bravest Polish patriots, the most devoted women and guiltless children, were either exiled far off to the ice and snow regions of Siberia, or imprisoned in the damp dungeons of the despots!

Subsequently, however, the despoilers of Poland, were deprived of a part of their acquisitions by Napoleon I, and out of the territory which they then lost has been formed what is now called "The Kingdom of Poland," and which is made to "belong" to Russia.

The pretended "order" and "peace" now reigned in Poland for a few years.

But the barbarous treatment of the Poles by the ruffian band of the hateful tyrants soon again awakened the depressed spirits of the people, and inspired them with valor to battle against the tremendous odds of miscreants in the year 1830—the memorable date of the Polish Revolution, which we this day commemorate.

Although again unsuccessful in their struggle for freedom, by being treacherously betrayed and unaided from abroad, the Poles still hopeful for their country and their country's cause, suffered and are suffering tortures beyond the power of description! While other nations that are not immediately concerned in the robbery and murder of Poland, are basely viewing all this with indifference! And in some countries even the costless expression of "Sympathy" with the unfortunate Poles is being denied to them!

But time has at last shown that the *interest* of other nations, as well as the *freedom* of the whole world, is indirectly involved in the Polish question—while the unfortunate Pole, moved by the inner spirit of liberty, consoles himself with singing "Jeszcze Polska nie zginela!" *Poland is not yet lost!* And an involuntary tear presses itself to his eye when reflecting upon the injustice and ingratitude done to his dear native land.

The unextinguishable love of liberty pent up in their breasts; the oppressive yoke under which the Polish people are withering; the agonizing cries of innocent children murdered in their mothers' laps, or torn from them and sent to colonize some far-off desert; the memories of the past glories; the blood-stained soil *beneath* which are resting the bones of men who flinched not from sabre's edge, and the blue canopy of heavens *above*, always reminding man that he is entitled to "life, liberty, and the pursuit of happiness"—again roused the patriots to shake off the bloody shackles of oppression! Now is the hour, and now is the time! The Poles have arisen to free themselves! Their battle-cry is "Liberty or death!" Long crushed and tortured, yet not dead!

> *Like leaves on trees the race of man is found,*
> *Now green in youth, now withering on the ground;*
> *Another race the following Spring supplies;*
> *They fall successive, and successive rise.*

Awake, O ye freemen of America! On Polish ground the battle of European freedom is now fighting! In that country the undaunted champions of liberty shall create a new era—a new bulwark of freedom! Aid them, or they will perish! Aid them *morally* with sympathies, *materially* with donations. Their cause is just, therefore, they must and shall succeed! Look at the bloody deeds of their despoilers, whose

Lawless force, with guilty stride,
Spreads desolation far and wide,
While peace and liberty lie bleeding!

Remember! that where honor is allied to humanity, truth to loyalty, piety to justice, there lies the dignity of human nature. If tyrants can league together to destroy free people and free nations, why should not a free nation aid another struggling for liberty? If you permit freedom to be crushed *abroad,* your own will share the same fate *at home.* Therefore, *aid the struggling Poles!*

(From the *Irish-American* (New York), December 1, 1863.)

BIBLIOGRAPHY

SECONDARY SOURCES

Books

Abbot, Lyman (ed.). *Henry Ward Beecher, A Sketch of His Career: With Analyses of His Power as a Preacher, Lecturer, Orator and Journalist, and Incidents and Reminiscences of His Life.* Hartford, Conn.: American Publishing Co., 1887.

Adams, Ephraim D. *Great Britain and the American Civil War.* 2 vols. New York: Longmans, Green & Co., 1925.

Alexandrov, Victor. *L'ours et la baleine L'histoire des relations extra-ordinaires Russo-Americaines.* Paris: Librairie Stock, 1958.

Bailey, Thomas A. *America Faces Russia, Russian-American Relations From Early Times to Our Day.* Ithaca, N. Y.: Cornell University Press, 1950.

Baker, George E. (ed.). *The Diplomatic History of the War For the Union, Being the Fifth Volume of the Works of William H. Seward.* Boston: Houghton Mifflin Co., 1884.

Basler, Roy P. (ed.). *The Collected Works of Abraham Lincoln.* 8 vols. New Brunswick, N. J.: Rutgers University Press, 1953.

Bemis, Samuel F. *A Diplomatic History of the United States.* New York: Holt, Rinehart and Winston, 1955.

Blumenthal, Henry. *A Reappraisal of Franco-American Relations, 1830–1871.* Chapel Hill, N. C.: University of North Carolina Press, 1959.

Boynton, Charles B. *English and French Neutrality and the Anglo-French Alliance in Their Relations to the United States and Russia,* Cincinnati: C. F. Vent & Co., 1864.

Butler, Benjamin F. *Private and Official Correspondence of General Benjamin F. Butler During the Period of the Civil War.* 5 vols. Norwood, Mass.: Plimpton Press, 1917.

Callahan, James M. *Russo-American Relations During the American Civil War.* West Virginia Studies in American History, Series 1, Diplomatic History, No. 1, Department of History and Political

Science, West Virginia University, Morgantown, W. Va., January, 1908.

————. *The Diplomatic History of the Southern Confederacy*. Baltimore: The Johns Hopkins Press, 1901.

Coleman, Arthur P., and Coleman, Marion M. *The Polish Insurrection of 1863 in the Light of New York Editorial Opinion*. Williamsport, Pa.: The Bayard Press, 1934.

Complimentary Banquet Given By the City Council of Boston to Rear Admiral Lessofsky and the Officers of the Russian Fleet at the Revere House, June 7, 1864. Boston: J. E. Farwell and and Co., 1864.

Curtis, George W. (ed.). *The Correspondence of John Lothrop Motley, D.C.L.* 2 vols. New York: Harper & Bros., 1889.

Czechowski, Michael B. *Poland, Sketch of Her History*. New York: Baker and Godwin, 1864.

————. *Thrilling and Instructive Developments! An Experience of Fifteen Years as a Roman Catholic Clergyman and Priest*. Boston: G. C. Rand and Avery, Cornhill, 1862.

Dictionary of American Biography. 20 vols. New York: Scribner, 1928.

Edwards, Henry Sutherland. *The Polish Captivity: An Account of the Present Position of the Poles in the Kingdom of Poland and in the Polish Provinces of Austria, Prussia and Russia*. 2 vols. London: Author, 1863.

Fischer, LeRoy H. *Lincoln's Gadfly, Adam Gurowski*. Norman, Okla.: University of Oklahoma Press, 1964.

Groniowski, Krzysztof. *Realizacja reformy uwlaszczeniowej 1864 r.* (Implementation of the 1864 Land Reform). Warsaw: Instytut Historii Polskiej Akademii Nauk (Institute of History of the Polish Academy of Sciences), 1963.

Gurowski, Adam. *Diary*. 3 vols.; Vol. 1, Boston: Lee & Shepard, 1862; vol. 2, New York: Carleton, 1864; Vol. 3, Washington: W. H. & O. .H Morrison, 1866.

————. *Russia As It Is*. New York: D. Appleton & Co., 1854.

Haiman, Mieczyslaw. *Historja udzialu polakow w amerykanskiej wojnie domowej* (History of the Participation of Poles in the American Civil War). Chicago: "Dziennik Zjednoczenia" (Alliance Journal, 1928.

————. *Polish Past in America, 1608–1865*. Chicago: The Polish Roman Catholic Union of America, 1940.

Hoelzle, Erwin. *Russland und Amerika, Aufbruch und Begegnung zweier Weltmächtes.* Munich: Verlag R. Oldenbourg, 1953.

Koberowa, Irena. *Polityka czartoryszczyzny w okresie powstania styczniowego* (The Policy of the Czartoryski Group at the Time of the January Insurrection). Warsaw: "Ksiazka i Wiedza" (Book and Knowledge), 1957.

Koht, Halvdan. *The American Spirit in Europe, A Survey of Transatlantic Influences.* Philadelphia: University of Pennsylvania Press, 1949.

Laserson, Max. *The American Impact on Russia—Diplomatic and Ideological— 1784–1917.* New York: The Macmillan Co., 1950.

Lerski, Jerzy J. *A Polish Chapter in Jacksonian America, The United States and the Polish Exiles of 1831.* Madison, Wis.: The University of Wisconsin Press, 1958.

Lonn, Ella. *Foreigners in the Confederacy.* Chapel Hill, N.C.: The University of North Carolina Press, 1940.

Malkin, M. *Grazhdanskaya voina v S.Sh.A i tsarskaya Rossiya* (The Civil War in the U.S.A. and Czarist Russia). Moscow-Leningrad: 1939.

Mildmay, Susan St. John, and Mildmay, Herbert St. John (eds.). *John Lothrop Motley and His Family, Further Letters and Records Edited By His Daughter and Herbert St. John Mildmay.* London: John Lane the Bodley Head, and New York: John Lane Co., 1910.

Monaghan, Jay. *Diplomat in Carpet Slippers, Abraham Lincoln Deals With Foreign Affairs.* Indianapolis-New York: The Bobbs-Merrill Co., 1945.

Mott, Frank L. *American Journalism, A History of Newspapers in the United States Through 260 Years: 1690 to 1950.* New York: The Macmillan Co., 1953.

O'Brien, William Smith, *Lecture on Poland Delivered in Dublin, Wednesday, July 1st, 1863.* Dublin: Goodwin, Son and Nethercott, 1863.

Osada, Stanislaw. *Historya Zwiazku Narodowego Polskiego i rozwoj ruchu narodowego polskiego w Ameryce Polnocnej* (History of The Polish National Alliance and the Growth of the Polish National Movement in North America). Chicago: Zwiazek Narodowy Polski (Polish National Alliance), 1905.

Owsley, Frank L. *King Cotton Diplomacy, Foreign Relations of the Confederacy.* Chicago: The University of Chicago Press, 1931.

Pierce, Edward L. *Memoir and Letters of Charles Sumner.* 2 vols. Boston: Roberts Bros, 1893.

Piotrowski, Rufin. *The Story of a Siberian Exile.* London: Longman, Roberts and Green, 1863.

Reddaway, W. F., et al. (eds.). *The Cambridge History of Poland.* 2 vols. Cambridge: Cambridge University Press, 1951.

Robertson, James R., *A Kentuckian at the Court of the Tsars, The Ministry of Cassius Marcellus Clay to Russia, 1861–1862 and 1863–1869.* Berea, Ky.: Berea College Press, 1935.

Smiley, David L. *Lion of Whitehall The Life of Cassius M. Clay.* Madison, Wis.: University of Wisconsin Press, 1962.

Sorokin, Pitirim A. *Russia and the United States.* New York: E. P. Dutton and Co., 1944.

Szygowski, Juliusz. *Powstanie polskie w.r. 1863 i Stany Zjednoczone* (The Polish Insurrection of 1863 and the United States). Paris: Ksiegarnia Polska (Polish Book Shop), 1961.

Tarsaidze, Alexandre. *Czars and Presidents, The Story of a Forgotten Friendship.* New York: McDowell, Obolensky, 1958.

Taylor, Bayard. *The Poems of Bayard Taylor.* Boston: Ticknor and Fields, 1866.

————. *Travels in Greece and Russia, with an Excursion to Crete.* New York: G. P. Putnam Sons, 1872.

Thomas, Benjamin P. *Russo-American Relations, 1815–1867.* Baltimore: John Hopkins University Studies in Historical and Political Science, Series XLVIII, No. 2, 1930.

West, H. R. *Contemporary French Opinion on the American Civil War.* Baltimore: Johns Hopkins University Studies in Historical and Political Science, Series LXII, No. 1, 1924.

Wieczerzak, Joseph W. *The Polish Insurrection of 1830–1831: A Brief Study of Reactions, Actions and Repercussions on the American Scene.* New York: New York University, 1958, (Unpublished Master's Thesis).

Williams, William A. *American-Russian Relations, 1781–1947.* New York: Rinehart & Co., 1952.

Wittke, Carl. *The Irish in America.* Baton Rouge, La.: Louisiana State University Press, 1956.

Woldman, Albert. *Lincoln and the Russians.* Cleveland and New York: The World Publishing Co., 1952.

Articles

Adamov, E. A. "Russia and the United States at the Time of the Civil War," *Journal of Modern History,* Vol. II, No. 4, December, 1930., pp. 586–602.

"An Example of Friendly Solidarity," *USSR,* July, 1961, pp. 54—55.

Bailey, Thomas A. "The Russian Fleet Myth Re-examined," *Mississippi Valley Historical Review,* Vol. XXXVIII, No. 1, June, 1951, pp. 81-90.

Blinn, Harold E. "Seward and the Polish Rebellion of 1863," *The American Historical Review,* Vol. XLV, No. 4, July, 1940, pp. 828–33.

Bobr-Tylingo, Stanislaw. "Stany Zjednoczone A. P. a Powstanie Styczniowe," (The United States of America and the January Insurrection), *Teki Historyczne* (Historical Papers) (London), Vol. XI, 1960–1961, pp. 133–47.

Davidson, Marshall B. "A Royal Welcome for the Russian Navy," *American Heritage,* Vol. IX, No. 4, June, 1960, pp. 32–43.

Duker, Abraham G., "Polish Political Emigres in the United States and the Jews, 1833–1865," *Publications of the American Jewish Historical Society,* No. XXXIX, Part 2, December, 1949, pp. 143–67.

Ellsworth, Edward W. "Sea Birds of Muscovy in New England," *The New England Quarterly,* Vol. XXXIII, No. 1, March, 1960, pp. 3–18.

Gilbert, Benjamin F. "Welcome to the Czar's Fleet, An Incident of Civil War Days in San Francisco," *California Historical Society Quarterly Review,* Vol. XXII, No. 1, March, 1947, pp. 13–19.

Golder, Frank A. "Russian Fleet During the Civil War," *American Historical Review,* Vol. XX, No. 4, July, 1915, pp. 801–12.

Heilprin, M. *"Nos Amis les Cosaques!" Continental Monthly,* Vol. V, No. 1, January, 1864, pp. 216–20.

Higham, Robin D. S. "The Russian Fleet on the Eastern Seaboard, 1863–1864," *The American Neptune,* Vol. XX, No. 1, January, 1960, pp. 49–61.

Kalussowski, Henryk K. "Tardy Truths," *Continental Monthly.* Vol. VI, No. 2, August, 1864, pp. 209–22.

Leavitt, Joshua. "Poland," *New Englander Magazine and Yale Review,* Vol. XXII, No. 2, April, 1864, pp. 276–95.

Lerner, Harold. "The Question of a Polish Legion and Polish Immigration During the Second Mexican Empire," *The Polish Review*, Vol. VI, No. 3, Summer, 1961, pp. 99–107.

Nagengast, William E. "The Visit of the Russian Fleet to the United States. Were Americans Deceived?" *Russian Review*, Vol. VIII, No. 1, January, 1949, pp. 46–55.

Orlowski, Leon. "Henryk Korwin-Kalussowski (1806–1894) Delegate of the Polish National Government in Washington," *Bulletin of the Polish Institute of Arts and Sciences, New York*, Vol. IV, 1945–1946, pp. 60–66.

Pomeroy, Earl S. "The Visit of the Russian Fleet in 1863," *New York History*, Vol. XXIV, No. 4, October, 1943, pp. 512–18.

Tochman, Gaspar. "Dr. Tochman's Reply to the Polish Democratic Societies," *Southern Literary Messenger*, Vol. XXIV, No. 5, May, 1862, pp. 321–26.

————. "Poland and Russia," *Southern Literary Messenger*, Vol. XXXVII, No. 12, April, 1863, pp. 222–40.

Wieczerzak, Joseph W. "American Opinion and the Warsaw Disturbances of 1861," *The Polish Review*, Vol. VII, No. 3, Summer, 1962, pp. 67–83.

————. "The Polish Insurrection of 1830–1831 in the American Press," *The Polish Review*, Vol VI, No. 1–2, Winter-Spring, 1961, pp: 53–72.

OFFICIAL DOCUMENTS

Printed

The Congressional Globe Containing the Debates and Proceedings of the First Session of the Thirty-Eighth Congress. Washington: Congressional Globe Office, 1864.

Lewak, Adam, (ed.). *Polska dzialalnosc dyplomatyczna w 1863–1864 r., zbior dokumentow* (Polish Diplomatic Activity in the years 1863–1864, a Collection of Documents). Vol I. Warsaw: Ministerstwo Spraw Zagranicznych (Ministry of Foreign Affairs), 1937.

Proceedings of the Board of Aldermen of the City of New York from July 2d, to September 30, 1863, Vol. XCI. New York: Edmund Jones & Co., Printers, 1864.

Richardson, James D. (ed.). *A Compilation of the Messages and Papers of the Confederacy, Including the Diplomatic Corres-*

pondence, 1861–1865. 2 vols. Nashville, Tenn.: United States Publishing Co., 1905.

United States Department of State, *Messages and Documents, 38th Congress, 1st Session,* 1863.

Manuscript

All of the following are located at the National Archives of the United States, Washington, D.C., Department of State Record Group 59.

Despatches:
>> Austria (1863)
>> France (1863)
>> Great Britain (1863)
>> Russia (1861, 1862, 1863 and 1864)
>> Sweden and Norway (1863)

Instructions:
>> France (1863)
>> Portugal (1863)
>> Russia (1861, 1862, 1863 and 1864)

Bukaty, Antoni. MS 2446 in the Library of the Polish Academy of Sciences, Kornik, Poland

Janowski, Jan N. MS 3685 in the Jagellonian Library, Cracow, Poland

Taylor, Bayard. MSS in Houghton Library, Harvard University, Cambridge, Mass.

NEWSPAPERS

Atlanta, Ga.:
>> *Memphis Appeal* (Forced to move its office from Memphis, Tenn.)

Boston:
>> *Boston Commonwealth*
>> *Boston Daily Courier*
>> *Boston Post*
>> *Daily Evening Traveller*
>> *The Liberator*
>> *The Pilot*

Charleston, S.C.:
  Charleston Courier
  Mercury
Cincinnati, Ohio:
  Daily Gazette
Columbus, Ohio:
  The Crisis
New York:
  Commercial Advertiser
  Courrier des États-Unis
  Daily News
  Echo z Polski [Echo from Poland] (name later changed to *Echo Polskie* [Polish Echo])
  Evening Express
  Evening Post
  Harper's Weekly
  Irish-American
  New York Herald
  New York Journal of Commerce
  New York Sun
  New York Times
  New York Tribune
  New-Yorker Staats-Zeitung
  Spectator
  World
Petersburg, Va:
  Daily Express
Philadelphia:
  North American and United States Gazette
  Philadelphia Inquirer
  Public Ledger
Richmond, Va.:
  Daily Dispatch
  Daily Richmond Enquirer
  Daily Richmond Examiner
  Richmond Daily Whig
  Sentinel
San Francisco:
  Daily Alta California
  Daily Evening Bulletin

Washington, D.C.:
  Daily National Intelligencer

Newspapers Published Abroad:
England:
  Glos Wolny (Free Voice), London
Germany:
  Ojczyzna (Fatherland), Leipzig, (later published in Bendlikon, Switzerland)
Poland:
  Czas (Time), Cracow)
  Dziennik Poznanski (Poznan Daily), Poznan

NOTES: *Introduction*

[1] Halvdan Koht, *The American Spirit in Europe. A Survey of Transatlantic Influences* (Philadelphia: University of Pennsylvania Press, 1949), p. vi.

[2] *The Federalist; A Commentary on the Constitution of the United States, Being a Collection of Essays written in Support of the Constitution agreed upon September 17, 1787 by the Federal Convention.* (New York: The Modern Library, 1954), IX, p. 119; XXIX, p. 243 and LXXV, p. 489.

[3] Mieczyslaw Haiman, *Polish Past in America, 1608–1865* (Chicago: The Polish Roman Catholic Union Archives and Museum, 1939), p. 49.

[4] There were at least eighteen American editions of *Thaddeus of Warsaw;* the first dating back to 1817, the last to 1911.

[5] Joseph W. Wieczerzak, "The Polish Insurrection of 1830–31 in the American Press," *The Polish Review*, Vol. VI, No. 1–2, Winter-Spring, 1961, pp. 53–72.

[6] Jerzy J. Lerski, *A Polish Chapter in Jacksonian America, The United States and the Polish Exiles of 1831* (Madison, Wisconsin: University of Wisconsin Press, 1958) pp. 56–73. Dr. Samuel Gridley Howe, physician, teacher of the blind, participant in the Greek Revolution of the 1820s, and husband of Julia Ward Howe who wrote the "Battle Hymn of the Republic" during the Civil War, was charged with the delivery of the American funds to the Polish insurgents. He was detained by Prussian authorities on his way to the front and freed from prison through the intercession of William Cabell Rives, the American Minister to France.

[7] Lerski, *op. cit., passim,* and Thomas Bailey, *America Faces Russia, Russian American Relations From Early Times to Our Day* (Ithaca, New York: Cornell University Press, 1950), pp. 56–57.

[8] *Messages and Addresses of the Presidents, Fillmore, 31st Cong., 2nd Sess.,* December 8, 1850.

[9] The reply to the protests of the Russian chargé, Baron von den Osten Sacken, is to be found in United States Department of State, Notes to Foreign Delegations, Russia, No. 3, December 4, 1831. Buchanan's reports are to be found in United States Department of State, Despatches, Russia, Buchanan to Livingston, No. 9, December 20, 1832, and No. 22, August 7, 1833.

[10] Stanislaw Osada, *Historya Zwiazku Narodowego Polskiego i rozwoj ruchu narodowego polskiego w Ameryce Polnocnej* (History of the Polish National Alliance and the growth of the Polish National movement in North America) (Chicago: Polish National Alliance, 1905), pp. 21–22, and Mieczyslaw Haiman, *Historja udzialu polakow w amerykanskiej wojnie domowej* (History of the participation of Poles in the American Civil War) Chicago: *Dziennik Zjednoczenia* (Alliance Journal), 1928), pp. 10–11.

[11] Haiman, *Historja udzialu. . .* , p. 15

[12] Bayard Taylor, *Travels in Greece and Russia, With An Excursion to Crete* (New York: G. P. Putnam & Sons, 1872), pp. 313–314.

[13] United States Department of State, Despatches, Russia, Pickens to Cass, No. 13, September 29, 1858.

NOTES: *Chapter I*

[*] This chapter originally appeared as an article entitled "American Opinion and the Warsaw Disturbances of 1861" in *The Polish Review*, Vol. VII, No. 3, Summer, 1962, pp. 67–83.

[1] United States Department of State, Despatches, Russia, Appleton to Black, No. 14, March 6, 1861.

[2] *Ibid.*, No. 15. March 8, 1861. Only six were killed.

[3] *Ibid.*

[4] *Ibid.*

[5] United States Department of State, Despatches, Russia, Appleton to Seward, No. 16, April 20, 1861.

[6] *Ibid.*

[7] *Ibid.* The extracts mentioned here have been lost.

[8] In his "Letter of a Polish Gentleman to Prince Metternich" which he wrote after the Austrian government had suppressed the 1846 risings in its Polish province, Galicia.

[9] United States Department of State, Despatches, Russia, Clay to Seward, No. 11, November 13, 1861. Seward replied that the laws of the United States did not authorize the setting up of such a post (Department of State, Instructions, Seward to Clay, No. 23, December 11, 1861). There was no American consulate in Warsaw until 1871.

[10] Biographical data on Tochman is included in Mieczyslaw Haiman, "Historja udzialu polakow w amerykanskiej wojnie domowej" (History of the Paritcipation of Poles in the American Civil War) (Chicago: *Dziennik Zjednoczenia* [Alliance Journal]), pp. 119–130.

His activities on behalf of the Confederacy are detailed in Ella Lonn, *Foreigners in the Confederacy* (Chapel Hill: The University of North Carolina Press, 1940), pp. 160–164. His reply to the Polish Democratic Societies was printed in the *Southern Literary Messenger*, Vol. XXIV, No. 5, May 1862, pp. 321–326.

[11] United States Department of State, Despatches, Russia, Clay to Seward, No. 20 *bis*, March 19, 1862.

[12] Max M. Laserson, *The American Impact on Russia—Diplomatic and Ideological—1784–1917* (New York: The Macmillan Co., 1950), p. 75, points out that Clay was "influenced by the official Russian position to a certain extent." However, he does not support his contention with any documentation. Ironically, his biographers James R. Robertson, *A Kentuckian in the Court of the Tsars, The Ministry of Cassius Marcellus Clay to Russia, 1861–1862 and 1863–1869* (Berea, Kentucky: Berea College Press, 1935), p. 23, and David L. Smiley, *Lion of Whitehall, The Life of Cassius M. Clay* (Madison: University of Wisconsin Press, 1962), p. 11, note that he studied French under Jesuit priests at the College of St. Joseph, Bardstown, Kentucky. The latter biographer most wrongly notes that this may have contributed to Clay's "tolerance" in religious matters.

NOTES· *Chapter II*

[1] E.g., the *New York Herald*, January 3, 1863 and the Philadelphia *Public Ledger*, January 2, 1863. The former deemed it an unnecessary, unwise, ill-timed and impractical war measure.

[2] *Congressional Globe*, 37th Cong., 3rd Sess., Part 1, pp. 207–208.

[3] The *Philadelphia Inquirer*, March 3, 1863, noted: "It is curious, if not instructive, to notice the course pursued by some of the leading men of Europe in their expressions of sympathy. GARIBALDI and VICTOR HUGO, for instance are zealous advocates for the Poles, although both pray for the success of the United States Government in its effort to crush the Southern Rebellion."

For Herzen's position on both issues see Laserson, *op cit.*, p. 208.

[4] The journals cited the London *Times* as their source for this information. My background material on the insurrection is taken from W. F. Reddaway *et al.*, eds., *The Cambridge History of Poland*. Vol. 11, 1697–1935, Chap. XVI "Poland Under Alexander II: The Insurrection of 1863," pp. 365–86. The author of the chapter is Arthur P. Coleman.

[5] This posture is indicated by analyses in H. Reed West, *Contemporary French Opinion on the American Civil War* (Baltimore: Johns Hopkins University Press, 1924), *passim*.

[6] *New York Tribune,* February 14, 1863.

[7] Two interesting coincidences: During the Dresden Uprisings of 1848 Mieroslawski was a comrade-in-arms of Carl Schurz, who became a major general in the Union Army. At first, Schurz had been considered for the post of Minister to St. Petersburg, but because the Czar found his republicanism too radical, Cassius Clay was sent as Lincoln's second choice (*vide,* United States Department of State, Despatches, Russia, Clay to Seward, No. 20, March 7, 1862).

[8] *New York Tribune,* February 14, 1863.

[9] Frank L. Mott, *American Journalism, A History of Newspapers in the United States Through 260 Years: 1690–1950* (New York: The Macmillan Company, 1950), pp. 341–42.

[10] *New York Sun,* February 14, 1863.

[11] *Ibid.*

[12] *Ibid.*

[13] *New York Times,* February 17, 1863.

[14] *Ibid.*

[15] *Ibid.*

[16] *Ibid.*

[17] Mott, *op cit.,* p. 260.

[18] *North American and United States Gazette,* February 19, 1863.

[19] Mott, *op cit.,* p. 260. The *Gazette* had several editorial writers on its staff.

[20] *North American and United States Gazette,* February 19, 1863.

[21] *Ibid.*

[22] *Ibid.*

[23] *Ibid.*

[24] *Ibid.* One of the "enlightened counsellors" was supposedly Prince Orloff, the Russian Minister to Brussels, who, according to the *Gazette,* "took trouble to proceed in all haste to Warsaw" and who "exerted all his eloquence to plead the cause of right and humanity" before his personal friend Constantine.

[25] *Ibid.*

[26] *Ibid.*

[27] *Ibid.*

[28] *New York Sun* and *New York Herald,* February 23, 1863.

[29] *New York Journal of Commerce,* February 23, 1863.

[30] *North American and United States Gazette,* February 28, 1863.

[31] *Ibid.*

[32] *Ibid.*

[33] *Ibid.*

[34] *Boston Daily Courier,* February 28, 1863. "Pleasures of Hope" is the title of a poem written early in the nineteenth century by the Scottish poet Thomas Campbell. Its line "And Freedom shrieked when Kosciusko fell" was frequently quoted by American orators and journalists. In 1831, Bostonians had presented the Polish insurgents with a banner.

[35] *Boston Daily Courier,* February 28, 1863

[36] *Ibid.*

[37] E.g., Mott, *op. cit.,* p. 357.

[38] *Ibid.*

[39] *Boston Daily Courier,* March 18, 1863.

[40] *Ibid.*

[41] One of its rivals, the *Boston Commonwealth* on March 30, 1863, cited a statement attributed to Italy's King Victor Emmanuel to the effect that were he not the Italian ruler, he would want to be a Polish insurgent; and noted in that connection: "Evidently he had not read the Boston *Courier* which applauds no insurrections except those against freedom."

[42] *The Crisis,* March 4, 1863. My search through the *Congressional Globe* for the remark proved fruitless.

[43] Mott, *op. cit.,* p. 356.

[44] *The Crisis,* March 4, 1863.

[45] *Daily Richmond Examiner,* February 17, 1863.

[46] *Richmond Daily Whig,* March 27, 1863.

[47] *Daily Express,* April 3, 1863.

[48] *Ibid.*

[49] *Daily Express,* April 3, 1863.

[50] *Ibid.*

[51] *Daily Richmond Examiner,* March 28, 1863.

[52] *Sentinel,* March 31, 1863.

[53] *Daily Richmond Enquirer,* April 1, 1863.

[54] Frank L. Owsley, *King Cotton Diplomacy, Foreign Relations of the Confederacy* (Chicago: The University of Chicago Press, 1931), pp. 494–95, tells the story of the Russell correspondence and the British consuls.

[55] *The Pilot,* April 11, 1863.

[56] *Ibid.* The term "Dalemations" (Dalmatians) for the Poles, though poetic, is erroneous. The proper appellation is "Sarmatians."

NOTES: *Chapter III*

[1] The Cincinnati *Daily Gazette* (April 4, 1863) identified her as "Madame Pustowozoff" and gave her age as eighteen. Actually, her name was Henryka Pustowojtow.

[2] *World*, March 3, 1863.

[3] *Ibid.*

[4] *World*, March 13, 1863.

[5] *New York Times*, March 7, 1863.

[6] *New York Times*, March 13, 1863.

[7] *New York Herald*, March 7, 1863.

[8] *New York Herald*, March 14, 1863.

[9] *New York Herald*, March 17, 1863.

[10] *North American and United States Gazette*, March 14, 1863.

[11] *Ibid.*, March 17, 1863.

[12] *Ibid.*

[13] A general discussion of Russia's attitude towards mediation in the Civil War, all of which clearly indicates that it was not governed by any altruistic considerations, is to be found in Albert A. Woldman, *Lincoln and the Russians* (Cleveland and New York: The World Publishing Company, 1952), pp. 84–103.

[14] *North American and United States Gazette*, March 17, 1863.

[15] *Ibid.* "Gurowski" was a wishful misspelling of "Kurowski." See pp. 159–160.

[16] *North American and United States Gazette*, March 17, 1863.

[17] *North American and United States Gazette*, March 18, 1863.

[18] *Ibid.*

[19] *Ibid.*

[20] *Ibid.* The Convention was signed in 1833.

[21] *Ibid.*

[22] *Ibid.*

[23] *Ibid.*

[24] *North American and United States Gazette*, March 21, 1863.

[25] *North American and United States Gazette* (Philadelphia), March 25, 1863.

[26] *Ibid.* See footnote 15.

[27] *Daily National Intelligencer*, March 24, 1863.

[28] *Ibid.*

[29] *Ibid.*

[30] *Daily Evening Traveller*, March 24, 1863.

[31] *Daily Evening Traveller*, March 24, 1863.

[32] *Philadelphia Inquirer*, March 16, 1863.

[33] *Ibid.*

[34] *New York Sun*, March 13, 1863.

[35] *New York Sun*, March 14, 1863.

[36] *New York Sun*, March 18, 1863.

[37] *Ibid.*

[38] *New York Journal of Commerce*, April 15, 1863. According to Mott, *op. cit.*, p. 352, the *Journal* was named by a New York grand jury as one which "encouraged" the Southern rebels.

[39] *New York Sun*, April 7, 1863.

[40] *North American and United States Gazette*, April 8, 1863.

[41] *The Crisis*, April 15, 1863.

[42] *Spectator*, April 16, 1863.

[43] *North American and United States Gazette*, April 27, 1863. The full title of Edwards' work was *The Polish Captivity—An Account of the Present Position of the Poles in Austria, Prussia and Russia*. It was published in London by the W. H. Allen Co. in two volumes. Rufin Piotrowski's *The Story of a Siberian Exile*, written in the 1850's, was also published in a new edition in 1863 by Longman, Roberts and Green of London.

[44] *North American and United States Gazette*, April 27, 1863.

[45] *Ibid.*

[46] *Ibid.*

NOTES: *Chapter IV*

[1] *The Poems of Bayard Taylor* (Boston: Ticknor and Fields, 1866), p. 411.

[2] United States Department of State, Despatches, Russia, Taylor to Seward, No. 28, January 27, 1863.

[3] United States Department of State, Despatches, Russia, Taylor to Seward, No. 31, March 3, 1863.

[4] United States Department of State, Despatches, Russia, Taylor to Seward, No. 34, April 1, 1863.

[5] *Ibid.*

[6] Bayard Taylor, *Travels in Greece and Russia, with an Excursion to Crete* (New York: G. P. Putnam & Sons, 1872), pp. 313–314. The statement follows a report that the Poles were "gradually acquiescing in the rule of Russia."

[7] United States Department of State, Despatches, Russia, Taylor to Seward, No. 35, April 20, 1863.

[8] United States Department of State, Despatches, Russia, Taylor to Seward, No. 35, April 20, 1863.

[9] United States Department of State, Despatches, France, Dayton to Seward, No. 276, February 23, 1863.

[10] United States Department of State, Despatches, France, Dayton to Seward, No. 292, March 27, 1863.

[11] United States Department of State, Despatches, Great Britain, Adams to Seward, No. 337, February 26, 1863.

[12] United States Department of State, Despatches, Great Britain, Adams to Seward, No. 334, March 6, 1863.

[13] United States Department of State, Despatches, Sweden, Haldman to Seward, No. 28, April 24, 1863.

[14] United States Department of State, Instructions, France, Seward to Dayton, No. 328, April 8, 1863.

[15] United States Department of State, Instructions, France, Seward to Dayton, No. 336, April 24, 1863.

[16] United States Department of State, Instructions, Portugal, Seward to Harvey, No. 116, April 24, 1863.

[17] Samuel F. Bemis, *A Diplomatic History of the United States* (New York: Holt, Rinehart and Winston, 1955), p. 367. The memorandum was dated April 1, 1861. As Bemis points out, (p. 368) "Lincoln quietly pigeonholed the document, for historians to bring to light long afterward."

[18] George W. Curtis, ed., *The Correspondence of John Lothrop Motley, D.C.L.* (New York: Harper and Bros., 1899), Vol. II, p. 119.

[19] *Ibid.*

[20] Susan St. John Mildmay and Herbert St. John Mildmay, eds., *John Lothrop Motley and His Family, Further Letters and Records Edited by His Daughter and Herbert St. John Mildmay* (London: John Lane the Bodley Head, and New York: John Lane Co., 1910), pp. 176–77.

[21] Bayard Taylor to his wife, May 2, 1863, MS in Houghton Library, Harvard University.

[22] Bayard Taylor to his wife, May 6, 1863, MS in Houghton Library, Harvard University.

[23] Bayard Taylor to his mother and sisters, July 4, 1862, MS in Houghton Library, Harvard University.

[24] Bayard Taylor to his wife, April 24, 1863, MS in Houghton Library, Harvard University.

[25] James D. Richardson, ed., *A Compilation of the Messages and Papers of the Confederacy, Including the Diplomatic Correspondence, 1861–1865* (Nashville: United States Publishing Co., 1906), Vol. II, p. 435, No. 18, Hotze to Benjamin.

[26] James D. Richardson, ed., *A Compilation of the Messages and Papers of the Confederacy, Including the Diplomatic Correspondence, 1861–1865* (Nashville: United States Publishing Co., 1906), Vol. II, p. 437, No. 41, Mann to Benjamin, March 13, 1863.

[27] Richardson, *op. cit.*, p. 439.

[28] Richardson *op. cit.*, p. 437, No. 41, Mann to Benjamin, March 13, 1863.

[29] Richardson, *op. cit.*, pp. 440–441, No. 31 Mason to Benjamin, March 19, 1863.

[30] Richardson, *op. cit.*, pp. 456–457, Slidell to Benjamin, No. 29, March 21, 1863.

[31] Richardson, *op. cit.*, p. 460, Benjamin to Slidell, No. 14, March 24, 1863.

[32] Richardson, *op. cit.*, p. 367, Benjamin to Lamar [not numbered], November 19, 1862.

[33] Richardson, *op. cit.*, p. 455, Lamar to Benjamin [not numbered], March 20, 1863.

[34] United States Department of State, Despatches, Russia, Clay to Seward, No. 3, May 7, 1863.

NOTES: *Chapter V*

[1] United States Department of State, Despatches, France, Dayton to Seward, No. 297, April 9, 1863.

[2] United States Department of State, Instructions, France, Seward to Dayton, No. 299, April 27, 1863.

[3] United States Department of State, *Messages and Documents,* 38th Cong., 1st Sess., 1863, p. 829.

[4] United States Department of State, *Messages and Documents,* 38th Cong., 1st Sess., 1863, p. 829.

[5] United States Department of State, *Messages and Documents,* 38th Cong., 1st Sess., 1863, p. 830.

[6] *Ibid.*

[7] *Ibid.*

[8] United States Department of State, Instructions, France, Seward to Dayton, No. 342, May 11, 1863. The entire text of the document is included as Appendix A.

[9] United States Department of State, Instructions, France, Seward to Dayton, No. 342, May 11, 1863.

[10] United States Department of State, Instructions, France, Seward to Dayton, No. 342, May 11, 1863.

[11] *Ibid.*

[12] E. g., Bailey, *The United States Faces Russia,* pp. 74–75 and Laserson, *The American Impact on Russia,* pp. 233–35. The most complete discussion by an American historian of the problem is in

Harold E. Blinn, "Seward and the Polish Rebellion of 1863," *The American Historical Review*, Vol. 45, No. 4, July, 1940, pp. 828–33.

[13] E. g., Alexandre Tarsaidze, *Czars and Presidents, The Story of a Forgotten Friendship* (New York: McDowell, Obolensky, 1958), p. 192. Henry Blumenthal, *A Reappraisal of Franco-American Relations, 1830–1871* (Chapel Hill, N. C.: University of North Carolina Press), p. 147, cites a statement which had been made by Gorchakov to the French Ambassador to St. Petersburg, Fournier, in 1862, that "In case of European complications, America is an ally of Russia without the necessity of an alliance."

[14] United States Department of State, Despatches, Russia, Clay to Seward, No. 4, May 19, 1863.

[15] United States Department of State, Despatches, Russia, Clay to Seward, No. 4, May 19, 1863.

[16] United States Department of State, Despatches, Russia, Clay to Seward, No. 6, May 25, 1863.

[17] United States Department of State, Despatches, Russia, Clay to Seward, No. 7, May 29, 1863.

[18] United States Department of State, Despatches, Russia, Clay to Seward, No. 8, June 2, 1863. The Secretary of State's suggestion to make the contents of the note "informally" known to Gorchakov had been made in United States Department of State, Instructions, Russia, Seward to Clay, No. 8, May 11, 1863.

[19] United States Department of State, Despatches, Russia, Clay to Seward, No. 9, June 7, 1863. The translation is Clay's.

[20] United States Department of State, Despatches, Russia, Clay to Seward, No. 8, June 2, 1863.

[21] United States Department of State, Instructions, Seward to Clay, No. 24, June 30, 1863.

[22] United States Department of State, Despatches, Clay to Seward, No. 10, June 17, 1863.

[23] United States Department of State, Despatches, Russia, Clay to Seward, No. 10, June 17, 1863.

[24] United States Department of State, Despatches, Russia, Clay to Seward, No. 15, July 23, 1863.

[25] United States Department of State, Despatches, Russia, Clay to Seward, No. 17, August 5, 1863.

[26] *Ibid.*

[27] United States Department of State, Despatches, Russia, Clay to Seward, No. 18, August 13, 1863.

[28] United States Department of State, Despatches, Russia, Clay to Seward, No. 18, August 13, 1863.

[29] *Daily National Intelligencer*, June 30, 1863.

[30] *Spectator*, June 8, 1863.

[31] *Spectator,* June 8, 1863.

[32] *Richmond Daily Whig,* June 23, 1863.

[33] *Richmond Daily Whig,* June 23, 1863.

[34] *Richmond Daily Whig,* June 27, 1863.

[35] *Daily Richmond Examiner,* July 26, 1863.

[36] *Ibid.*

[37] *Daily Richmond Examiner,* July 26, 1863.

[38] *North American and United States Gazette,* August 4, 1863.

[39] *New York Times,* August 19, 1863.

[40] *Ibid.*

[41] *New York Times,* August 19, 1863.

[42] *Philadelphia Inquirer,* August 25, 1863.

[43] Adam Lewak, ed., *Polska dzialalnosc dyplomatyczna w 1863–1864 r.* (Polish Diplomatic Activity in the Years 1863–1864) (Warsaw: Ministry of Foreign Affairs, 1937), Vol. 1, p. 131. My translation.

NOTES: *Chapter VI*

[1] *Philadelphia Inquirer,* April 9, 1863, The letter is dated April 8.

[2] *Ibid.*

[3] See pp. 169–171.

[4] C.f. my master's thesis, *The Polish Insurrection of 1830–1831s A Brief Study of Reactions, Actions and Reprecussions on the American Scene* (New York: New York University, 1958), Unpublished; and article, "The Polish Insurrection of 1830–31 in the American Press," *The Polish Review,* Vol. VI, No. 1–2, Winter-Spring 1961, pp. 53–72.

[5] See p. 42.

[6] *Philadelphia Inquirer,* April 12, 1863.

[7] *Philadelphia Inquirer,* March 11, 1863.

[8] *Philadelphia Inquirer,* March 16, 1863.

[9] *New York Sun,* March 18, 1863.

[10] *New York Herald,* March 15, 1863.

[11] The newspaper was the *Echo z Polski* (Echo from Poland). It published its first issue on June 1, 1863.

[12] According to Mieczyslaw Haiman, *Historja udzialu . . .* p. 35, Alexander Raszewski, an active member of the already organized "Democratic Society of Polish Exiles in America" *(Towarzystwo Demokratyczne Wygnancow Polskich w Ameryce),* set up the almost entirely Polish Company C of the 31st New York Infantry Regi-

ment; General Krzyzanowski, a subordinate of Carl Schurz, commanded the 58th New York Infantry Regiment; Karge commanded a regiment of New Jersey cavalry and during the Battle of Vicksburg was in temporary command of the Second New Jersey Cavalry Regiment. The names of all the original members of the Polish Central Committee are listed at the end of the committee's first address (see Appendix B). According to *Echo z Polski*, September 3, 1863, regular meetings were held every fifteen days at Pythagoras Hall.

13 *New York Herald*, March 15, 1863.

14 *New York Herald*, April 29, 1863.

15 *Ibid*. The complete text of the appeal is included in Appendix B.

16 The *Spectator* was a semiweekly publication of the *Commercial Advertiser*. Arthur P. Coleman and Marion M. Coleman, *The Polish Insurrection of 1863 in the Light of New York Editorial Opinion* (Williamsport, Penna.: The Bayard Press, 1934), p. 124, terms the *Commercial Advertiser* (also edited by Hall) "Republican and semi-religious." The same description would seem apt for the *Spectator*.

17 *Spectator*, May 7, 1863.

18 This was the populist *Zemlya i Volya* (Land and Liberty) group which operated clandestinely.

19 *Spectator*, May 7, 1863.

20 *Ibid*.

21 *New York Times*, May 22, 1863. The preliminary meeting of the American Ladies' Committee was held May 30 in the schoolrooms of the Episcopal Church of the Transfiguration on East 29th Street. *Echo z Polski*, July 10, 1863, records a meeting of a "Ladies' Polish Aid Society" held at the Cooper Institute. The president of the society was Mrs. Martha Walker Cook; its vice presidents were a Mrs. Mallison, a Mrs. Roys [*sic*], and Mrs. Rutkay, who was a sister of the Hungarian patriot Louis Kossuth. Mrs. Mary Crane is listed as treasurer. The society voted to call a mass meeting to awaken sympathy for Poland, but because of the Confederate invasion of Pennsylvania it was called off.

22 Mieczyslaw Haiman, *Historja udzialu*. . . . According to *Echo z Polski*, June 20, 1863, a separate appeal was issued to the Poles "of the Mosaic faith" on June 22, 1863. It resulted in the formation of a separate "Polish-Israelite" Committee, whose president, Moritz Markson Markowitz, was also a member of the Polish Central Committee. Later, the "Polish-Israelite" Committee placed itself under the control of the Central Committee (cf. *Echo z Polski*, August 22, 1863).

23 *Daily Evening Bulletin*, April 17, 1863.

[24] *Daily Evening Bulletin,* May 25, 1863.

[25] *Ibid.*

[26] *Daily Evening Bulletin,* May 30, 1863.

[27] *Daily Evening Bulletin,* September 4, 1863. The *Echo z Polski,* October 10, 1863, noted that $775 of this sum had been collected by Marcin Prag, "an Israelite."

[28] *Daily Evening Bulletin,* September 29, 1863.

[29] Mieczyslaw Haiman, *Historja udzialu . . .,* p. 154. An itemized financial report was printed in *Echo z Polski,* April 20, 1864. None of the other Polish Committees reached $1,000.

[30] Mieczyslaw Haiman, *Polish Pioneers of California* (Chicago: Polish Roman Catholic Union of America, 1940), Chapter VII. "California Poles and the January Insurrection," pp. 74–78. According to Abraham G. Duker, "Polish Political Emigres in the United States and the Jews, 1833–1865," *Publications of the American Jewish Society,* No. XXXIX, Part 2, December, 1949, p. 144, the synagogue's rabbi, R. A. Henry, was himself from Poland. In contrast to San Francisco, the Poles of New York commemorated the first anniversary of the insurrection with a low requiem mass at a parish church and hoped that a yet-to-be-organized American-Polish Committee would hold a large-scale meeting (cf. *Echo z Polski,* January 16 and 30, 1864).

[31] Mieczyslaw Haiman, *Historja udzialu . . .,* p. 136.

[32] Schurz eulogized Krzyzanowski in a speech delivered in Green Wood Cemetery, Brooklyn, New York, on January 30, 1887.

[33] See pp. 221–212 and 222.

[34] *New-Yorker Staats-Zeitung,* July 4, 1863.

[35] E.g., *Courrier des États-Unis,* March 30, 1863, where one paragraph reads:

Des manifestations en faveur de la Pologne ont lieu dans toutes les grandes villes de l'Italie, de même qu'en Suisse et en Suede. Un journal fait la remarque que la republique des Etats-Unis ne c'est point encore associée à ce mouvement unanime des nations liberales. Cela n'a rien d'étonnant. Les Americains du Nord, faisant au Sud une guerre d'extermination, pour le faire entrer dans l'Union malgré lui, ne peuvent pas, désormais, sympathiser sans inconsequence, ni avec les Polonais, ni avec les Venitiens, ni avec les Hongrois, qui sont, eux aussi des séparatistes.

[36] *The Irish-American,* July 4, 1863.

[37] *Ibid.*

[38] *Ibid.*

[39] *The Irish-American,* July 4, 1863. O'Brien also lectured on the insurrection in Dublin. Among the material at the National Library of Ireland is a pamphlet entitled *Lecture on Poland Delivered in*

Dublin, Wednesday, July 1st, 1863 (Dublin: Goodwin, Son and Nethercott).

[40] The abortive project for an "Irish Brigade" to defend the Pope was proposed in 1862.

[41] Smith O'Brien passed through the United States and Canada following his release from the British penal colony in Tasmania.

[42] *The Irish-American,* August 8, 1863.

[43] *The Irish-American,* October 17, 1863. A Polish translation of the letter was printed in the *Echo z Polski* on October 17 and 24, 1863.

[44] *The Irish-American,* October 17, 1863.

[45] *The Irish-American,* October 17, 1863.

[46] *The Irish-American,* November 11, 1863.

[47] *The Irish-American,* December 5, 1863.

[48] *The Irish-American,* December 5, 1863. See also Carl Wittke, *The Irish in America* (Baton Rouge, La.: Louisiana State University Press, 1956), p. 83 and pp. 135 ff.

[49] *The Irish-American,* December 5, 1863. The full text of the address is to be found in Appendix C.

[50] The friendship is traced in Le Roy H. Fischer, *Lincoln's Gadfly,, Adam Gurowski* (Norman, Okla.: University of Oklahoma Press, 1964), p. 52.

[51] Osada, *op. cit.,* p. 26.

[53] Leon Orlowski, "Henryk Korwin-Kalussowski (1806–1894) Delegate of the Polish National Government in Washington," *Bulletin of the Polish Institute of Arts and Sciences,* Vol. IV, 1945–1946, p. 64. The French text of the letter of appointment appeared in the *Echo z Polski,* August 22, 1863.

[54] Osada, *op. cit.,* pp. 29–30. Lewak, *op. cit.,* Vol. I, p. 406, contains a note from Wladyslaw Czartoryski to the National Government dated November 25, 1863, which presented the request for nomination of an agent to the United States.

[55] *Ibid.,* p. 30.

[56] Orlowski, *op. cit.,* p. 65. The Polish text of the February 12, 1864 letter was printed in *Echo z Polski,* May 14, 1864. The June 25, 1864 letter appeared in the July 30, 1864 edition.

[57] *Ibid.* Orlowski's article gives biographical data on Kalussowski. He had become a naturalized American citizen, had been employed by the Land Office and Treasury Department after some years as teacher of Latin and French. He was instrumental in founding the Polish National Alliance, a fraternal organization still in existence in the United States. Unfortunately, his archives and entire library perished in a fire at Alliance College, Cambridge Springs, Pennsylvania, in 1939.

[58] Mieczyslaw Haiman, *Historja udzialu* . . ., pp. 153–154. Martha Walker Cook was the editor of the *Continental Monthly*. The *Dictionary of American Biography*, Vol. IV, p. 377, notes:

Her admiration for the music and literature of Poland, her sense of outraged justice in the political sufferings of that country and of the debt of America for the services of Polish *émigrés* in the Revolution made her a warm if occasionally a somewhat sentimental advocate of Poland's cause. She was ready at all times with sympathy and with practical assistance and advice in aid of Polish emigrants, thus rendering a service which endeared her name to Poles at home and in America.

Ironically, Martha Walker Cook's brother, Robert Walker, ex-Governor of Kansas, had lobbied for Russia in negotiating the purchase of Alaska.

NOTES: *Chapter VII*

[1] *New York Herald*, September 29, 1863.

[2] For a discussion of sources consulted in connection with this study, see the Historiographical Note at the end of this chapter.

[3] An English translation of the sealed orders to the "fleet's" commander, Vice Admiral Lessovsky, signed by the Executive Secretary of the Ministry of Marine, Adjutant-General N. Krabbe, is printed in Alexandre Tarsaidzé, *op. cit.*, pp. 353–58. Lessovsky was instructed to drop anchor in New York or another United States port and "there await the outcome of negotiations on the Polish Question" (Remark II, 5). In the event of a peaceful solution of the question, the ships were to be "directed to a destination in a foreign station" about which he was to receive requisite notification in "proper time" (Remark II, 5). Wladyslaw Zbyszewski, who had commanded a Russian frigate, had deserted and later on commanded the privateer *Kosciuszko* purchased by the Czartoryski group in Paris, revealed the Russian plan to the French Ministry of Marine. This was recently discovered in the Ministry records and noted by Stanislaw Bobr-Tylingo, "Stany Zjednoczone A. P. a Powstanie Styczniowe," (The United States of America and the January Insurrection), *Teki Historyczne* (Historical Papers) (London), Vol. XI, 1960–1961, p. 153.

[4] Arthur P. Coleman and Marion M. Coleman, *op. cit.*, p. 120.

[5] *New York Sun*, September 15, 1863.

[6] *New York Sun*, September 25, 1863

[7] *Evening Post*, September 25, 1863.

[8] *New York Herald,* September 26, 1863.

[9] *New York Herald,* September 26, 1863.

[10] *New York Sun,* September 26, 1863; *World,* September 26, 1863.

[11] *New York Herald,* September 27, 1863.

[12] *New York Herald,* September 28, 1863.

[13] *New York Herald,* September 29, 1863.

[14] *New York Sun,* September 29, 1863.

[15] *New York Sun,* September 30, 1863.

[16] *New York Sun,* September 30, 1863.

[17] *Proceedings of the Board of Aldermen of the City of New York from July 2d to September 30th, 1863,* Vol. XCI, New York: Edmund Jones & Co., Printers, 1864, p. 526 (text of the resolution) and p. 462 (message of Mayor Opdyke). One of the speakers at the reception was the *Tribune's* Editor, Horace Greeley.

[18] *Commercial Advertiser,* October 2, 1863.

[19] *New York Journal of Commerce,* October 2, 1863.

[20] Arthur P. Coleman and Marion M. Coleman, *op. cit.,* p. 124.

[21] *Evening Post,* October 5, 1863.

[22] *Evening Post,* October 28, 1863.

[23] Lyman Abbot, ed., *Henry Ward Beecher, A Sketch of His Career: With Analyses of His Power as a Preacher, Lecturer, Orator and Journalist, and Incidents and Reminiscences of His Life* (Hartford, Conn.: American Publishing Co., 1887, pp. 538–39. The *Commercial Advertiser,* October 10, 1863, stated that Beecher's statements were "unfortunate."

[24] Reported in the *New York Herald,* November 4, 1863.

[25] Reported in the *New York Tribune,* September 11, 1863. Sumner was viciously attacked by Cassius Clay (United States Department of State, Despatches, Russia, Clay to Seward, No. 24, October 7, 1863) for being "on the side of Catholic, intolerant, reactionary, aristocratic Poland, repudiating democratic aid, even in her death throes, so much more odious than Muscovite tyranny." Clay singled out the phrase "liberal institutions," and acidly commented: "Liberal institutions"!—where the people are ignored—the democratic idea openly denounced—freedom of religion repudiated—cruelty reduced to a science—and assassinations organized into a system!"

[26] Edward L. Pierce, ed., *Memoir and Letters of Charles Sumner* (Boston: Robert Bros., 1893), Vol. II, p. 146. The letter was written October 6, 1863.

[27] Adam Gurowski, *Diary, from November 18, 1862 to October 18, 1863* (New York: Carlton, 1864), p. 320, entry for September 11, 1863.

[28] *Ibid.,* p. 337, entry for October 4, 1863. Gurowski's *Russia As*

It Is (New York: D. Appleton and Company, 1854), which gave American readers an introduction to the concept of Panslavism was probably read and re-read at this time. Harvard University's copy has the acquisition date April 20, 1863 entered on the bookplate.

[29] The only book-sized biography of Gurowski is Le Roy Fischer, *Lincoln's Gadfly, Adam Gurowski* (Norman, Okla.: University of Oklahoma Press, 1964). Fischer deals with Gurowski's attitude towards Gorchakov on page 212, and towards the visit on page 203. He utilizes a letter which Gurowski wrote to the exile leader Jan Nepomucen Janowski in Paris, found in the Janowski Correspondence, Jagellonian Library, Cracow, MS 3685, Vol. II, 335–36, dated October 25, 1863, but he presents an inaccurate and incomplete translation on p. 35. Gurowski wrote: "The bloody strife now spreading itself in Poland shocks me deeply, and though I view this struggle from the same standpoint that I chose for myself in the years 1834–35, I often fall into despair. *Victus aut Victor* Poland as a country, Poland as a people (what is more as a nation) will be so destroyed that a century will scarcely heal her wounds, will lessen her misery. . . ." In a subsequent paragraph (which Fischer does not cite) Gurowski tried to explain the attitude of his American compatriots. He noted that the Civil War "as a political struggle" placed Americans in contact with foreign nations and obligated them to search for friends and "external alliances," and as if to justify the saying that opposites attract, he noted, "Russia is America's *only* friend."

In a letter which Henryk Kalussowski wrote Janowski on January 21, 1864 from Washington D. C. (Janowski Correspondence, Jagellonian Library, MS 3685, Vol. IV, 344–345) the former indicated that he had seen Gurowski, that he had a lengthy conversation with him, and that he read Kalussowski's Polish newspapers to obtain news "about things Polish." Then he noted that "neglected today by his friends of a short while ago," Gurowski "felt offended and sharply latched on in the journals to the mission and the Muscovite sailors." It would seem from this that Gurowski had a belated change of heart.

[30] *Harper's Weekly*, October 17, 1863. Thomas, *op. cit.*, p. 138, indicated that "Paris and London were naturally perturbed" by the possibility of a formal Russo-American alliance. Felix Aucaigne, a French publicist, discussed the possibility that a secret alliance did exist in a widely read monograph entitled *L'Alliance Russo-Americaine* (Paris, 1863). The London *Times* editorialized on it in its editions of October 15, 24 and 27. However, the final word came from Seward who wrote on October 5 to Dayton in Paris: "Any statesman who has observed how inflexibly this government adheres to the policy of peace and non-intervention, would not need to be

informed that the report of an alliance by us with Russia for European war is an absurdity." (*vide*, George E. Baker, ed., *The Diplomatic History of the War for the Union, Being the Fifth Volume of the works of William H. Seward* (Boston: Houghton Mifflin Company, 1884), p. 404.

[31] *New York Herald,* October 5, 1863.

[32] *New York Herald,* October 7, 1863. See also pp. 140–141.

[33] *New York Tribune,* October 7, 1863.

[34] *New York Sun,* October 9, 1863. The San Francisco *Evening Bulletin,* October 26, 1863, noted that there were twenty foreign ships in New York harbor of which eight to ten were Russian. The British had sent a three-decker, Admiral Charles Milne's flagship, from Halifax, Nova Scotia. There were a number of French gunboats and one Spanish frigate. The same report noted that the city's old people talked of intervention but its younger ones were "looking forward to delightful flirtations with gold lacebedizened officers."

[35] *New York Times,* October 11, 1863.

[36] *New York Times,* October 18, 1863.

[37] *New York Times,* October 18, 1863.

[38] *New York Herald,* October 10, 1863.

[39] *New York Tribune,* October 11, 1863.

[40] *New York Tribune,* October 14, 1863.

[41] *New York Herald,* October 15, 1863.

[42] *New York Herald,* October 23, 1863.

[43] A complete list of members was printed in the *New York Herald* on November 1, 1863. Theodore Roosevelt, father of the future President Theodore Roosevelt, was chairman.

[44] Tarsaidze, *op. cit.,* pp. 204–207, supplies the colorful and statistical details relative to this event.

[45] *World,* October 21, 1863.

[46] *New York Herald,* October 24, 1863.

[47] *World,* November 6, 1863.

[48] *New York Journal of Commerce,* November 6, 1863.

[49] *Evening Post,* November 6, 1863.

[50] *New York Herald,* November 12, 1863.

[51] *New York Herald,* November 12, 1863.

[52] *New York Herald,* November 18, 1863.

[53] Tarsaidze, *op. cit.,* p. 207.

[54] *New York Tribune,* November 1, 1863.

[55] *New York Sun,* October 30, 1863.

[56] *New York Journal of Commerce,* November 19, 1863.

[57] *New York Times,* December 1, 1863. Judge John W. Edmonds, a Tammany man, presided. The account also names as vice presidents of the meeting: Peter Cooper (a wealthy merchant descended

from America's first railroad man of the same name), William Curtis Noyes, Robert Emmet (an Irish exile leader descended from the Irish national hero of the same name), "Herr" Ottendorfer, Frederick Kapp, another prominent German immigrant, and Joseph Hoxie. Jerzy J. Lerski, *A Polish Chapter in Jacksonian America, The United States and the Polish Exiles of 1831* (Madison, Wis.: University of Wisconsin Press, 1958), p. 21, identifies Hoxie as a member of a Polish Committee formed in New York in 1831 to give financial support to the November Insurrection.

The *Times* estimated that three-fourths of the audience at the Cooper Institute meeting was native American, while the remaining one-fourth consisted of Poles and other exiles.

[58] *Commercial Advertiser*, December 1, 1863. The same editorial appeared in the New York *Spectator*, December 3, 1863. According to *Echo z Polski*, Smith had donated $1,000 to the Poles.

[59] *Commercial Advertiser*, December 1, 1863. .

[60] *Ibid.*

[61] *Ibid.*

[62] *Ibid.*

[63] *Philadelphia Inquirer*, October 29, 1863.

[64] *Ibid.*

[65] *Philadelphia Inquirer*, November 13, 1863. The letter is dated November 9, 1863.

[66] *Philadelphia Inquirer*, November 21, 1863. The "organ of Archbishop Hughes" was probably the *New York Freeman's Journal,* a newspaper which was alleged to be owned by the Catholic prelate.

[67] Occasionally, the Northern journals would reprint the complete text of the editorials in their major Southern counterparts. (E.g., the editorial "Alexander II and Abraham I" which appeared in the Richmond *Dispatch* (see footnote 69) was reprinted in the *New York Herald*, November 3, 1863.

[68] Richmond *Daily Whig*, September 10, 1863.

[69] *Daily Dispatch*, October 7, 1863.

[70] *Daily Richmond Examiner*, October 5, 1863.

[71] Richmond *Daily Whig*, October 3, 1863.

[72] Richmond *Daily Whig*, October 7, 1863. John Randolph of Roanoke, Virginia, was briefly (for a few months in 1830) United States Minister to St. Petersburg.

[73] *Memphis Appeal*, November 21, 1863. Mott, *op. cit.*, p. 364, notes that this journal was given the nickname "Moving" *Appeal* as it had to move its presses before the advancing Union armies and had set them up in ten towns in four different states.

[74] *Daily Richmond Examiner*, October 23, 1863.

[75] *Ibid.*

[76] *Memphis Appeal,* December 7, 1863.

[77] E.g., on October 10, 1863, the *Daily Examiner* took Earl Russell to task for his utterances which had been in favor of Poland while denying the Confederacy "the smallest crumb of comfort in the way of recognition." It noted that his appeal to the Vienna Treaty was belated because it was not made during the Poles' period of oppression and then added: "To his [Russell's] disordered optics the 'order that reigns' in New Orleans seems to be as pleasing as that of Warsaw is disgusting."

[78] Tarsaidze, *op. cit.,* pp. 214–19. Bobr-Tylingo, *op. cit.,* p. 141, notes that Popov was alerted in April, 1863 to await orders. He also indicates that the British Navy in the Far East had been strengthened through Russell's intervention because of fears that the United States would hire Japanese vessels as privateers to harass British shipping (p.143).

[79] Tarsaidze, *op. cit.,* p. 219. Tarsaidze notes that the Russians were very pleased with one visitor, a Dr. Chapka, as he "had none of the rudeness which they found in most Californians." They made him their guest of honor but were later informed by San Francisco authorities that he was "a sort of male mid-wife, with a most unsavory reputation." Among the members of the San Francisco Polish Committee was a Hungarian physician named Dr. Czapkay. I would venture to guess that Dr. *Chapka* and Dr. *Czapkay* were one and the same.

[80] San Francisco *Evening Bulletin,* November 18, 1863.

NOTES: *Chapter VIII*

[1] *Daily National Intelligencer,* December 14, 1863 and December 18, 1863. Seward reported the reception to Cassius Clay (United States Department of State, Russia, Seward to Clay, No. 52, December 8, 1863. Clay had also been keeping Seward apprised of the exhilarating effects which the welcome given the Russian visitors had on the Russians at home. In one dispatch (No. 29, November 8, 1863) he commented that "the Russian reception in American waters, is the subject of conversation in all circles: and the gentry and the common people seem alike to feel the friendly demonstration made at this time; when France, England and Austria are attempting, under the pretense of National justice, to put them under the ban of Christianity for defending the integrity of their Empire."

In a later dispatch (No. 38, 1864) Clay noted that the Grand Duke, the Czarina, and the Czar himself had expressed gratitude for the hospitality shown the officers. The same dispatch included copies of the *Invalide Russe,* sent him by its editor by order of the Minister of War. The journal contained an editorial expressing Russian sympathy with America and equating the Polish and Confederate Insurrections!

[2] Roy B. Basler, ed., *The Collected Works of Abraham Lincoln* (New Brunswick: Rutgers University Press, 1953), Vol. VII, p. 93.

[3] *Ibid.* Taylor's reply is dated December 28, 1863. He was lecturing in Washington at the time. Woldman, *op. cit.,* p. 146, notes that Admiral Lessovsky and several of his officers heard the lecture one evening and that the President himself also went to hear Taylor. Taylor's New York appearance had been made on December 9, 1863, at the Cooper Institute.

[4] *Boston Daily Courier,* January 14, 1864. The lecture was delivered at the Tremont Temple on January 13.

[5] *New York Herald,* October 7, 1863.

[6] *New York Herald,* November 1, 1863.

[7] *Commercial Advertiser,* November 21, 1863.

[8] *New York Herald,* November 28, 1863.

[9] *New York Journal of Commerce,* November 11, 1863.

[10] *New York Sun,* December 19, 1863.

[11] *Philadelphia Inquirer,* December 4, 1863.

[12] *Boston Post,* December 29, 1863.

[13] *Ibid.*

[14] *Ibid.*

[15] *Boston Post,* December 29, 1863.

[16] W. F. Reddaway, *et al., op. cit.,* pp. 382–83. Details of the program are discussed by Krzysztof Groniowski, *Realizacja reformy uwlaszczeniowej 1864 roku* (Implementation of the 1864 Enfranchisement Reform) (Warsaw: Instytut Historii Polskiej Akademii Nauk [Institute of History of the Polish Academy of Sciences] 1963).

[17] Ellsworth, *op. cit.,* p. 15.

[18] *Ibid.,* and Woldman, *op. cit.,* p. 269.

[19] Tarsaidze, *op. cit.,* p. 209.

[20] *Complimentary Banquet Given By the City Council of Boston to Rear Admiral Lessofsky and the Officers of the Russian Fleet at the Revere House, June 7, 1864* (Boston: J. E. Farwell and Co., 1864), p. 10. Hereafter referred to as *Complimentary Banquet.* . . .

[21] *Complimentary Banquet.* . ., pp. 23–24. The text of the address was also carried in the *Boston Daily Evening Transcript,* June 8, 1864, 1864. Alison wrote the *History of Europe from the Battle of Waterloo to the Accession of Louis Napoleon.*

[22] *Complimentary Banquet.* . . ., p. 24.

[23] *Ibid.*

[24] *The Pilot,* June 4, 1864.

²⁵ Higham, *op. cit.*, p. 58; Haiman, *Historja udzialu* . . ., pp. 154–155; Irena Koberdowa, *Polityka czartoryszyzny w okresie powstania styczniowego* (The Policy of the Czartoryski Group During the January Insurrection) (Warsaw: "Ksiazka i Wiedza" ["Book and Knowledge"]), 1957, p. 170, states that 87 seamen fled from vessels of the Atlantic Squadron during its American visit and that a sizeable number of them were Poles. Butler's correspondence has been published in Benjamin F. Butler, *Private and Official Correspondence of Benjamin F. Butler During the Period of the Civil War* (Norwood, Mass.: Plimpton Press, 1917), Vol. III, pp. 502–93, 563, 595. The expression "hunt him up" is Butler's own (p. 502). See footnote 89.

²⁶ *Echo z Polski*, June 18, 1864.

²⁷ *The Congressional Globe Containing the Debates and Proceedings of the First Session of the Thirty-Eighth Congress* (Washington: Congressional Globe Office, 1864), pp. 3156:-3157:1. The account appeared in the *Echo z Polski*, June 11, 1864. Reverdy Johnson had been a law firm partner of the renegade Gaspar Tochman (see pp. 38–39).

²⁸ *Echo z Polski*, July 8, 1864. This development was reported in a letter from Kalussowski to the editor, dated at Washington June 30, 1864.

²⁹ *Echo z Polski*, September 10, 1864. The translation is mine.

³⁰ *Ibid.*

³¹ *Echo z Polski*, June 11, 1864. The September 3, 1864 edition noted that a Czech newspaper had reported the existence of a Czech-Polish "Frémont Club" in St. Louis.

³² *Echo Polskie* (Polish Echo—The new name of the *Echo z Polski*), October 8, 1864. Subsequent issues of the newspaper point to friction between the two immigrant groups. There were charges and countercharges that one or the other wanted to play a dominant role.

³³ Tarsaidze, *op. cit.*, discusses the roots of the movement (p. 150 and pp. 223 ff.). The *Dziennik Poznanski* (Poznan Journal), April 13, 1863, noted that an Orthodox service was held in Trinity Episcopal Church, New York, to celebrate the anniversary of Alexander II's accession to the throne.

³⁴ Tarsaidze, *op. cit.*, p. 150. Boynton's biography is in the *Dictionary of American Biography*, Vol. II, pp. 536–37.

³⁵ Charles B. Boynton, *English and French Neutrality and the Anglo-French Alliance in Their Relations to the United States and Russia* (Cincinnati: C. F. Vent and Co., 1864), p. 307.

³⁶ *Ibid.* pp. 552–53.

³⁷ The other titles are: *The Navies of England, France, America*

and Russia (1865), and *The Four Great Powers: England, France, Russia and America: Their Policy, Resources and Probable Future* (1866).

[38] Leavitt's biography is in the *Dictionary of American Biography,* Vol. XI, pp. 84–85.

[39] Joshua Leavitt, "Poland," *New Englander Magazine and Yale Review,* Vol. XXII, No. 2, April, 1864, pp. 3–4.

[40] *Ibid.,* p. 4.

[41] *Ibid.,* p. 4.

[42] *Ibid.,* p. 5.

[43] *Ibid.,* p. 8.

[44] *Ibid.,* p. 11.

[45] *Ibid.,* p. 18.

[46] *Ibid.,* p. 18. He was referring to Archbishop Hughes of New York.

[47] *Ibid.,* p. 19.

[48] *Ibid.,* p. 19.

[49] *Ibid.,* p. 19.

[50] *Ibid.,* p. 19.

[51] *Ibid.,* p. 20.

[52] *Ibid.,* pp. 21–22.

[53] *Poland, Sketch of Her History,* p. 8.

[54] *Ibid.,* p. 14.

[55] *Ibid.,* p. 25.

[56] *Ibid.,* p. 33.

[57] *Ibid.,* p. 37.

[58] *Ibid.,* p. 40.

[59] *Ibid.,* p. 42.

[60] *Echo z Polski,* October 3, 1863.

[61] Czechowski to Janowski, October 30, 1863. MS 3685, Vol. I, 411–12 in the Janowski Papers, Jagellonian Library, Cracow. I am indebted to Professor Stefan Kieniewicz of Warsaw University and the Institute of History, Polish Academy of Sciences, for calling my attention to the existence of this and other letters in the Janowski Collection. Mrs. Krystyna Murzynowska of the Institute of History, Polish Academy of Sciences, gave me invaluable assistance in deciphering Czechowski's handwriting. It should be added that in this letter Czechowski expressed disappointment that the "devilish visit of the Russian fleet" had completely halted the sale of his books for several months.

[62] Czechowski to Janowski, February 12, 1864. MS 3685, Vol. I, 413–14 in the Janowski Papers, Jagellonian Library, Cracow. The *Goniec* (Messenger), (Lwow) July 18, 1863, describing the first issue of the *Echo z Polski* (which I have been unable to locate), noted that

Kalussowski had planned to publish works entitled *A Hundred Years of the Struggle of Poles for Independence (Stuletnia walka polakow za niepodleglosc)* and *The Faults and Virtues of the May Third Constitution (Wady i zalety konstytucyi 3 maja).* The letter also alluded to Geritt Smith, whose article on the Civil War had been sent to Janowski for use in presenting the case for the North to the European press.

[63] Kalussowski to Janowski, January 21, 1864. MS 3685, Vol. IV, 344–45 in the Janowski Papers, Jagellonian Library, Cracow.

[64] Czechowski to Janowski, March 20, 1866, MS 3685, Vol. I, 599, in the Janowski Papers, Jagellonian Library, Cracow. The letter was sent from Grandson, Vaud Canton, Switzerland.

[65] *Echo z Polski,* October 10, 1863. The same edition also announced the resignation of Michael Heilprin, member of a well-known Jewish family, from his position as Secretary of the Washington Polish Committee (whose president was Kalussowski) "because of weakness" *("z powodu slabosci").*

[66] In one of his dispatches (No. 42, April 8, 1864) Cassius Clay wrote to Seward about a letter that had appeared in the Paris *La Presse* on March 25, 1864. The writer was described as Lucien Fogue, a "commandant-major" in the Polish insurrectionary army from April to September, 1863. Clay took special note of Fogue's conclusion that "the Polish nation consists of some thousands of nobles—whose fanatical ideas are absolutely retrograde, antiliberal, and opposed to civilization: whilst the ideas of the thoughtful 'elite' of Russia are positively democratic." Clay added that Fogue had provided more proof that the Polish struggle "ran on all fours" with the Southern rebellion, and this explained why England, France, and Austria were naturally sympathetic to both.

"Fogue" and "Fouquet" were undoubtedly the same person.

[67] Henryk K. Kalussowski, "Tardy Truths," *Continental Monthly,* Vol. VI, No. 2, August, 1864, p. 209. To differentiate Muscovite Russia from the earlier Kievan Russia (Ruthenia), Kalussowski spelled the name of the former "Rossia." This was an approximation of Polish terminology in which Muscovite Russia is *Rosja* and Kievan Russia is *Rus.* He explained this to his readers on p. 216 of the article.

[68] Henryk K. Kalussowski, *op. cit.,* p. 210.

[69] *Ibid.,* p. 211.

[70] *Ibid.,* p. 213.

[71] *Ibid.,* p. 214.

[72] *Ibid.,* p. 215.

[73] *Ibid.,* p. 219. According to Orlowski, *op. cit.,* p. 63, Kalussowski had been married in a Protestant Episcopal Church.

[74] Kalussowski, *op. cit.*, p. 221.

[75] *Ibid.*, pp. 215–16.

[76] *Ibid.*, pp. 221–22. The manifesto was an extremely anti-Western document drawn up by the Panslavists.

[77] *Ibid.*, p. 209. Earlier, Michael Heilprin, former Secretary of the Washington Polish Committee, did utilize the *Continental Monthly* to criticize New York's welcome of the Russian "fleet" (*vide:* M. Heilprin, *"Nos Amis les Cosaques!" Continental Monthly,* Vol. V, No. 1, January, 1864, pp. 216–20).

[78] Haiman, *Historja udzialu . . .*, p. 153. My translation. The mention of gold is probably in reference to several hundreds of dollars which the Russian officers donated to the poor of New York.

[79] Lonn, *Foreigners in the Confederacy*, pp. 225–28. Lonn identifies the four delegates as Colonel J. Smolinski, Colonel A. Lemkiewicz, Major A. Brunicki, and Chaplain J. Mayewski. *Ojczyzna* (Fatherland) January 4, 1865, printed their correspondence and identified them as Colonel Józef Smolinski, Colonel Aleksander Lenkiewicz, Major Zygmunt Bujnicki and Chaplain Józef Majewski. The mission was delayed by Lenkiewicz's illness. (He died of yellow fever.)

[80] Lonn, *op. cit.*, pp. 224–25. Before the mission was organized, Smolinski wrote two letters from London to his friend Antoni Bukaty in Paris. He offered little in the way of explanation. I found the letters in the Kórnik Library (MS 2446, 112, dated June 7, 1864, and MS 2446, 115, dated June 11, 1864).

[81] *Ibid.* According to the same source (pp. 223–24) a similar scheme had been suggested by Confederate Colonel Valerian Sulakowski, a veteran of the November Insurrection, who was chief engineer to General Magruder. Sulakowski proposed to bring over 5,000 Polish volunteers in time for the fall campaign. The funds were to be raised from the sale of cotton or Confederate bonds sold to "patriotic and discreet citizens." The troops would have been mercenaries paid $2,000 to $4,000 apiece, armed from Garibaldi's alleged store of muskets. Sulakowski's cotton-carrying schooner, which was to be exchanged with its cargo for a steamer in Cuba, was captured by the Union Navy, and he ended up in Matamoras. He was later involved in a scheme to secure Polish volunteers for Maximilian. (Cf. Harold Lerner, "The Question of a Polish Legion and Polish Immigration During the Second Empire," *The Polish Review,* Vol. VI, No. 3, Summer, 1961, pp. 102–106.)

[82] *Charleston Courier,* September 25, 1864.

[83] United States Department of State, Instructions, Austria, Seward to Motley, No. 99, October 15, 1864. Seward noted that the Confederates proposed to have fast European-built steamers get

through the blockade at Wilmington, Delaware, with the troops. The other American diplomats in Europe received copies of the instructions.

84 United States Department of State, Despatches, Great Britain, Adams to Seward, No. 810, November 10, 1864.

85 United States Department of State, Despatches, Austria, Motley to Seward, No. 82, November 8, 1864. In Despatch No. 47, March 7, 1864, Motley discussed the state of siege and sent Seward a copy of the Austrian government order which put it into force.

86 E.g., *Glos Wolny*, July 31, 1864, *Echo Polskie*, October 8, 1864, and *Ojczyzna*, January 4, 1865.

87 *The New York Times* of August 28, 1864 tersely concluded its news report of the event with the words: " . . . and so closes the bloody tragedy of the late Polish Revolution."

88 United States Department of State, Despatches, Russia, Clay to Seward, No. 61, November 14, 1864. A month before, Clay had requested the recall of Bayard Taylor's successor, Henry Bergh, in a private letter dated October 17, 1864. Several reasons were enumerated (e.g., refusal to call upon officers of the Russian government, refusal to call on foreign legations, not allowing Clay access to archives, not buying a carpet for the legation, etc.). Reason No. 4 was that "He habitually denounces this government for the suppression of the Polish rebellion; and ridicules the Emperor, and the nation." Bergh's post-diplomatic career did not include any lecturing on Russia or Poland. He founded the American Society for the Prevention of Cruelty to Animals.

89 State Department Records (Record Group 59, National Archives) contain the following: A note from Stoeckl to Seward, dated February 8, 1864, complaining that a seaman Ragochin who had been abducted by recruiting brokers and enrolled in a New York artillery regiment had not been delivered to him despite orders from the War Department; Seward's reply of February 13 noting that the Secretary of War's attention was called to the matter; Seward's note of the same date to Stanton re Ragochin; a letter dated March 10 from Assistant Adjutant General Canby to Seward on Butler's attempts to find Ragochin alias Alexander Myklovski [sic]; and Seward's March 11 note to Stoeckl informing him that the search was unsuccessful. [Material contained in footnote 89 was received too late for inclusion in footnote 25, where it logically belongs].

INDEX

254